THE RELIGIOUS THOUGHT OF ST. JOHN

THE
RELIGIOUS THOUGHT
OF ST. JOHN

By

EDWIN KENNETH LEE, M.A., M.Litt.

Vicar of Lofthouse, Leeds

LONDON

S · P · C · K

1950

First published in 1950
by S.P.C.K.
Northumberland Avenue, London, W.C. 2

Printed in Great Britain by
T. and A. Constable Ltd., Hopetoun Street,
Printers to the University of Edinburgh

TO

PETER

AND

ROSEMARY

CONTENTS

CONTENTS

CHAPTER 8

ETERNAL LIFE

CHAPTER 9

THE APPROPRIATION OF ETERNAL LIFE

CHAPTER 10

THEOLOGY AND ETHICS

PREFACE

THE Johannine interpretation of religion has increasingly come into its own in recent years. St. John is astonishingly modern in his outlook, or perhaps one ought to say that theology is more appreciative of the Johannine outlook upon religion now than twenty-five years ago when theologians were preoccupied with the Synoptic Gospels and the Jesus of History. This is the reason for attempting in this volume to present the teaching of St. John as contained in the Gospel and the Epistles as an organic whole. This will have the effect of displaying the richness and profundity of his thought more than the separate treatment of the different subjects can ever do. We shall see that the many subjects touched upon in his writings may be subordinated to a few dominant ideas which are closely related to one another. Furthermore, modern research has made us familiar with the idea that a true understanding of any part of the Gospel records can only be reached when we consider its *Sitz im Leben*, or what Dibelius calls the "place in the stream of life". What has proved to be so valuable in examining the literary forms of the Gospel records is here applied in seeking to interpret the mind of St. John. The distinctive characteristics of the Johannine writings did not rise *in vacuo*, but were influenced by the intellectual and religious atmosphere in which the author lived. In this book an attempt has been made to estimate the significance of certain points of contact between the teaching of St. John and contemporary philosophical and religious thought. The conclusion to which such an investigation leads us is that St. John was one of the greatest of those Christians who, in the telling phrase of Dr. Glover, "out-thought" the pagan and Jewish world.

The following summary will serve to emphasize the unity of Johannine thought. We begin with a consideration of the peculiar characteristics of the Johannine writings (Chapter 1). In these writings God is thought of as Light, Truth, and Father (Chapter 2).

So close is the relationship between the Father and the Son, which is revealed in the self-witness of Jesus (Chapter 3), and the title Logos, that Jesus may also be called the Light of the World (Chapter 4). In contrast to this conception of God as Light, the world is regarded as Darkness (Chapter 5). The Light shines in this Darkness when the Word is made flesh. The glory of God is made manifest in the historic mission of Jesus. Christ reigns from the tree (Chapter 6). The purpose of this manifestation is the Salvation of the World. An important element in this work of salvation is the separation of the children of God from the world: the constitution of the New Israel. In this work of salvation the Death of Christ occupies an essential place (Chapter 7). The blessing of salvation is Eternal Life. The abiding of Jesus with his disciples, upon which depends the possibility of eternal life, is continued by the coming of the Comforter (Chapter 8). The appropriation of eternal life depends on believing and knowing Jesus (Chapter 9). The Sacraments of Baptism and Holy Communion are the visible channels by which this eternal life is communicated to the faithful (Chapter 7). The ethics of John are derived from his theological principles. The New Commandment is closely related both to the New Covenant in his Blood and to brotherly love. Prayer and worship are integral parts in the life of fellowship with God and with one another. The unifying principle of Johannine thought is his conception of God as love (Chapter 10). It will thus be seen that the main divisions of John's teaching dovetail into one another and cannot be understood apart from the whole.

Throughout this work I am indebted to Walter Lowrie's book, *The Doctrine of St. John*, and I am especially grateful to Messrs. Longmans, Green, Inc. of New York for their permission to use material from this book. My obligations to others will be evident from the footnotes and bibliography. But no doubt I am indebted to many whose names have not been mentioned. I ask them to accept this general acknowledgement of what I owe to them. My thanks are also due for the help and guidance I have received from the late Canon N. D. Coleman, formerly Lecturer in Hellenistic Greek in the University of Durham, The Rev.

F. N. Davey, Editorial Secretary of the S.P.C.K., and Mr. J. A. Porter, B.A.

The Vicar of a colliery parish does not have the opportunity for quiet study which should lie behind such a book as this. There must be many points which have not been adequately discussed or have been omitted altogether. I ask my readers to forgive these deficiencies which are inevitable in attempting to write a book in the midst of a busy parish life. It is the outcome of many years' work. I hope that what I have written may help some to appreciate more fully the profound and deeply spiritual contribution that St. John has made to Christian thought.

E. K. L.

ABBREVIATIONS
MODERN LITERATURE

D.C.G.	*Dictionary of Christ and the Gospels.*
Ency. Bib.	*Encyclopaedia Biblica.*
E.R.E.	*Encyclopaedia of Religion and Ethics.*
H.D.B.	Hastings' *Dictionary of the Bible.*
I.L.N.T.	*Introduction to the Literature of the New Testament,* by J. Moffatt.
J.T.S.	*The Journal of Theological Studies.*
T.W.z.N.T.	*Theologisches Wörterbuch zum Neuen Testament.* Editor, G. Kittel.

RABBINIC LITERATURE

Aboth	*Aboth de R. Nathan.* Ed. S. Schechter, 1887.
Lev. R.	*Leviticus Rabbah* in *Midrash Rabbah,* Wilna, 1878.
Mekh.	*Mekhilta.* English Trans. by Lauterbach, *Mekilta,* 1933-1935.
Mishnah	*The Mishnah.* English Trans. by H. Danby, 1933.
Sifre 'Ekebh.	*Sifre Deuteronomy, 'Ekebh.* Ed. Friedmann, 1864.
Tanh. B.	*Tanhuma.* Ed. S. Buber, Wilna, 1885.
Targums	*The Targums.* English Trans. by Etheridge, 1862.
T.B. 'Ab. Zar.	*Babylonian Talmud, 'Abhodhah Zarah* in *Der Babylonische Talmud.* German Trans. by L. Goldschmidt, 1897-1936. English Trans. by M. L. Rodkinson, 1896-1903. Another English translation is being prepared, entitled *Babylonian Talmud,* by various writers, Ed. Rabbi I. Epstein, 1935-
T.B. Bab. Bath.	*Babylonian Talmud, Baba Bathra.*
T.B. Keth.	*Babylonian Talmud, Kethubboth.*
T.B. Sanh.	*Babylonian Talmud, Sanhedrin.*
T.B. Šuk.	*Babylonian Talmud, Šukkah.*
T.J. Sabbath	*Jerusalem Talmud, Sabbath* in *Le Talmud de Jérusalem.* French Trans. by M. Schwab, 1871-1889.

I

INTRODUCTORY

i. *Introduction*

No apology is needed to-day for an essay in Biblical theology. Divers circumstances have combined to give it an importance which is likely to increase in the future. There has been a revulsion from metaphysical dogmatism and detailed exegesis, and this has encouraged the study of the Bible as a whole. No doubt immense service has been done in the past by the detailed work of exegetical scholars; especially by work in which, for a time and for a purpose, the direct influence of theological preconceptions has been laid aside. But it is only up to a certain point that this is either desirable or possible. Such work is too detailed to be creative. The time has come for the detailed work of exegetical scholars to be gathered into one whole, and there is evidence that this is being realized.

Biblical theology stands midway between exegesis and systematic theology. Its special mark is that it studies separately the several Biblical documents, in relation to the individual authors, with the aim of reproducing the standpoint of each writer. This in no wise prejudices the fact that there is a substantial unity of doctrine throughout the New Testament; and it is by the method of Biblical theology that such a fact is established. The study of the author's thought throws back a flood of light upon the several items of exegetical enquiry, and it is in this that Biblical theology attains its characteristic expression.

There are two characteristics of Biblical theology. In the first place, it is not directly concerned with the bearing of Biblical truths upon the religious life; it is history rather than homily. It seeks to learn what was the meaning of the author. In the second place, it does not seek to go beyond the historical standpoint of

A   1

the author. It does not attempt to extract universally valid propositions, or to extend by inference the sphere of his idea. It does not seek to translate the author into equivalent terms of modern thought, but to interpret him in the terms of his own philosophic method.

These characteristics of Biblical theology will be kept in mind in this particular study. It will be our purpose to give such an exposition of the thought of John that not only will it comprise his theology, in the sense that every topic of that theology will be discussed, but it will display his theology as a whole, as a system. The profundity of Johannine thought will thereby be revealed. Small minds are a jumble of unrelated and discordant ideas; big minds remain true to a few central and fundamental beliefs. These beliefs are expressed in different ways; conveying thus the impression of the complexity and manifoldness of life itself. But variety of expression does not bespeak discordance of ideas. An underlying unity is revealed in the fabric to whose meaning the many strands of diverse colours have gone. It will be the purpose of this book to reveal that unity in the Johannine writings.

It is not difficult to arrange the several topics of Johannine theology under the familiar headings and discuss them separately. But it is no easy task to arrange the teaching of John according to a system which will reflect the fulness of his rich mind, which will show how one part of his thought dovetails into another and which will display the unity of the many ideas which comprise the Johannine conception of Christianity. It demands not only a minute inspection of the single texts in order to rise to an apprehension of the author's thought as a whole, but also an imaginative faculty which will co-ordinate the scattered details into a constructive reproduction of the author's thought. Dr. Maurice Goguel has said: "It is on psychology that in the last analysis must rely every attempt to understand the life of Jesus".[1] This is especially true of the Fourth Gospel. And some attempt will be made to arrive at a sympathetic insight into the mind of John in this book.

[1] *Vie de Jésus*, p. 196.

ii. *Author*

For the purpose of this study the Fourth Gospel and the three Johannine Epistles are regarded as having been written by the same author. This is the opinion of Canon Streeter, who says that "the three Epistles and the Gospel of John are so closely allied in diction, style, and general outlook that the burden of proof lies with the person who would deny their common authorship . . . we are forced to conclude that all four documents are by the same hand".[1] It is not of great importance to determine who the actual author was. The external evidence for the Apostolic authorship of the Fourth Gospel as worked out by Westcott in his classical commentary,[2] and the internal evidence discussed by Scott Holland,[3] appear convincing to some scholars. But the references to John the Elder cannot be set aside.[4] The view which appears to do fullest justice to the evidence is that the writer of the Fourth Gospel is John the Elder, who was an intimate disciple of John the Apostle; that he records the teaching of John the Apostle with great fidelity; that the Apostle is the "witness" to whom reference is sometimes made, and is also the "disciple whom Jesus loved". It may be that the Apostle actually dictated to the Elder parts of what now constitutes the Gospel; but parts are the Elder's own recollections of the Apostle's teaching and parts are his own comment. By adopting this view one may argue that the author of the First Epistle is also the actual writer of the Fourth Gospel, while also admitting the differences in style and content to which most scholars call attention.[5] The author of the Epistle speaks with authority and belongs to the apostolic company of those whose fellowship is with the Father and the Son. But that is all we know about him. If he is not the writer of the Fourth Gospel he must have been either a personal disciple of the Evangelist or thoroughly versed in his writings and teaching. In any case, he is a reliable witness to the teaching of John.

[1] *The Four Gospels*, p. 460.   [2] *The Gospel of St. John*, pp. v-xxviii.
[3] *The Fourth Gospel*.
[4] This evidence is fully discussed by Moffatt, *Introduction to the Literature of the New Testament*, pp. 596-619.
[5] Cf. Temple, *Readings in St. John's Gospel*, i, p. x.

The differences between the two writings have led some scholars to affirm that they were written by different authors. Dr. Moffatt, for example, arrives at the conclusion that the writer of the First Epistle, while belonging to the general Johannine school of thought, occupies a slightly different ground from that of the Fourth Gospel.[1] It is of course agreed that some of the differences are due to the different purposes for which the Gospel and the Epistle were written. Although full allowance is made for this, Prof. C. H. Dodd is convinced that the Epistle was written by a different author, who was far less profound than that of the Gospel.

Prof. Dodd has collected together all the evidence on the subject which can be derived from the vocabulary, style, and content of the Epistle, as compared with the Gospel. He summarizes the differences in style and vocabulary as follows: "There is surely to be felt in the Fourth Gospel a richness, a subtlety, a penetrating quality of style to which the Epistle cannot pretend. While the rhythm of both is slow and regular, in the Gospel it is subtly varied, within the limits imposed by its general character; but in the Epistle regularity often descends to monotony. The language of the Gospel has an intensity, a kind of inward glow, a controlled excitement, which the reader does not feel, or seldom feels, in the Epistle. The language of the Epistle is generally correct Greek, though not always as lucid as might be wished; it is sometimes forcible and epigrammatic; but it does not suggest the pen of a ready writer. It does not persuade the reader (as does the Fourth Gospel) that here is a man who, with a relatively small vocabulary and narrow range of grammatical idiom, had genuine power of style ".[2]

It is, however, extremely difficult to form an objective judgement about the style of an author, especially when the aim and

---

[1] *I.L.N.T.*, pp. 589-593 ; see also Schmiedel, *The Johannine Writings*, pp. 201-211 ; E. F. Scott, *The Fourth Gospel*, pp. 88 ff. ; but cf. *Literature of the New Testament*, p. 261.

[2] *The Johannine Epistles*, p. xlix. For detailed proof see *The First Epistle of John and the Fourth Gospel*. Prof. Dodd shows that there are *measurable* differences in idiom and vocabulary between the two writings. These may be explained by the hypothesis that the person described in John 21. 24 as ὁ γράψας ταῦτα is the author of the Epistle as distinguished from ὁ μαρτυρῶν περὶ τούτων.

circumstances of the two writings compared are so different as those of the Fourth Gospel and the First Epistle of John. It has, for example, been argued by Dr. A. E. Brooke, with detailed examples, that there are so many close affinities between the two documents in grammar, style, phraseology, and thought, that, in his opinion, the author of the Epistle was also the author of the Gospel.[1] And so acute a critic of Greek style as Dr. J. H. Moulton held that "in every consideration of style" the Johannine Epistles form with the Fourth Gospel "a literary unity".[2]

Prof. Dodd also points out that "the Epistle represents a theological outlook nearer than that of the Gospel to primitive or popular Christianity".[3] This is a more serious matter if we are going to use the Epistle to supplement the evidence from the Gospel in our enquiry into the religious thought of John. The examples Prof. Dodd quotes are as follows:

(a) In the Epistle the *Parousia* is expected in the immediate future, whereas in the Gospel, although the belief in the Judgement Day is retained, it has been attenuated. The promise of our Lord's return has been fulfilled by his resurrection and the coming of the Paraclete. The author of the First Epistle, says Prof. Dodd, knows nothing of this reinterpretation of the Advent hope.

It is admitted that popular conceptions are more prominent in the Epistle than in the Gospel. But it seems too much to say that in the Epistle there is no evidence of this spiritual reinterpretation which is characteristic of the Gospel. The spiritualization of the Antichrist is at least as complete as the spiritualization of the popular eschatology in the Gospel. This is recognized by Prof. Dodd, who says: "The real Antichrist is for him not a person, whether human or supernatural. It is an idea—an idea no doubt embodied in persons who promulgate it, but essentially an idea, with power to poison the minds of men and pervert them from the truth".[4] Furthermore, the *Parousia* which the writer

---

[1] Brooke, *The Johannine Epistles* (I.C.C.), pp. i ff. ; cf. Charles, *Book of Revelation* (I.C.C.), i, pp. xxiv ff.

[2] *Grammar of New Testament Greek*, ii, p. 31.

[3] *The Johannine Epistles*, p. liii.

[4] Ibid., p. 50.

of the Epistle expected to take place in the near future is represented as a spiritual fact rather than an apocalyptic display. In the Epistle, as in the Gospel, eternal life is a present possession, and also an object of hope. The difference in emphasis may be explained by the near approach of the Antichrist, which had the effect of bringing into prominence the more primitive conception of the impending Day of Judgement.

(*b*) Prof. Dodd says that the teaching of the Epistle about the death of Christ scarcely goes beyond the terms of the Apostolic preaching. He summarizes the teaching of the Gospel about the death of Christ as follows:) The Evangelist's distinctive doctrine, he says, is that the dying Christ both accomplished the final "descent" of the Son of God from heaven, and was "lifted up" in glory, thereby frustrating the powers of evil, releasing the life that was in him to dwell in believers, and drawing all men into the unity of the divine love. Of all this, affirms Prof. Dodd, there is nothing in the Epistle.[1]

There is nothing in the Epistle to correspond with the Evangelist's teaching about exaltation in death. The word δόξα does not occur in the Epistle, nor the distinctive doctrine associated with the word. But the other ideas mentioned by Prof. Dodd are found in the Epistle, although they are expressed in different ways, as one would expect in a letter having a different purpose from the Gospel. It is a characteristic of the Epistle that the powers of evil are frustrated by the manifestation of Christ (3. 8). It can hardly be doubted that this manifestation of Christ included his death as well as his life. Especially is this the case when the writer of the Epistle says that "the blood of Jesus cleanseth us from all sin" (1. 7). The whole manifestation of Christ in the world, but in some signal way his death, is regarded as a victory over the powers of darkness.

In the Epistle there is also the idea that life was released by the death of Christ in order that it might be shared by the believers. In 1 John 5. 6 we are told that "this is he who came by water and blood, even Jesus Christ; not with the water only, but with the water and with the blood. . . . For there are three who

---

[1] *The Johannine Epistles*, p. liv.

bear witness, the Spirit, and the water, and the blood: and these three agree in one". In the context the author is alluding to the frustration of the powers of evil. As the water symbolizes purification and the blood life released in death, the meaning is that both the purity of Jesus' life and his death upon the cross are the sources of victory over evil. They are the means by which eternal life is bestowed, and the effective symbols of this are Baptism and Holy Communion. The two Sacraments are the means by which the life released in death is communicated to men throughout the ages. As Prof. Dodd says, "The Church possesses a counterpart to the baptism of Christ, in the Sacrament of Baptism, and a counterpart to his sacrificial death, in the Sacrament of the Eucharist. Both Sacraments attest and confirm to believers the abiding effect of the life and death of Christ".[1] This is exactly the teaching of the Fourth Gospel (John 6 and 19. 34).

It is also said that there is no evidence in the Epistle for the Evangelist's idea that the death of Christ was the means by which men were drawn into the unity of the divine love. This idea is to be found in the Epistle, though in a different form. For what is the barrier to such fellowship with God? It is sin. Therefore if the unity of the divine love is to be shared by men, sin must be removed. And it is a characteristic of the Epistle that sin is removed by the death of Christ (1. 7; 2. 1; 3. 5; 4. 10). This act is especially related to the love of God (4. 10; 3. 16). The power of sin is neutralized by the death of Christ, and one result is that fellowship with God is made possible. To be within the light, to have fellowship with God, is to be pure from sin. "Such purity", says Prof. Dodd, "belongs to believers, not through their own moral achievement, but by virtue of the death of Christ." [2] The death of Christ and fellowship with God are thus intimately related. It is the same conception as that found in the Fourth Gospel, although the idea is represented in different terms. The Gospel and the Epistle together give richness to the same idea.

(c) The conception of the Holy Spirit is quite different in the two writings. In the Epistle Christ's advocacy is exercised

---

[1] *The Johannine Epistles*, p. 131.
[2] Ibid., p. 21.

in heaven. In the Gospel the sphere of Christ's advocacy is on earth, and is consequent on the withdrawal of the bodily presence of Christ. As Prof. Dodd observes, the ideas associated with the Holy Spirit in the Epistle correspond to a more primitive theology. In the Acts the Spirit is regarded primarily as a gift granted to the prophets which enabled them to proclaim the Gospel. Similarly, in the Epistle the presence of Christ is confirmed by the manifestation of the Spirit in an individual's life. There is nothing in the Epistle to correspond to the Evangelist's teaching that the Holy Spirit, as the Paraclete, is the representative of Christ in whom he himself returns to his flock. Nevertheless the two conceptions do not exclude one another, and, for a balanced doctrine of the Holy Spirit, both writings must be taken into consideration. There is no reason why both conceptions should not be included in the teaching of one man. It is significant that only in the Johannine writings does the word "Paraclete" occur.

There are, then, these differences to be found between the Gospel and the Epistle. To some they are indications that the two documents cannot have been written by the same author. We have tried to show that the differences are not fundamental. In any case, those who affirm that there were two authors are agreed that there is an underlying unity between the two works which is more significant than the differences. Prof. Dodd, for example, quotes with approval the following opinion of Dionysius of Alexandria taken from the *Ecclesiastical History* of Eusebius (vii. 25. 18-21):

"The Gospel and the Epistle agree with one another. They begin alike . . . (John 1. 14; 1 John 1. 1-3) . . . and he deals with the whole matter by way of the same topics and terms, some of which I shall briefly enumerate. Anyone who attends attentively will find in each writing, life largely, light largely, and the repudiation of darkness; truth continually, grace, joy, the flesh and blood of the Lord, judgement, the forgiveness of sins, God's love for us, and the mutual love enjoined upon us: that we must keep all the commandments; the condemnation of the world, the devil, and Antichrist; the promise of the Holy Spirit; God's adoption of us as sons; the absolute faith demanded of us; the

Father and the Son everywhere. To characterize them generally all through, one may observe one and the same complexion in the Gospel and the Epistle." [1]

This is our justification for drawing upon both the Gospel and the Epistle for our study of Johannine theology. Our experience has been that of Sir Edwyn Hoskyns. He says that the themes of the Gospel and the Epistle are expressed in language so identical that it is difficult to interpret the Epistle without constant reference to the Gospel in order to elucidate obscure points and to reinforce the general meaning. Hoskyns's conclusion is that the two works come from the same hand and were originally written for the same group of Christians.[2] In the exposition that follows we shall, therefore, use both the Gospel and the Epistle on the grounds that they are mutually illuminating and both give us an insight into the religious thought of John. When important differences in teaching occur they are noted in the proper place.

Different strata have been observed in the Fourth Gospel, due perhaps to an oral stage, so that some of it seems like narratives taken straight from the Tradition, with little or no change; some also taken from the original Tradition, but so interwoven with interpretation that we cannot recover the original form; and some free writing in accordance with the known habits of Hellenistic religious authors of the period.[3] Nevertheless the book has a deeper unity than is suggested by either chronology or topography.[4] The end is in view from the beginning (1. 29; 19. 36); the divisions of the subject are clearly marked; there is a steady climax in the events, a growing revelation of Jesus and of his Father by the Son; we watch his "hour" all the time, as it delays, approaches, and arrives. As a detailed example of this we may point out the logical connexion between the first six chapters. It is the Evangelist's purpose in the first four chapters to give a series of witnesses to the truth as it is in Jesus. After the witness of John the Baptist there comes the witness of the

---

[1] The Johannine Epistles, p. xlviii.

[2] The Fourth Gospel, i, p. 54.

[3] Stanton, The Gospels as Historical Documents, pt. iii, pp. 17-76; Jackson, The Problem of the Fourth Gospel, pp. 97-123.

[4] Cf. Strachan, The Fourth Gospel, p. 81.

disciples. After that comes the witness of a Pharisee (3). And then follow the two witnesses, of the Woman of Samaria and of the Nobleman of Capernaum (4). There is nothing haphazard in this arrangement. It is an account of an ever-widening circle of witnesses.[1] From the Forerunner to the intimate disciples, from the intimate disciples to the Jerusalem Pharisee, from the Jerusalem Pharisee to the Samaritan woman, from the Samaritan woman to a Gentile Nobleman. Then comes the idea of the Life-giving Word which takes the reader to the end of chapter 6. Many attempts have been made to transpose chapters 5 and 6 on the ground that the connexion between 4. 42 and 6. 1 is more natural. But for this there is no MS. authority and it is essential that 5 comes before 6, as 5 defines the Son as adequate to give the Life-giving Bread in 6. This is not to deny that there may be some passages which have apparently been misplaced.[2] Such misplacements are probably due to the accidental disarrangement of leaves in the original MS. or to editorial revision. Nevertheless such theories of displacement assume a topographical, chronological, or logical sequence which may not have been present in the mind of the author.[3]

Archbishop Bernard's Commentary [4] has been criticized because it introduces into a Gospel which is all of one piece a distinction which destroys the unity both of the whole and of each section. Bernard distinguished between the Witness and the Evangelist in too sharp a manner. The Gospel, according to Bernard, is history and interpretation, whereas it is history interpreted. Thus the unity of the whole is lost and no skill in exegesis can compensate for the loss. For example, chapter 4 is one complete whole in which the narrative is carefully built up to reach the confession of the Samaritans. The words of Nicodemus in chapter 3 are set in a framework controlled by the

[1] A reverse process is to be found in 6. There the circle grows progressively smaller as the chapter proceeds. The audience is reduced from the multitudes to the Jews, from the Jews to many of his disciples, from the many disciples to the Twelve. See *The Message and Mission of Jesus*, p. 720.

[2] See Moffatt, *I.L.N.T.*, pp. 552 ff.

[3] For a full discussion see F. W. Lewis, *Disarrangements in the Fourth Gospel*, and F. R. Hoare, *The Original Order and Chapters of St. John's Gospel*.

[4] See *Theology*, March 1930, article by Sir Edwyn Hoskyns.

significance of water. It seems impossible, therefore, to treat
the words "of water" as a gloss, or to detach the confession of the
Samaritans as though it were added to a record complete without
it. Hoskyns does not fall into this error in his Commentary.
According to this scholar: "He has forged his book into one
whole, its unity being secured by a steady revolution round one
central theme, indeed round one point where the author had
seen the truth manifested in the darkness. . . . His work therefore
contains no fragments, no isolated, scattered bits of information,
no detached or detachable doctrines or dogmas, no independent
rites or ceremonies ".[1]

It may be objected that the Gospel, which is by far the most
abundant source for our study, gives, not primarily John's teaching, but the teaching of Jesus. Does this mean that we are
restricted, for the special purpose of this study, to the more
obvious comments of the author ? We need not be reduced to
this extremity. The question of the historicity of the speeches of
Jesus in the Fourth Gospel, vital as it is for religious interests, is
not one of immediate concern in a book on Johannine theology;
we are here exclusively concerned with the doctrines of the author.
We have already suggested that there are various strata in the
Fourth Gospel, but these are so interwoven with each other that
it is almost impossible to separate them. And without the least
prejudice to the substantial authenticity of these reports it requires
but slight familiarity with the contrast between the Synoptic
Gospels and the Fourth Gospel to convince one that they are not
verbatim reports, but rather reflect the peculiarities of the author,
who puts into the mouth of the Jews, the Baptist, and of Jesus

---

[1] *The Fourth Gospel*, p. 43 ; cf. Bauer, *Das Johannes Evangelium*, p. 229 : " One
and the same man wrote the entire book". See also Streeter, *The Four Gospels*,
p. 377. The three main theories that have been put forward regarding the unity of
the Fourth Gospel are : (*a*) Partition theories, which disentangle a more or less
genuine *Grundschrift* from the subsequent editorial revisions. (*b*) Revision theories,
which explain the phenomena of the Canonical Gospel by positing an editor who,
not only in the appendix but elsewhere, recast the Gospel for his own purposes.
(*c*) Both these theories may be combined with the hypothesis of dislocations in the
text. But whatever may be the evidence for these theories, the Gospel has a sequence
and one dominating aim which stamp upon it a unity of thought which justifies the
statement in the text. See Moffatt, *I.L.N.T.*, pp. 551 ff.

himself, the same characteristic language which we find him employing in his Epistles. The speeches of Jesus as recorded in the Fourth Gospel contain only what the author has completely assimilated and made his own, and consequently the Fourth Gospel is, as we call it, the Gospel according to St. John.[1]

This is the general opinion of modern scholars. Dr. J. E. Carpenter expresses the fact by maintaining that the members of the Johannine circle represent Jesus "as speaking by anticipation in their name".[2] In a long chapter Dr. Percy Gardner argues that the Evangelist gives the teaching of Jesus as Plato gives the teaching of Socrates.[3] Dr. B. H. Streeter thinks that the original readers would not have supposed the author to mean that the doctrine propounded in the discourses was verbally identical with what Jesus actually taught in Palestine, "but rather that it was organically related to what Christ taught in such a way as to be the doctrine which Christ would have taught had he been explicitly dealing with the problems confronting the Church at the time when the Gospel was written".[4] Dr. W. F. Howard holds that "it is the Evangelist's manner to take a saying of Jesus and render it into an idiom that is rich in meaning for his own contemporaries".[5]

iii. *Philosophical and Religious Affinities*

There are certain widely accepted claims in respect of the philosophical and religious affinities of the Fourth Gospel which must be considered in the course of this study. There are some who say that the Gospel is an extension of the characteristic teaching of St. Paul; others that Greek philosophical thought is the key to the understanding of the Gospel; others that the Hellenistic Mystery Religions, with their stress upon union with the Deity, ideas of birth, light, and life, have left their mark upon the Evangelist's mind; others that the key is to be found

---

[1] That is, the Gospel of which the Elder is the writer but of which the Apostle is the true author. For a defence of the theory that the Johannine discourses contain much of the original teaching of Jesus see W. F. Howard, *The Fourth Gospel in Recent Criticism*, pp. 215 ff. and 267 f.

[2] *The Johannine Writings*, p. 225.   [3] *The Ephesian Gospel*, pp. 100 ff.
[4] *The Four Gospels*, p. 371.   [5] *The Fourth Gospel in Recent Criticism*, p. 221.

in the Old Testament literature and other influences which operated within the borders of Judaism during the first and second centuries A.D. It will be convenient to discuss some of these claims now.

(*a*) Dr. B. W. Bacon says: "The supreme key to the Gospel is the absolute loyalty to Paulinism. Its author is the ' Vindicator' (*goël*) of Paul, accomplishing after Paul's death that 'unity of Spirit' in the universal church which was the supreme aim of Paul's life". The Greek metaphysic which some find in the Logos doctrine is there, according to Dr. Bacon, because Paul has met the author half-way in Hellenistic cosmology and anthropology. If Paul had written the Gospel, the Logos doctrine would have been given the same prominence as in the Johannine Gospel. In the Epistles of St. Paul there are expressed, though in a somewhat incidental way, all the elements of the Logos doctrine found in the Prologue of the Fourth Gospel. "He is before all things." Jesus is the creating and sustaining force of the world. He is the centre of all life, physical and spiritual. He is the Enlightener. He is in the world from the beginning, though the world had not recognized him. He was the spiritual Rock which had followed the Israelites. He is the Revealer of the invisible God. Thus, says Dr. Bacon, "Paulinism", to the author of the Fourth Gospel, "is much more than an influence. We should call it rather his universal solvent in which all elements of mere historical tradition are held in solution until precipitated in his own moulds of thought".[1] Deissmann [2] says that "the greatest monument of the most genuine understanding of Paul's mysticism is the Gospel and Epistles of John".

On the other hand, Prof. A. Schlatter, after many years' study of the second-century Rabbinic commentaries on the Old Testament, comes to the conclusion that the Fourth Gospel is thoroughly Jewish in language and outlook. This is the assumption upon which his commentary *Der Evangelist Johannes* (1930) is based. In the preface he says: "It has been said that John Hellenized the message of Paul. Is it possible to make the thought

---

[1] *The Fourth Gospel in Research and Debate*, pp. 281 ff.
[2] *Paul* (Eng. Trans.), p. 155.

and purpose Greek without the words becoming Greek?   Then is
the language of John Hellenized?   John has been called a mystic.
Was there ever mystical life without mystical language?   He calls
himself a disciple of Jesus who accompanied our Lord from Jordan
to the Cross.   If he was a native of Palestine, who thought in two
languages, so widely different from each other, only specialized
training could prevent his Greek from betraying its origin".[1]

The great contrast between St. Paul and John is that of the
God-mysticism of John and the Christ-mysticism of St. Paul.[2]
St. Paul never speaks of union with God or of "being in God"
as John does, and this appears to undermine the thesis of Dr.
Bacon at its most important point.   Furthermore, St. Paul dwells
upon the suffering, the humiliation, and the death of Christ.
The earthly life of Jesus was, according to St. Paul, primarily
an act of grace; according to John, it was a declaration of divine
truth.   The difference may, perhaps, be expressed by saying that
according to St. Paul the earthly life of Jesus was the supreme act
of God's love, whereas, for John, the earthly life was the uniquely
true symbol or expression of God's love.   The Fourth Evangelist
sees in all the steps of the earthly life of Jesus a glory as of the only
begotten Son of the Father which shines out in works such as no
other man did, and in words which no other man spake, and
supremely in the death on the cross.   Nevertheless it would be
strange if such a powerful thinker as St. Paul had no influence
on the Evangelist, especially as they were both concerned to
recommend the Christian Gospel to the Gentile world.

(b) In the detailed account of John's thought we shall notice
the close relation to Old Testament conceptions; at this point it
will be sufficient to draw attention to the Aramaic characteristics
of John's style.   Even if we consider that Dr. Burney[3] failed to
establish the case for an Aramaic original afterwards translated

---

[1] *Der Evangelist Johannes*, p. viii.

[2] See Schweitzer, *Die Mystik des Apostels Paulus*, p. 361.

[3] *The Aramaic Origin of the Fourth Gospel*.   For a criticism of Burney's position see
Colwell, *The Greek of the Fourth Gospel*.   Dr. Matthew Black has recently re-examined
the problem in *An Aramaic Approach to the Gospels and Acts*.   His conclusion is that the
Gospel is not a direct translation from an Aramaic original, but that the Evangelist
used an Aramaic source which contained some sayings of Jesus.

into Greek, we can still distinguish, through the Greek, characteristics of the Hebrew language. The most general signs of
it are: the simple and unperiodic structure of the sentences;
the monotonous connexion of the sentences by "and", "but",
"then", to the neglect of the rich store of particles which in
Greek served to express the logical relation of the clause; the
circumstantiality and monotony of the expressions and the fond-
ness of antithesis and parallelism. Dr. Burney has made it
clear that the three notes of Semitic poetry are constantly found
in the Fourth Gospel, namely, parallelism, rhythm, and rhyme,
and that the Prologue has many of the characteristics of a Hebrew
poem. Dr. E. A. Abbott [1] finds in the Johannine method of
recording Christ's sayings an example of the way in which the
sacred text was treated in the Jewish schools of the last few
centuries B.C. "The Fourth Gospel", he says, "asserts that all
Christ's sayings, while he lived, were in need so to speak of a
Targum. They were proverbs, requiring the interpretation that
would be given them after his death by the Holy Spirit in order
to apply them to practice. . . . To us it seems a contradiction in
terms to speak of an 'inspired Targum'. Yet that is what the
Fourth Gospel is". Dr. Israel Abrahams [2] finds in John 7. 22,
where Jesus defends his general position from the analogy of
circumcision, another instance of the Fourth Gospel's close
acquaintance with Hebraic traditions. Dr. Hugo Odeberg [3] has
marshalled a mass of evidence to show that John has close
affinities with Rabbinic theology. He points out that within the
environment of Rabbinical Judaism there was a mystical Judaism,
and suggests that many of the religious ideas of the Fourth Gospel
receive their inspiration from this environment.[4] This is a
significant suggestion, for it implies that the language and
thought of the synagogue in the Diaspora were influenced by
Hellenistic thought much more than has been formerly realized.
Greek philosophical terms were not adopted merely to make

[1] *The Son of Man*, p. 411.
[2] *Studies in Pharisaism and the Gospels*, i, p. 135.
[3] *The Fourth Gospel interpreted in its relation to Contemporaneous Religious Currents
in Palestine and the Hellenistic-Oriental World* (1929).
[4] Op. cit., p. 5.

Judaism intellectually respectable in a Hellenistic environment. They had become an integral part of the theological outlook of an influential group of people within Rabbinic Judaism. The dialogues and disputes recorded in the Fourth Gospel reflect ideas that had been developed in this way in the Synagogues of the Diaspora, where Greek influences were active.[1] These literary features suggest that the author thought in the Semitic vernacular, and his references to the Old Testament reveal a greater familiarity with the sacred text than it seems reasonable to expect from a Greek convert.[2] Dr. C. C. Torrey[3] says: "All the quotations in this Gospel are from the Hebrew . . . the quotations are all made from memory, and with the customary freedom of choice and arrangement ".

(c) It was inevitable that comparisons should be drawn between the works of Philo and the Johannine writings.[4] The brooding fulness of thought which fills the Fourth Gospel demands for its interpretation a constant sensitiveness, especially as to the deeper meanings which prompted the methods which are characteristic of the Alexandrian Jewish philosophy as represented by Philo. Moffatt[5] says that the differences between Philo and John only serve to bring out the latter's familiarity with the Philonic methods and materials. The most obvious resemblances are to be found in Philo's conception of the Logos as a mediator between the transcendent God and the material universe, and as the agent of divine activity in creation and revelation. These will be discussed more fully when we come to consider John's choice of the term Logos.[6]

Other points of contact may be found in John 1. 18, for Philo

---

[1] Cf. Strachan, *The Fourth Gospel*, p. 22.

[2] Schlatter argues that as the Evangelist was more at home with Hebrew than with Greek it is unlikely that he was influenced by Greek ideas (*Der Evangelist Johannes*, viii).

[3] *The Four Gospels : A New Translation*, p. 330. According to Dr. Torrey, the Fourth Gospel was written in Aramaic prior to the year A.D. 70, and " was carried out of Palestine by one of the Christian fugitives to be translated and put into circulation at a later day ".

[4] For the works of Philo see L. Cohn and P. Wendland, *Philonis Alex. opera quae supersunt*. The English translation, in the Loeb Classical Library, by Colson and Whitaker, takes account of the emendations suggested by Cohn and Wendland.

[5] *I.L.N.T.*, pp. 523 ff.   [6] See pp. 87 ff. below.

also protests against the idea of God being seen (*De Mut. Nom.* 2). The miracle of turning the water into wine (2. 2-11) finds a parallel in Philo's Melchizedek who ἀντὶ ὕδατος οἶνον προσφερέτω καὶ ποτιζέτω καὶ ἀκρατιζέτω ψυχάς (*Leg. Alleg.* 3. 26). The six water-pots from which the wine is drawn correspond to the Philonic principle that "six is the most productive of numbers" (ἑξάδι τῇ γονιμωτάτῃ, *De Decal.* 30). The unceasing activity of the Father in 5. 17 reflects Philo's assertion: παύεται γὰρ οὐδέποτε ποιῶν ὁ θεός (*Leg. Alleg.* 1. 3). The disciples' relation to Christ as friends rather than as slaves (15. 15) may be compared with Philo's comment on Genesis 18. 17: οὐχὶ δεσπότης ἢ κύριος· φίλον γὰρ τὸ σοφὸν θεῷ μᾶλλον ἢ δοῦλον (*De Sobr.* 55). We find other possible parallels as follows: 1. 5=*Q. in Gen.* 1. 3; 1. 9=*Quod Deus sit imm.* 6 and *De Mun. Op.* 7; 1. 16=*De Post. Cain.* 43; 1. 38= *Quod det. pot. ins. sol.* 8; 1. 50=*Q. in Gen.* 32; 1. 51=*De Somn.* 1. 22; 3. 14=*Leg. Alleg.* 2. 19; 3. 19=*Q. in Gen.* 2. 22; 4. 10=*Leg. Alleg.* 2. 21; 4. 42=*Quod Deus sit imm.* 34; 5. 32=*De Sacr. Ab. et Cain.* par. 28; 8. 12=*De Sapien.* 24; 11. 51=*De Const. Princ.* 8; 15. 2=*De Somn.* 2. 19; 19. 3=*In Flacc.* 6; 19. 31=*In Flacc.* 10.

These parallels are sufficient to show that there is enough agreement both in literary methods and religious speculation to suggest that the Fourth Evangelist was deeply influenced by the Philonic spirit, but whether he was directly aware of the works of Philo remains uncertain.

(*d*) In the time of the Ptolemies, Thoth, the god of Hermopolis, became very popular among certain groups of Alexandrians under the name of Hermes Trismegistos. These groups did not attempt to set up rival schools of philosophy. They were drawn together by a common desire to find "salvation" for themselves. They were earnest seekers after God, and only occasionally were they moved to write about their speculations. Examples of their writings are to be found in the literature known as the *Hermetica*. They consist of a number of Tractates by a series of unknown writers, attached to no definite locality, but presenting a common view of God, the world, and human nature under the name Hermes Trismegistos.[1]

---

[1] *E.R.E.*, article "Hermes Trismegistos", vi, p. 626.

B

Since the publication of the *Poimandres* in 1904 by Prof. Reitzenstein of Strasburg, and of the *Hermetica* in 1925 by Mr. Walter Scott, many scholars have noticed close parallels between these Tractates and the Fourth Gospel. Loisy,[1] for example, says: "The conception, religious and mystical, of our Logos is much more strictly and directly related to Egyptian theosophy, which, using on one side the assimilation of the Logos to Hermes in the Stoic preaching, and on the other identifying Hermes with the God Thoth, saw in Thoth-Hermes, not only the Logos organ of creation, but the mediator of the divine revelation and of regeneration for immortality, and worked, like our Gospel, with the mystic terms of 'truth', 'light', 'life'." Because of this apparent connexion between the Fourth Gospel and the ideas contained in the *Hermetica*, Loisy thinks that the Evangelist was "one converted from Paganism" and a "master of *gnosis* rather than an apostle of faith".[2]

The verbal parallels can be appreciated only in the original language, and the following examples may be quoted:

POIMANDRES	THE FOURTH GOSPEL
ὁ δὲ ἀγαπήσας τὸ ἐκ πλάνης ἔρωτος σῶμα, οὗτος μένει ἐν τῷ σκότει πλανώμενος, αἰσθητῶς πάσχων τὰ τοῦ θανάτου. (Par. 19; Scott, i. 124.)	καὶ ἠγάπησαν οἱ ἄνθρωποι μᾶλλον τὸ σκότος ἢ τὸ φῶς. (3. 19.) ἵνα πᾶς ὁ πιστεύων εἰς ἐμὲ ἐν τῇ σκοτίᾳ μὴ μείνῃ. (12. 46.)
ἅγιος ὁ θεὸς ὃς γνωσθῆναι βούλεται, καὶ γινώσκεται τοῖς ἰδίοις. (Par. 31; Scott, i. 130.)	εἰς τὰ ἴδια ἦλθε. (1. 11.) γινώσκω τὰ ἐμὰ καὶ γινώσκουσί με τὰ ἐμά. (10. 14.)
διὸ πιστεύω σοι καὶ μαρτυρῶ εἰς ζωὴν καὶ φῶς χωρῶ. εὐλογητὸς εἶ, πάτερ· ὁ σὸς ἄνθρωπος συναγιάζειν σοι βούλεται, καθὼς παρέδωκας αὐτῷ τὴν πᾶσαν ἐξουσίαν. (Par. 32; Scott, i. 132.)	μαρτυρῶ (*passim*). πάτερ, ἐλήλυθεν ἡ ὥρα· δόξασόν σου τὸν υἱόν, ἵνα ὁ υἱὸς δοξάσῃ σε, καθὼς ἔδωκας αὐτῷ ἐξουσίαν. (17. 1.)

[1] *Le Quatrième Évangile*, 2nd Ed., p. 89.
[2] Ibid., p. 66.

These verbal parallels may not be of great significance, but there are also to be found in this literature many ideas and terms which recall some of the leading conceptions of the Fourth Gospel. The ultimate essence of the universe is conceived as archetypal Light. From this proceeds Mind and Truth and all things. God may be defined as the creator of Mind and Truth: "Thou art Mind in that Thou thinkest, Father in that Thou createst, God in that Thou workest, and God as maker of all things" (*Corp. Herm.* 5. 11). God is represented as perpetual energy with the result that "there is nothing which is not in God, and nothing in which God is not" (*Corp. Herm.* 9. 9). From the Light comes forth the Logos who is designated Son of God. In a hymn of praise to God, Hermes sings: "Holy art Thou who by Logos hast constructed all things that are; Holy art Thou, of whom all nature is an image" (*Corp. Herm.* 1. 31). The writer asks, "from what womb can a man be born again?" (*Corp. Herm.* 12. 1), and he describes the reborn as a "Son of God".

Here then is a body of literature containing such Johannine phrases as "Life", "Light", "Logos", "Truth", and such typical Johannine doctrines as the never-ceasing energy of God, and rebirth. These phrases were apparently current coin among the people for whom John wrote. In the opinion of Miss M. R. Ely [1]: "The *Poimandres* represents the expression of a rather long development of religious speculation, whose origin was certainly pre-Christian, but whose literary expression is probably contemporaneous with early Christianity, and perhaps partly anterior to it". The literature, therefore, gives us a glimpse into one of the many workshops in which Christianity was fashioned. John may well have had these pure seekers after God in mind when he wrote, and some may have found in his unique message of the "Word made flesh" the fulfilment of their yearnings.

(e) Prof. Walter Bauer in his commentary *Das Johannes Evangelium* (1925), and Dr. Hugo Odeberg in the work already mentioned, have shown that there are many striking parallels between the Fourth Gospel and the Mandaean literature. The Mandaeans are the surviving representatives of a Gnostic move-

[1] *Knowledge of God in Johannine Thought*, p. 101.

ment of the second century. They possess a large collection of scriptures, the contents of which are of great antiquity. The largest and most interesting portion of these writings is liturgical and mythological in character. The myths relate to the origin and nature of the world, of the gods and of men. In the opinion of Dr. W. Brandt,[1] they cannot be dated earlier than the first century A.D. Amid a strange medley of Jewish, Chaldean, and Persian elements we find some typical Johannine phrases such as: "I am a word", "the light of Life", "the worlds do not know thy names, nor understand the Light".[2]

We may also compare the following: John 17. 21, "That the world may believe that thou hast sent me", with "The Sent of the Light am I, whom the Great One has sent into the World" (*Ginza, or Treasure House, Right*, 2. 64). John 17. 2, "Thou gavest him authority over all flesh", with "The Great One has . . . given authority to thee over everything" (*Ginza, R.*, 3. 73). John 8. 12, "I am the Light of the world: he that followeth me shall not walk in the darkness but shall have the light of life", with "Manda d'Hayye revealed himself to all the children of men and delivers them from darkness to light, from obscurity to the light of life" (*Ginza, R.*, 5. 3).

Prof. Bultmann,[3] in seeking an explanation for these parallels, traces them to the disciples of John the Baptist. The Mandaean texts give prominence to the River Jordan, the rite of Baptism, and John the Baptist. And it may be that the Mandaeans trace their origin to the disciples of the Baptist. These texts, therefore, according to Bultmann, incorporate the substance of the teaching of John the Baptist. Jesus was at first associated with this movement, but later broke away and formed a community of his own. The Fourth Gospel reproduces more faithfully than the Synoptic Gospels this gnostic element in the teaching of Jesus derived from the Baptist. A consequence of this theory is that Johannine Christianity is really older than the Synoptic tradition. The Jerusalem community represents a secondary development

---

[1] *E.R.E.*, viii, p. 386 a.
[2] Bauer, op. cit., pp. 8-31.
[3] See Carpenter, *The Johannine Writings*, pp. 288, 289.

produced by Judaizing reaction, probably due to Peter. It is doubtful whether the arguments in favour of the earlier presentation of Christianity contained in the Synoptic Gospels can be overcome by such slender evidence as this. Dr. W. Brandt [1] thinks that the theory that the Mandaeans were originally a Jewish or Judaeo-Christian sect is at variance with certain characteristics in their literature. After an examination of these characteristics he says: "The inevitable inference is that the Mandaeans had been throughout complete strangers to the religious traditions of the Jews". Prof. Lietzmann, after a careful study of the Mandaean liturgy, has come to the conclusion that the notices of John the Baptist belong to a later stage of the tradition and have no other basis than the canonical Gospels. There is nothing to connect the Mandaeans, he says, with conjectural followers of John the Baptist. He believes that the Mandaean Baptismal rite is actually derived from the Nestorians, even to the use of the word Jordan in the sense of Baptismal water. [2] We may conclude, therefore, that any parallels between the Mandaean literature and the phraseology of the Fourth Gospel are due to the influence of the Jewish and Christian beliefs on the later development of Mandaeism.

In regard to all these instances of parallelism between pagan literature and the Fourth Gospel there is no need to assert a dependence of one upon the other. Their relationship might be collateral in the sense that both might be independent products of the same psychological factors. The researches of anthropologists seem to show that man everywhere tends to satisfy the same instincts in the same way. Similar myths, rites, customs, tabus, have sprung up to all appearance independently in diverse lands in response to the same social or individual needs, and there is no need to postulate a "monophyletic" origin even for so wide and elaborate a system as totemism. The basic human need which Christianity and the pagan religions alike claimed to satisfy was the craving of the sick soul for "salvation". And as it is common to the religious mind to desire purity and strength,

[1] E.R.E., article "Mandaeans", viii, p. 386.
[2] See Church and Gnosis, by F. C. Burkitt, p. 114; cf. J.T.S., xxix, pp. 225 ff.

it was natural that the rites common to all should have taken the form of a cleansing bath and of a sacred meal. In regard to verbal parallelism, Bernard points out [1] a very close similarity between a passage in the *Timaeus* of Plato (92 *c*) and the Johannine doctrine of a υἱὸς μονογενής. As there can be no direct contact between the writings of Plato and the Fourth Gospel, Dr. Bernard says that it is thus highly precarious to build up community or similarity of doctrine upon coincidences of language between two writers.[2]

iv. *The Fourth Gospel and the Synoptics*

It should furthermore be observed that John is dominated neither by the literature of his day nor by the movements of his time. His mind is too great and original to direct his attention to the task of blending various tendencies with Christianity or refuting opposing ideas. A man of genius preserves his identity amid a welter of competing interests, motives, and ideals which surround him. Any references to current movements are always strictly subordinate to his main purpose. And the Fourth Gospel impresses one with its coherent and unified presentation; it does not reveal a mind of unreconciled and contending beliefs, but one which has attained mental, moral, and spiritual maturity.

Nevertheless it is necessary to know the atmosphere of thought and religion in which the Fourth Gospel was written. A presentation of Christianity emerging from Ephesus about A.D. 100 will not be conceived in the same vein as a record of traditions that were current in Jerusalem half a century earlier. It will lay emphasis upon aspects of truth previously hardly in sight. Its terms and its phrases will be influenced by the intellectual outlook, the current jargon, the religious controversies. The literature which we have been discussing reveals the beliefs and opinions of the non-Christian world in Ephesus at the time the Fourth Gospel was written. As Dr. Gardner remarks,[3] Ephesus

---

[1] *St. John*, p. cxli.

[2] Commenting on the use of the term μονογενής by Plato, Dr. A. E. Taylor remarks that "it is very hard not to suspect some, perhaps far-away, influence" in the use of the word by the Evangelist in the Prologue (*A Commentary on Plato's Timaeus*, p. 649).

[3] *The Ephesian Gospel*, p. 17.

was the preordained place for the writings of John. "His teaching fell on a soil rich alike with the learning of Jewish Hellenists, the wisdom of Greek philosophy, and the enthusiasm of Phrygian mystics." These conditions no doubt prompted the chief themes of the Fourth Gospel and influenced its vocabulary. The circumstances were very different from those in which the Synoptic Gospels were written, and it is this that causes the chief difference between the Fourth Gospel and the other three.

The proposition that the author of the Fourth Gospel was acquainted with at least those of Mark and Luke is so generally accepted that there is no need to argue it out here,[1] but we must estimate its significance for our presentation of the religious thought of John.

The real connexion of the Fourth Gospel with its predecessors lies not in vocabulary but in ideas, and should be tested not on stylistic grounds but on historical and doctrinal grounds. For example, at almost every point where the orbit of the Fourth Gospel coincides with that of the Synoptic tradition, the former can be shown to represent a more developed stage of Christian reflexion upon the facts. Sir Edwyn Hoskyns, in the illuminating discussion on the "Historical Tension of the Fourth Gospel" in his Commentary, draws attention to the way John draws isolated sayings in the Synoptic Gospels into the very centre of his theological scheme. An example of this may be given in the Markan saying: "I will destroy this Temple that is made with hands, and in three days I will build another." In the Fourth Gospel the Jews are made out to take this literally, but the readers of the Gospel and the disciples are meant to see a much deeper meaning in the saying, for "he spake of the temple of his body" (2. 21). Thus, "Far from merely providing an improbable and inadequate accusation, the Saying now utters a resounding challenge that confidently anticipates the supreme act by which Judaism will be superseded and the true worship of the Father

---

[1] See, e.g., Bacon, *The Fourth Gospel*, p. 366 ; Stanton, *The Gospels as Historical Documents*, iii, p. 214 ; Streeter, *The Four Gospels*, ch. xiv. Mr. Gardner-Smith, however, does not think that John had read any of the Synoptic Gospels ; see *St. John and the Synoptic Gospels*.

inaugurated, namely the resurrection of Jesus from the dead. The Saying has become inseparable from the major theme of the Gospel".[1] There are also examples of similar treatment of non-Markan material which has found its way into Matthew and Luke.

Nevertheless the day is over when the Fourth Gospel and the Synoptists could be played off against each other. The problem is too delicate and complex for such crude methods. Dr. Rawlinson has shown in his *New Testament Doctrine of Christ* that there was a "cult" of the Lord Jesus from the earliest days and that this is reflected in all the documents of the New Testament. Even in the most primitive assertion of Messiahship, the Person of Jesus is represented as possessing an absolute and final significance. The difference between the Fourth Gospel and the Synoptic Gospels arises from the fact that the circumstances in which they were written are different. They are addressed to different audiences living in a different intellectual atmosphere. John "sets out to interpret the Christian story and Christian experience to the new world of Hellenism by translating the Gospels into a form intelligible to Greek modes of thought".[2] In the Greek-speaking world in which John lived a new technique was required. The Messiah, which was the name under which Jesus had been preached to the Jews, was meaningless when the Gospel was carried from Palestine to the Gentile world. There is evidence that the Jews themselves appreciated this difficulty in proclaiming their faith. For some of the Rabbis substituted the term Logos for the Messiah in order to be "intellectually respectable in Gentile circles".[3]

At Ephesus this need for reinterpreting the Christian Gospel into the terms of Hellenistic culture would be obvious to every thinking Christian. The Evangelist had probably lived at

---

[1] *The Fourth Gospel*, p. 77.

[2] B. W. Bacon, *The Gospel of the Hellenists*, p. 112.

[3] W. L. Knox, *Some Hellenistic Elements in Primitive Christianity*, p. 41, n. 2. When, however, Dr. Knox says that the sole *raison d'être* for the use of the term Logos was to make Judaism intellectually respectable in Gentile circles, he underestimates the extent to which Greek philosophical terms had been assimilated by the Judaism of the Diaspora.

Ephesus for some considerable time and consequently imbibed much of the surrounding culture. We get a glimpse of the conditions under which Christian teachers must have worked at Ephesus in the passing reference in the Acts to the discussions which were held by St. Paul in the school of Tyrannus (Acts 19. 9). At this school such cultured people as the Alexandrian Apollos must have gathered for discussion.[1] St. Paul's Epistles to the Ephesians and the Colossians also indicate how much Christianity must have become permeated with the philosophic spirit of Hellenistic culture. The warnings against the dialectical subtleties of superficial *gnosis* are highly significant in view of the speculation that was rife at Ephesus. The population of Ephesus was made up of the most diverse elements. East and West met in the market-places and argued in the schools. In such a mixture of elements the Evangelist proclaimed the Christian Gospel. In view of this background "our Gospel can be understood only as the Evangelist's attempt to interpret the faith to the Church of his own day".[2]

v. *Characteristics of the Fourth Gospel*

The aim of the Gospel is accurately represented in John's own declaration: "Many other signs therefore did Jesus in the presence of his disciples, which are not written in this book: but these are written, that ye may believe that Jesus is the Christ, the Son of God; and that believing ye may have life in his name" (John 20. 30, 31). The Messianic title is here linked with another one; side by side we have the Jewish and Greek outlooks, the national and the universal. One bears witness to the organic connexion of Christianity with Judaism, the other indicates the liberation of Christianity from Jewish limitations. Thus we may see the process of transition written even on the professed purpose of the Gospel.

This valuation of Jesus' Person is particularly expressed in relation to the "signs" which he did. But it is not the signs only;

[1] La Piana's *Foreign Groups in Rome* (Harvard Theological Studies) gives a picture of similar groups at Rome.

[2] Macgregor, *The Gospel of John*, p. xxvi ; see also Scott, *The Fourth Gospel*, pp. 10, 11, and W. Manson, *The Incarnate Glory*, p. 37.

it is also his teaching which in the Fourth Gospel has a special reference to his Person.   There is a tendency to obliterate the features of surprise, ignorance, mistake, and disappointment. Everything is made to hinge upon the appreciation or rejection of Jesus, upon belief or disbelief in him, upon men's ability to see, or their blindness to, God's manifestation in him.   In contrast to the Synoptic account, Jesus is represented as frequently referring to himself in the first person singular. He says, "I am the bread of life" (6. 35, 48), "the light of the world" (8. 12), "the door of the sheep" (10. 7-9), "the good shepherd" (10. 11, 14), "the resurrection and the life" (11. 25), "the true vine" (15. 1, 5), "the way, the truth, the life" (14. 6).   In a similar manner he says, "I am from above . . . I am not of this world" (8. 23); "I am in the Father, and the Father in me" (14. 11); "Before Abraham was, I am" (8. 58).   E. Norden thinks that such self-proclamation is analogous to the way in which those who claimed that they were divine referred to themselves in Hellenistic circles.[1] Stauffer, however, after a thorough examination of the ego-style in ancient religions, contends that the idea that the ego-sayings in the Fourth Gospel are derived from Hellenistic sources cannot be substantiated.[2] It is possible, therefore, that the use of the first person singular was based upon the Old Testament title of Yahweh, "I am that I am" (Ex. 3. 14).   In the LXX this is rendered ἐγώ εἰμι ὁ ὤν.[3] It was certainly the intention of the Evangelist to emphasize the authority of Jesus. And the use of this title would have the effect not only of emphasizing the divine nature of his mission, but also of drawing attention to the central place he himself occupied in that mission.

This stress upon the Person of Jesus has led some to think that the author was a speculative mystic of the Alexandrian type. Miss Evelyn Underhill, for example, says [4]: "It is not even the memory of the disciple, even the beloved disciple whose reminiscences, if he be not a purely symbolic figure, may well have

[1] *Agnostos Theos*, pp. 177 ff. and 207 ff.
[2] *T.W.z.N.T.*, article " ἐγώ ", i, pp. 350-352.
[3] Cf. Rawlinson, *The New Testament Doctrine of Christ*, p. 208.
[4] *The Mystic Way*, pp. 229 and 234 ; cf. Inge, " The Theology of the Fourth Gospel ", in *Cambridge Biblical Essays*, p. 254.

coloured the Ephesian traditions after Jesus' death, but the vivid
first-hand knowledge, the immovable certitude of the mystic
'in union' with the Object of his adoration, which supplies
material for this unearthly picture of the earthly life of Jesus". In
Miss Underhill's opinion the temporal background of the historic
life receives the projection of the author's spiritual experiences.
"He selected, from the huge and quickly growing Christian
legend, those events which seemed to him like the types, the
dramatic representations, of the great wonders and changes
which had been wrought in his soul."

At first sight it does appear as though John were only interested in the moral effectiveness of the revelation made by
Jesus. Great emphasis is laid upon the subjective significance of
Christ's Person. But he contends just as emphatically for the
objective reality of the things narrated.[1] The comparison with
St. Paul is instructive in this connexion. For St. Paul, the
objective reality of the great dogmatic facts of Christ's life is of
essential importance. St. Paul, however, abstracts the dogmatic
element from the lively unity of its personal and ethical connexion. The death and resurrection of Christ are the indispensable basis of his dogmatic scheme. John, on the other hand,
looks upon the life of Jesus as a whole, finding in it the basis
of his dogmatic inference and in its subject the highest revelation. It is for this reason that he regards the Incarnation
as the central fact in his thought. It is not that John's emphasis
lay upon the Incarnation in a narrow sense, as a particular
moment in the life of Jesus, or as a separate dogma. "The word
was made flesh" (1. 14) is rather an expression for the total
manifestation of Christ. It denotes both the dogmatic fact and
the significance of Christ as the revealer of God (1. 18). This
characteristic of John runs throughout his presentation and has
led to the erroneous opinion that the death, the resurrection, and
the ascension of Christ have no dogmatic importance in the
Fourth Gospel.

---

[1] Kundsin, in *Topologische Ueberlieferungsstaffe im Johannes Evangelium*, regards the
topographical details in John as far more accurate than those in Mark. He regards
the Gospel as the first witness to the stream of tradition found in Pilgrim-literature.

John's treatment of the "works" of Jesus throws light on this characteristic. The miraculous works are shown to be "signs" not only by this name but by his constant representation of them as expressions of Christ's mission. As wonders, they prove that his mission is from God (3. 2), and, as symbols, they reveal the character of his mission (6. 2). In the first point of view it is the greatness of the miracle which is significant (5. 20); in the second it is its kind (10. 32). The resurrection of Lazarus owes its importance not merely to its character as a wonder, but also because it manifests Jesus as the Resurrection and the Life. As signs Jesus' works are practically words; but it must not be overlooked that work and word are constantly contrasted; that each is in a certain sense the supplement of the other, each being in its own special way a ground of faith. A mere talking Christ does not help the world; the Son therefore manifests himself (and the Father) as a worker (5. 17). The works have for John a special importance in that they reveal the will and the might to perform what is promised in the word. It is not the speech but the deed of Christ which is the ground of faith (10. 37). It is not true, therefore, to say that the "historical element is a mere setting similar to that which we find in the Hermetic writings and in the Platonic dialogues".[1] The historical details are an essential part of the message of Christ. The works of Christ have at one and the same time the significance of a deed done in all objective actuality, and of a revelation whose importance lies in its subjective appreciation. "The non-historical factor penetrates our supposed historical data, and the historical factor is woven into what is manifestly non-historical."[2]

It is probably true that the Evangelist has selected some of his material because of its symbolical significance. For example, the feeding of the five thousand leads to the discourse on the Bread of Life, the healing of the blind man presents Jesus as the Light of the World, the raising of Lazarus teaches that Jesus is the Resurrection and the Life, the coming out of water and blood from his side symbolizes that not only the ministry of Jesus saves,

---

[1] Knox, Some Hell. Elements in Prim. Christianity, p. 61.
[2] Hoskyns, The Fourth Gospel, p. 120.

but also his death. The attempt, however, to carry through allegory in every detail leads to some strange results.[1] It is better to accept the historical accuracy of the many lifelike touches in the Fourth Gospel, unless there are cogent reasons to the contrary.

The fact that the references to Baptism and the Holy Communion are recorded in complete detachment from the practice or institution of either has led to a similar emphasis upon the subjective element in the Fourth Gospel.[2] Commenting on the discourse in the sixth chapter, Bernard cites Lightfoot as saying: "Faith is the flesh, the substance of the Christian life; love is the blood, the energy coursing through the veins and arteries".[3]

cc
see
p 27

But John's insistence upon the fact that "the Word was made flesh" should make us hesitate before adopting the idea that John thought little of the external character of the Sacraments. What he does is to guard against any isolation of God's activity in the world. The Word of God is active and present everywhere. The Sacraments represent and focus a principle at work far beyond themselves, and it is this wider truth that John would have us learn.[4] In the hard saying (6. 52-59) we are compelled to recognize a reference to the Sacrament of the Lord's Supper, and, after every attempt to rationalize it in terms of revelation and spiritual communion, there remains a residuum of absolutely objective character, or else Christ was needlessly offensive to his disciples.[5]

John's doctrine, therefore, cannot be evaporated into a mere subjective system of revelation, faith, knowledge, and life. The real and objective importance of Christ's descent from heaven (6. 38), his death (6. 51), and his ascension (6. 62), is not nullified because they are at the same time vehicles of revelation. It is a characteristic of John's thought that while grasping the material fact he finds in it a deep spiritual import. He is truly sacramental

[1] For examples see E. A. Abbott's article "Gospels" in the *Ency. Bib.*

[2] It should be noted that the omission of the Institution of the Holy Communion in the Fourth Gospel is in common with the original texts of all the Gospels.

[3] *St. John*, p. clxxv.

[4] Cf. Westcott, *The Gospel of St. John*, pp. 112 ff.

[5] According to Dr. Odeberg, the offence is that Jesus declares himself to be the Bread from Heaven and has nothing to do with the eating and drinking (*The Fourth Gospel* etc., pp. 267 ff.).

in outlook. In the words of Baron von Hügel [1]: "The Church and the Sacraments, still predominantly implicit in the Synoptists, and the subjects of the costly conflict and organization in the Pauline writings, here underlie as already fully operative facts, practically the entire profound work". This judgement is important, for in the opinion of von Hügel the method and form of the Fourth Gospel "are pervadingly allegorical; its instincts and aim are profoundly mystical".[2]

A further characteristic of John's thought is that it is profoundly contemplative and intuitional. Nothing can be further from the truth than to call him speculative. He never speculates: he sees.[3] He sees a drama: the conflict of the powers of light with the darkness, and their final victory; and he simply writes what he sees. He sees the earthly manifestation of the Son of God; and he pictures it in the Gospel:

> To me that story — ay, that life and death,
> Of which I wrote "it was", — to me it is;
> — Is, here and now; I apprehend nought else.

He sees in Jesus the light of the glory of God, and in the full inspiration of that sight he imparts, in his Epistle, the practical significance, the moral result, of that manifested life. Logical analysis, dialectical method in general, was quite foreign to John. His thought moves in the sphere of a few profound facts whose significance he develops by contrast. The antithetical method of expression so characteristic of his writings is based upon the parallelism of Hebrew literature. What appear at first sight to be disconnected antitheses contain a real progression of thought.[4]

---

[1] *Essays and Addresses*, i, p. 84.

[2] *Ency. Brit.*, Ed. 11, xv, p. 455.

[3] Cf. ὃ ἑωράκαμεν . . . ὃ ἐθεασάμεθα in 1 John 1. 1, where the distinction is either (*a*) as between the external sight of miracles and the spiritual beholding of the glory of Christ, or (*b*) as between the sight which has simply knowledge for its result and that fuller and more entranced gaze that rejoices in the object contemplated. He who contemplates is sufficiently struck to stop and gaze. See also John 6. 36-40 where " beholdeth " in verse 40 is an intentional advance upon " having seen " of verse 36. See also Abbott, *Johannine Vocabulary*, pp. 110, 111. Bultmann observes that θεωρία is the characteristic element in the Greek idea of knowledge. The Greek observes (θεωρεῖ) the object of knowledge from a distance and endeavours to ascertain its essential qualities (*T.W.z.N.T.*, article "Γινώσκω", i, p. 691).

[4] John 3. 17-18; 4. 20-21; 7. 37-38; and 1 John 1. 6-7; 5. 18-19; 2. 4, 5, 6.

But antithesis is for John far more than a literary form. It is the expression of his deepest thought. He sees everything in its essential character and in fundamental contrast. The contrast between God and all that is not of God he names according to its different aspects; light and darkness, life and death, love and hate. The Logos is no gnostic mediator in this contrast.[1] He was manifested to destroy the works of darkness; the darkness is to be abolished and is already passing away before the shining of the true light.

In spite of the fact that John sees things in their fundamental contrast as light and darkness, he does distinguish different stages of development. He sees in the germ the promise of the full fruit. Eternal life is actually possessed by the believer now, though its full fruition is to be expected in the hereafter. Appreciation of Christ's Person is called faith in every stage, from the lowest to the highest, and at every stage it works eternal life. We have even now a true knowledge of God though we shall be perfectly like him only "when we see him as he is".

The dominant characteristics of John's thought are therefore the principle of contrast which is expressed by light and darkness and the whole series of related antitheses; the intuitive faculty which represents stages of development pictorially, dramatically, and in terms of vision, rather than argumentatively and logically; the blending of subjective and objective, spiritual and historical, without denying the real importance of either; the colouring of Jewish and Greek thought which determines the conception of God and of the world and the specific content of salvation in a new relation to God within the community of the chosen brotherhood, the New Israel. It will be our purpose in the following pages to bring out and to illustrate these characteristics of the religious thought of John.

[1] The fifth chapter is especially adapted to reject the erroneous idea of a δεύτερος θεός.

2

GOD

i. *God is Light*

John justifies the name Theologian. For, although the Gospel is a history of the Life of Jesus and the Epistle is concerned with the problems of Christian brotherhood, his teaching is essentially a theology. The history he records is in every detail the revelation of God, and his ethics are resolved into the imitation of God. If there is any ethical question to solve, he finds his answer in the nature of God. He judges every practical problem before the judgement throne of God. If there is a lack of harmony among the brethren, he looks into the face of God as revealed in Jesus and he knows that "he that loveth not knoweth not God, for God is love". If any Christian is tempted to sin, the rebuke comes with a directness and absoluteness which is inconceivable except from this point of view: "He that sinneth hath not known God". The exalted conception of Christ's Person which is characteristic of the Fourth Gospel is set in its right place by his profession of Christ as being one with the Father (10. 30). The significance of Jesus depends upon his relation with God. The supreme demand which Jesus made of his disciples was that they might believe that "I am in the Father, and the Father in me; he that hath seen me hath seen the Father" (14. 9-10).

It is noticeable that it is this Gospel, which expresses most clearly the union of Christ with the Father, that is most emphatic in the subordination of the Son as son. The assertion that "the Father is greater than I" is not an anomaly; it is an essential fact in the self-witness of Jesus.[1] The Evangelist is concerned less

[1] This phrase has been explained mainly in two ways: (*a*) The eminence of the Father lies in the fact that the Son has the divine essence by communication. (*b*) That the eminence of the Father lies in his relation to the Son as Incarnate and not yet glorified. For explanations given by the early Fathers see Westcott, *St. John*, additional note to 14. 28.

with the relation between Father and Son than with the relation between Father and Son and the disciples. The witness of Jesus is to the Father, and to himself only as the Way to the Father. Through faith in Jesus the believer has access to the Father. Since, therefore, the Father is always regarded as the ultimate good, he is greater than the Son.[1] In accordance with this, Jesus himself testifies to the derivation of all his power from the Father. It is the Father who sent him (12. 49; 6. 39; 8. 16); his life and death are in accordance with the purpose of God (15. 10; 10. 18); he came not to do his own will but the Father's (5. 30); his works are the Father's and done in his name (10. 25, 37); he speaks only what he has seen (8. 38), heard (15. 15), and learnt (8. 28) from the Father; his very life is derived from the Father (5. 26; 6. 57); and his position in the world is characterized by this: "I am come in my Father's name" (5. 43).

It is clear, therefore, that God is the centre of John's thought. There is no intention of instituting a separate cult of Jesus. We are thus led up to the proclamation of the Good News in Christ by a single proposition about God: "God is light, and in him is no darkness at all" (1 John 1. 5). The importance which John attaches to this utterance is shown both by its immediate introduction: "This is the message which we have received from him and announce to you", and also by the position which it occupies at the beginning of the Epistle.[2] The introductory verses make it plain that the message which he here summarizes is the epitome of his whole knowledge about God in Christ. The central position occupied by God in Johannine thought is here demonstrated by the fact that the saving revelation of Christ finds its highest and most exclusive expression in a proposition, not about man, but about the character of God. It is eminently characteristic of the author's symbolic use of language that he is able to pack the whole Gospel message into one sentence. The very richness of his

---

[1] Hoskyns points out that in the Fourth Gospel the phrase " greater than " means of greater power and authority (*The Fourth Gospel*, ii, pp. 546 f.).

[2] ἀπαγγέλλομεν. The preposition here has the sense of increasing and strengthening as well as repetition. It is always used of solemn teaching with a character of authority about it. In the LXX it is almost a sacerdotal word (Deut. 24. 8; Is. 52. 15). See also Schniewind in *T.W.z.N.T.*, i, pp. 64, 65.

C

symbolism prevents us from being satisfied with a simple explanation of his use of the term "light" as descriptive of the character
of God.[1]

It is to be noticed that, in the Gospel, light is used as a description of the Logos rather than an attribute of God. It may
be that the Evangelist was unwilling to define God by a term
which was a characteristic of the current religious philosophy,
whereas the author of the Epistle was less guarded.[2] But in
general it may be said that, in the Gospel, Christ is usually represented as the connecting link between God and the world,
whereas in the Epistle the direct relation between the Father
and the brethren is more prominent. This is mainly a matter of
emphasis. In the Gospel the direct relation of the Father with
the disciples is to be found, for example, in 16. 27, "the Father
himself loveth you". On the other hand, in the Epistle fellowship
with the Father is conceived as realized in and through Christ:
"Our fellowship is with the Father, and with his Son Jesus
Christ". The difference is probably because the Gospel is chiefly
concerned about who and what Christ is, whereas the Epistle
was written to assure the brethren of their fellowship with God
in his Son Jesus Christ. It was natural, therefore, that he should
describe the Father as light in the Epistle. No fundamental
difference is implied.

The commonest use of the word light is also the simplest and
most obvious. When Jesus says, "I am the light of the world"
(8. 12; 9. 5), the term is apparently used with the same simplicity
as in Matthew 5. 14, "Ye are the light of the world", denoting
the pervading moral worth of pure influence, it being the attribute
of light that it shines and gives light to all that are in the house.
This simple application of the figure in the sense of moral revelation is still clearer in 12. 35, 36: "Yet a little while is the light
among you. Walk while ye have the light, that the darkness

---

[1] In the words of Godet : " This profound term designates perfect moral goodness,
combined with blissful consciousness of his sanctity, in the sphere of the highest life,
where luminous clearness of the Divine wisdom also rules as opposed to the world ".

[2] See Dodd, *The Johannine Epistles*, p. 19. In view of the Evangelist's adoption of
the term " Logos " it is unlikely that he would hesitate to use the term " light " of
God for this reason.

overtake you not; and he that walketh in darkness knoweth not whither he goeth". The most obvious use of it in this sense is in 3. 20, 21: "For every one that doeth ill hateth the light, and cometh not to the light, lest his works should be reproved. But he that doeth the truth cometh to the light, that his works may be manifest, that they have been wrought in God". In John 13. 30 Judas is represented as passing from the light of the world into the outer darkness, "and it was night".[1]

It is evident, however, that this simple definition falls short of the many uses of the term by John. In the passage just quoted the terms "light" and "darkness" acquire a purely ethical significance as the spheres, or even the principles, of good and evil. In this sense St. Paul uses them (Ephes. 5. 8, 9; 2 Cor. 6. 14). And that this is an element in John's use of the term is suggested by his use of darkness in an active sense and as a positive concept (1. 5; 12. 35; cf. 1 John 2. 11). In this sense light denotes a state of undisturbed happiness and of salvation, just as darkness means a state of perdition. As an extension to this meaning John uses light as a condition not only of happiness (5. 35) but of life itself (8. 12). The term thus assumes a more positive content: light works a change in objects as well as reveals their character.

Even so, we do not exhaust the meaning which John gives to the word light. The phrase, "God is light" (1 John 1. 5), means something more than that God is very clear and intelligible, or that self-revelation is his very nature. John's use of the word is so emphatic that it seems reasonable to interpret all other uses of the term by means of this. It seems that all that John found in Jesus as the revelation of God should be included in this term. For, regarding light primarily in its simplest form as that which reveals, and also having in mind that Christ is the manifestation of the light (1. 12), John could not fail to think also of the content of the revelation: holiness, power, justice, love. The term may, therefore, be extended to mean the inherent quality of God. Although this whole store of ideas may not be immediately

---

[1] Cf. Origen's comment on this verse. He says we must regard the visible "night" as a symbolic one, suggesting "that the night which came in the soul of Judas was the darkness which moves upon the face of the deep, namely Satan entered into him" (Lommatzsch's ed. of the *Works of Origen*, ii, p. 460).

apparent in the term light itself, it is a word with which the whole
sum of the Gospel and the essential nature of God can be
associated.   The message is one of good tidings, one of joy and
life, one in which there "is no darkness at all" (1 John 1. 5).
And it was natural to speak of light as the element in which God
lives, and of darkness as the element in which the world lives.
It is furthermore characteristic of John to express so much in
little; and so far from being a solitary use of the term as a description of God, it is rather the climax of his whole thought about
God, and we must read back, even into the simplest uses of the
term, something of the pregnancy of this summary of theology
that "God is light".

ii. *God as Light in Contemporary Literature*

John would be aware that in the Hebrew Scriptures God had
been called the Light of the world (Dan. 2. 22) and that the
Psalmist had referred to him as "my light and my salvation"
(Ps. 27. 1).   Israel was also called the Light of the Nations
(Is. 42. 6).   In Rabbinic literature we find a development of this
Old Testament conception.   For example, Bar Quappara in
the second century A.D., commenting on Psalm 18, said: "The
Holy One said to men: thy lamp is in my hand to kindle the
perpetual lamp.   The Holy One said: if thou lightest my lamp,
I will light thine" (*Lev. R.* 31. 4).   Adam was specifically named
by the Rabbis as the "Lamp of the world" (*T.J. Sabbath* 2. 8).
Teachers of the Torah were also called "Lights of the world,
for the commandment is a lamp and the lamp is light" (*T.B.
Bab. Bath.* 4 *a*).   The phrase "I am the light of the world", from
the standpoint of the Rabbis, could only be uttered by God or
by the Torah.   Jesus' adoption of the title "the light of the
world" therefore corresponds to the Jewish designation of God
as the light of the world.   It was characteristic of later Jewish
writers to use the twin images of life and light to describe the
effects of obedience to the wisdom of God revealed in the Mosaic
law (1 Bar. 4. 1: 2 Bar. 59. 2; 77. 16: 4 Ezra 14. 20, 21).[1]   In

[1] For an analysis of the ideas connected with light in Jewish literature see Kohler
in *Jewish Ency.*, viii, p. 83.

the New Testament generally the two terms are transferred to describe not obedience to the Law but the Grace of God that had been made known in Jesus Christ (Matt. 4. 16; Luke 2. 32; Acts 3. 15; 2 Tim. 1. 10, etc.). In the Fourth Gospel the transference is complete: it is as Life of the world that Jesus raises Lazarus from the dead (11) and as Light of the world that he heals the man born blind (9).

Though Jewish thought and phrases are in the background, it is probable that John was also influenced in his choice of the term light as a description of God by the frequency with which the terms life and light appear in contemporary pagan religions. Bauer says that "there seems to have been a fixed formula by which the Deity introduced itself: I am the light".[1] In the *Poimandres* "God is the first light" (*Corp. Herm.* 1. 21). A boundless expanse of light is a symbol of God. The first Mind is "light and life". From the light comes forth the Logos (*Corp. Herm.* 1. 5, 6, 12, 21; 13. 9, 18). Hermes bids mankind to "rid yourselves of darkness, and lay hold of light". When Hermes realizes his own attainment of the abode of Truth, he says: "Wherefore I believe and bear witness that I enter into life and light" (*Corp. Herm.* 13. 7, 8, 9).

The Mandaeans in their liturgies and the *Book of John* have a similiar *gnosis* of life and light, though the particular phrase "I am the light of the world" does not occur. Of the many examples that might be quoted the following is typical: "This one is the light of life, which was revealed, and men of proved faith praised it. And Manda d'Hayye said to them: I am come in order to dwell with you and I shall establish you in the light of life. I have separated you from the nations and the generations, I will establish you in the love of Truth, and you shall be truthful ones before me in the light of the life" (*Ginza, R.*, 5. 2, 179, 22-27; cf. John 7. 28).

Philo also has some impressive parallels with Johannine thought on this matter. He writes: "First God is light . . . and he is not only light, but the archetype of every other light, nay, more ancient and higher than every archetype. For the pattern

[1] *Das Evangelium Johannes*, p. 116.

was the Logos which contained all his fulness—light, in fact; for as the Law-giver says, God said, 'Let light come into being', whereas he himself resembles none of the things which have come into being" (*De Somn.* 1. 75). This association of the light with the Logos is striking, but Philo does not appear to bring light into conjunction with life in the same manner as the Hermetic and Mandaean literature. It is the opinion of Dr. Julius Grill, who has made a special study of the Fourth Gospel in relation to Philo, that "one cannot for a moment maintain that these two ideas have a specific role assigned to them in the Philonic doctrine of the Logos, and that they have become fundamental notions and catchwords, in the same way as in the Fourth Gospel".[1]

iii. *The True God*

John, like the other writers in the Bible, had no interest in the proposition that "God is" as opposed to the proposition that "God is not". But he laid great emphasis upon the fact that God is the source of all existence. He probably included this idea in the conception of God as light, as the positive reality opposed to negative darkness. But he had in the word true, with the substantive and adverb, truth and truly (ἀληθής, ἀληθινός, ἀλήθεια, ἀληθῶς), a more definite expression for it. As Bultmann says: " ἀληθινός is used as an attribute of God in the sense of actual, real in contrast to the nothingness of the heathen gods, and this meaning is determined by '*emĕth*".[2] The description of God as "the true" should, therefore, be interpreted to include the idea of God as the ground of the confidence of faith, though Dr. W. F. Howard thinks that John was influenced more by the Hellenistic connotation of the word.[3]

The common connotation of the words "true" and "truth" is, like the root meaning of the corresponding Greek words, a relative idea; it denotes the correspondence of an object with its idea, or of an idea with its expressed reality. On the other

---

[1] *Untersuchungen über die Entstehung des vierten Evangeliums*, i, pp. 225 f.
[2] *T.W.z.N.T.*, i, p. 250.
[3] *Christianity according to St. John*, p. 184 ; cf. Strachan, *The Fourth Gospel*, pp. 141-143, and Dodd, *The Bible and the Greeks*, pp. 65 ff.

hand, the root words in Hebrew thought (*'ōmen*, *'emĕth*) are similar
to the root meaning of our English words. As "true" and "truth"
are akin to troth and trust, so in the Hebrew the words express
faithfulness, reliability, and even faith itself.[1] The Greek words
have an intellectual cast, they have to do with ideas and their relation to facts; the Hebrew words deal primarily with persons and
things, and they describe them as realities which may be leaned
upon and trusted.[2] The Hebrew use of the words has influenced
John's use of the corresponding Greek words. The Hebrew
meaning is superadded to the Greek, though the words do not
thereby lose altogether their intellectual connotation. These
two meanings appear in John's use of the two adjectives ἀληθής
and ἀληθινός. The former abides more closely to the idea of
the true as distinct from that which is mendacious; it remains
a relative idea demanding another subject in regard to
which the person is true. The latter describes the subject in
question in its absolute nature, and thereby describes the object
in its essential character. The contrast which defines ἀληθής is
generally that between veracity and falsehood; while that
suggested by ἀληθινός is between essential reality and deceptive
appearance.[3]

Bultmann observes an important development in the meaning
of ἀληθινός which affects our interpretation of the Johannine use
of the word. He says that "in Hellenistic Greek ἀληθινός means
'genuine' no longer in the general sense, but means an attribute
of divine objects, the only really being, the Eternal".[4] He
therefore discerns a certain ambiguity in the Johannine use of
ἀληθινός, due to the fact that both meanings are implied by the
Greek word. He says: "If the purely formal meaning of
'genuine' (*echt*) still appears in John 4. 23 (οἱ ἀληθινοὶ προσκυνηταί),
it is nevertheless already referring to the fact that such genuine
worshippers are such because of their association with God. In the

---

[1] See Abbott, *Johannine Vocabulary*, p. 22, par. 1469, and Quell, *T.W.z.N.T.*, i,
p. 234.
[2] True men—Gen. 42. 11 ; true words—2 Sam. 7. 28 ; true God—2 Chron. 15. 3.
[3] Cf. Schlatter, *Der Evangelist Johannes*, p. 14: "ἀληθινός means in John whatever is
real and genuine as opposed to whatever is a deceitful show and a pretentious claim ".
[4] *T.W.z.N.T.*, i, p. 250.

word pictures in which Jesus is represented as φῶς ἀληθινόν (1. 9)
and as the ἄμπελος ἀληθινή (15. 1), ἀληθινός has chiefly the sense of
real or genuine (*wirklich=echt*), but this 'genuine' means at the
same time *divine* in contrast to *earthly* reality".[1] When Jesus,
therefore, claims to be the true light and the true vine, the word
used by John would suggest to his readers that he was able to
claim these titles for himself because he possessed *divine* reality.
Such a suggestion would be entirely in harmony with Jesus' claim
to possess a unique fellowship with the Father and the witness of
John that "the Word was God".

It is with this in mind that we approach the expression "full
of grace and truth" in 1. 14. Its place in the Prologue, and the
way in which John uses it to show the contrast between Christ's
manifestation and the Old Testament revelation, show that he
placed great emphasis upon this phrase. It is significant also
as the only instance of the phrase in the New Testament for the
Hebrew formula "loving kindness and truth", so often used of
God's revelation of himself (*hĕsĕd we mĕth*: Ex. 34. 6; 2 Sam. 2. 6;
Ps. 25. 10; 9. 10; 86. 15; 115. 1; 138. 2). This pair of ideas
appears in the Synoptists in the form "mercy and truth", as the
qualities to be exercised by men. But John finds in "grace and
truth" precisely the Hebrew idea of the qualities displayed by
God.

In Exodus 34. 6 God reveals his name as full of mercy and
truth. In the Prologue of the Fourth Gospel this solemn designation is transferred to the Logos. It is there used as an expression
of the glory of Jesus as the only begotten from the Father. The
ancient Law was but an imperfect revelation of God because it
represented him only in terms of such injunctions as could be
practically enforced in the society of that day; whereas the more
perfect revelation which was in old time merely "proclaimed"
was first "beheld" in the Word made flesh. That which is God's
peculiar character and glory is also Jesus' possession. Jesus
himself is therefore "the truth" (14. 6), because the sum of the
qualities hidden in God is revealed in him. He reveals God as
the true in the sense of the faithful and absolutely real. Further-

---

[1] *T.W.z.N.T.*, i, p. 251.

more, it is in harmony with this Hebrew conception that the truth does not come into being through perception, but exists in perfect completeness above and apart from any intellectual appreciation by men. Only within the world can there be ascribed to it a "becoming" (ἐγένετο).

Just as life and light are a unit and belong peculiarly to God, so John regards the truth as an undivided unity; God is the only true (17. 3). Truth, however, can be known (1 John 5. 20); God's word is truth (17. 17); and so, like light, it represents God's nature in terms of an active force and in relation to his rational creation.[1] It is in this connexion that the spirit and the truth are brought into relation (4. 23). The Spirit is the Spirit of the truth (14. 17; 15. 26; 16. 13); "the Spirit is the truth" (1 John 5. 7).[2] In this connexion, too, truth and life are brought together (1 John 5. 20), and in their union constitute the way to God (14. 6).[3]

As God is the "only true", John sees that all things in the world have reality in the deepest sense only as they partake of it from God. As Bultmann says, ἀληθινός is an attribute of God indicating divine reality in contrast to earthly reality.[4] Hence John speaks of "the true light" (1. 9; 1 John 2. 8); "the true bread" (6. 32); "the true food" and "drink" (6. 35); "the true vine" (15. 1). John speaks of that which is "truly love" (1 John 2. 5; 3. 18) as distinct from love that is merely pretence, and of the "true worshippers" (4. 23) and of being "truly disciples" (8. 31). The opposite of truth is a lie, which indicates not merely conscious deception, but mere appearance, and empty symbol. As the truth belongs to God, so the lie characterizes Satan (8. 44), and he who in his inmost being is dependent upon him has him for "father". The truth, as being God's nature, is the root of all worthy existence; a man may be

---

[1] Life is frequently associated with truth in non-Christian literature. See, e.g., the passage from Mandaean literature quoted above on p. 37 and the following passages in Philo : *Quod deus sit immut.* 96 ; *Leg. Alleg.* 3. 45 ; *De Jos.* 68 ; *De Fug. et Inv.* 139.

[2] The article should be preserved in translating these passages.

[3] The source of this great utterance is probably Jer. 10. 10.

[4] See above, p. 39.

"of the truth" (18. 37 ; 3. 19) as he may be "of God"; and both conceptions coincide in 18. 37 and 8. 47.

We see, therefore, that when John describes God as the true he thinks of him not only as veracious and faithful, but as the essential reality. He describes him not only as the true God in contradistinction to "idols", but as the "alone true", in contrast to the nothingness of the heathen gods and emptiness of every other claim to divinity. This knowledge enables us to appreciate the solemnity of the final utterance of the Epistle, in which John expresses the absolute confidence of his faith: "And we know that the Son of God is come, and hath given us an understanding, that we know the True, and are in the True, in his Son Jesus Christ; this is the true God and eternal life".[1] In the words of Dr. A. E. Brooke[2]: "The God who completely fulfils the highest conceptions of Godhead is the God who has been revealed in Jesus Christ, as contrasted with all false conceptions of God, against which the readers are warned in the next verse"—"My little children, guard yourself from idols." Even the Greek word εἴδωλα conveys the suggestion of unreality and was used in the LXX of the images of the heathen, the counterfeit gods, in contrast to the one real God. No doubt John is here thinking of "all false or counterfeit notions of God such as lead to the perversion of religion against which he has written".[3]

iv. *The Father*

That John thought of God as "personal" is a sure deduction from the Hebrew cast of his thought; but it is also determined by the fact that God revealed himself in a person, Jesus Christ. Therefore, in spite of all the use he made of such abstract terms as light and truth, terms which may have been determined by contemporary religion, and which may equally describe an impersonal deity, his favourite name for God is "the Father".

John does not use the word "create" ($\pi o\iota\epsilon\hat{\iota}\nu$) in the Prologue; but ἐγένετο has practically that meaning in 1. 3; and we might almost say that this verse—"without him", i.e. the Logos, "was

---

[1] Moffatt in his translation of the N.T. renders τὸν ἀληθινόν by "the Real God".
[2] *The Johannine Epistles*, p. 152.
[3] Dodd, *The Johannine Epistles*, p. 141.

not anything made"—is expressly formulated to leave room for the superior activity of God. The close parallel, which we shall later study,[1] between the Prologue and the first chapter of Genesis, puts it beyond doubt that John thought of God as Creator; but he goes beyond Genesis in thinking of creation as a continuous process (5. 17).[2] In Rabbinic speculation on the continual activity of God discussion was limited to the concomitant idea of the Divine Sabbath rest from the work of creation. For example, in *Mekhilta*, 37 *b*: "In six days the Lord made heaven and earth, and on the seventh day he rested and was refreshed (Ex. 31. 17). From what did he rest? From his work of creation or from judgement? The scripture says 'and was refreshed', teaching that judgement does not cease before him for ever. And in the same sense it says (Ps. 89. 14): 'Justice and judgement are the habitation of Thy throne! mercy and truth shall go before Thy face', and it says (Deut. 32. 4): 'the Rock, his work is perfect for all his ways are judgement'".

Because of this continued activity in judgement as set forth in Rabbinic literature, Dr. Odeberg is convinced that 5. 17 is based on the same Jewish notion. It signifies, he says, that Jesus stands in the same relation to the Sabbath as God and is continually active in the same work as his Father, namely that of Judgement.[3] This interpretation suits the context, in which Jesus is described as being engaged upon the divine work of conferring life and executing judgement, and is in harmony with John's slight interest in the physical world as such.

A distinction is to be observed between God as Father in a real sense (ὁ γεννήσας) and as Father in an ethical sense. The doctrine that God is the Father of all men in virtue of their material creation is not a Biblical idea at all.[4] There is only one passage in the whole of the New Testament which can be claimed to support the idea. This is the passage in the Acts when St. Paul at the Areopagus quoted from "certain of your poets",

---

[1] Pp. 113 ff.

[2] Cf. Strachan, *The Fourth Gospel*, pp. 168 ff.

[3] *The Fourth Gospel* etc., p. 202.

[4] πατήρ is occasionally used in the more general sense of Creator—Jas. 1. 17; Heb. 12. 9.

"For we are also his offspring" (Acts 17. 28). And even this probably means no more than "made in the image of God".[1] It is in fact a pagan idea, and is to be distinguished from the Christian idea chiefly because it is not capable of the same depth of meaning which we find attached to God's Fatherhood in the New Testament, and especially in the Fourth Gospel.

v. Ideas of New Birth

While, therefore, John does not follow contemporary thought in thinking that God's children are his offspring in the carnal sense, he has points of contact with Greek and Jewish thought in his teaching on the "new birth". The important passage in this connexion is 3. 5 ff. : "Except a man be born of water and the Spirit, he cannot enter into the kingdom of God". We shall discuss later the question whether this passage refers to Baptism[2]; at the moment we are concerned with the nature of the new birth. The context suggests that there is a contrast to be seen between the two worlds of the spirit and the flesh in accordance with the contrast between τὰ ἐπουράνια and τὰ ἐπίγεια. Thus the expression ἐξ ὕδατος καὶ πνεύματος should be put in contrast with εἰς τὴν κοιλίαν τῆς μητρὸς αὐτοῦ δεύτερον εἰσελθεῖν καὶ γεννηθῆναι. Upon this supposition it may be argued that ἐξ ὕδατος καὶ πνεύματος means primarily ἐκ σπέρματος πνευματικοῦ in contrast to earthly seed. The expression thus means that the spiritual man or members of the Kingdom of God owe their existence as such to the procreative power of God symbolized by the sacrament of Baptism.[3] It follows that such a new birth involves much more than just a moral change in a man : just as one must be born as a physical organism in order to enter into the physical world, so one must be born as a spiritual organism in order to enter into the divine world. This involves also a new standard of values,

[1] See Rackham, *The Acts of the Apostles*, p. 317 ; cf. Luke 11. 13, where the earthly father of children is parallel with the heavenly Father.

[2] Odeberg maintains that there is no reference here to Baptism, but to the procreative power of the Spirit (*The Fourth Gospel* etc., p. 48). But both Baptism and the procreative power of the Spirit are implied ; see further, pp. 188 ff.

[3] A symbol is that which partakes of the nature of the thing symbolized.

for the new realm entered is the realm of truth in contrast to falsehood, of light in contrast to darkness.[1]

Such teaching would not be strange to the first readers of the Gospel, for they would be familiar with the ideas of παλιγγενεσία of the Hermetic literature.[2] To become divine was the object of the Hermetic mysteries, and passages in the *Corpus Hermeticum* throw valuable light on the ideas current in John's time. For example, it is asserted that "no one can be saved until he be born again" (*Corp. Herm.* 13. 1). In the experience of rebirth the soul is bathed in a spiritual laver; and a heavenly messenger cries: "Wash yourselves in this laver if ye can, believing that ye shall ascend to him from whom it came" (*Corp. Herm.* 4. 4). In *Tractate* 13, which bears the title Λόγος ἀπόκρυφος περὶ παλιγγενεσίας, Hermes tells his son Tat that the world has been made by God with Reason, and man's function is to contemplate his works, and thus come to know his maker. To this end God filled a great bowl with Mind and sent it down to earth and bade a herald summon men to baptize themselves therein. As many as thus partook of the heavenly gift became immortal as the gods. In the discourse on rebirth Tat is puzzled to know from what womb a man may be born again and from what seed. The womb, he is told, is wisdom, the begetter is God, and the ministrant is some man who is a son of God. But rebirth cannot be taught; it can only be experienced. He to whom it is given feels within himself a form fashioned of immaterial substance; he passes out of himself into an immortal body. He who would be born again must cleanse himself of irrational torments of matter. Then the powers of God, truth, good, life, light, come and build up the body of reason. And at last Tat exclaims: "Father, God has made me a new being, and I perceive things now, not with bodily eyesight, but the working of mind.... I see myself to be the All. . . . I am present everywhere", and he breaks into a hymn of praise: "I have seen that which I seek; I

---

[1] Cf. Odeberg, *The Fourth Gospel* etc., pp. 48 ff. The use of ἄνωθεν in this passage suggests both the birth that is from above and the newness or completeness of the life that comes from God; see Schlatter, *Der Evangelist Johannes*, p. 87, and Büchsel, *T.W.z.N.T.*, i, p. 378.

[2] See Büchsel, *T.W.z.N.T.*, i, pp. 685 ff.

have found rest according to thy purpose; by thy will I am born again".[1]   In the opinion of W. Scott,[2] "the group of Hermetists to which the author of *Tractate* 13 belonged probably got this conception either from Christians, or from some pagan mystery-cult in which men were reborn by a sacramental operation".

In the *Metamorphoses* of Apuleius [3] we have a most exhaustive account of the Isiac initiation which gives us an insight into the ceremonies associated with rebirth in the mystery religions.   The candidate Lucius undergoes a bath and ceremonial lustration to prepare him for his enlistment in the service of the goddess.   After the baptism Lucius was clad in a mystic's robe and set on a dais beside the image of the goddess, revealed to the worshippers as divine, owing to his union with the goddess.   A three days' celebration of the initiate's new birth followed, and Lucius returned to Rome uttering a solemn thanksgiving.[4]   A striking parallel to Christian initiation is to be found in the *taurobolium* or *criobolium* which admitted men to the mysteries of Cybele and Attis; and sepulchral inscriptions have been found which testify to the belief that those who received this rite thereby become "eternally regenerate".[5]   The earliest date for such an inscription is, however, A.D. 376.   There cannot, therefore, be any connexion between this belief and the Christian conception.

In the Mithras Liturgy rebirth is brought about by the vision of the great god Helios.[6]   After the appearance of the great god the worshipper is bidden to "gaze upon god, and bellow long, and greet him thus: 'Hail, Lord, Master of the water; Hail, founder of earth; Hail, ruler of the Spirit.   Lord, born again am I, and so in my exaltation depart; and being exalted die.   Born in life-giving birth and dissolved in death, I go my way as thou

---

The above account is based on *Libellus*, 13 (Scott, i, pp. 239-255).   According to A. D. Nock in *Conversion*, p. 11, this Tractate describes "a curious sacrament of auto-suggestion".   Scott, *Hermetica*, ii, p. 373, gives an exhaustive list of periphrases for rebirth in the *Hermetica*.

[2] Scott, op. cit., ii, p. 374.

[3] *Metamorphoses*, 11. 23, in Loeb Classical Library, No. 44.

[4] W. L. Knox, in *Some Hell. Elements in Prim. Christianity*, p. 91, doubts whether this passage affords evidence for regeneration.

[5] See S. Angus, *The Mystery Religions and Christianity*, ch. 3.

[6] Printed in *The Vision of God*, by K. E. Kirk, p. 473.

hast ordained and as thou hast commanded and hast made
mystery'". It should be noticed that this account of rebirth is
found in a magic papyrus (*Par. Pap.* 574) which dates no earlier
than the beginning of the fourth century A.D., although it may
contain earlier material.

The metaphor of divine begetting is frequently found in
Philo. He equates γεννᾶν with ποιεῖν and applies it to the creation
of the Logos, of the world, and even of plants and animals. In
De Ebr. 30 he says: "The Architect who made this universe was
at the same time the father of what was thus born, whilst its
mother was the knowledge possessed by its maker. With this
knowledge God had union, not as men have it, and he begat
created being. And knowledge having received divine seed, when
her travail was consummated, bore the only beloved son, who is
apprehended by the senses, the world which we see". Other
relevant passages are as follows: *De Virtut.* 204; *De Confus. Ling.*
63; *De Cherub.* 43; *De Vit. Moys.* 1. 270; *De Mut. Nom.* 63;
Leg. Alleg. 2. 47; 3. 180; *De Migr. Abr.* 31, 35, 142; *De Post. Cain.*
135; *Quis rer. div. haer.* 62, 2000; *De Mund. Op.* 84; *De Somn.* 1.
181; *Quod deus sit imm.* 47; *De Spec. Leg.* 1. 329. But Philo
limits the metaphor of begetting to God's creative activity or his
endowment of men with spiritual, ethical, and religious gifts. In
his use of παλιγγενεσία he restricts himself to the cosmological
sense, and he does not conceive of God begetting man anew, but
only something in man.

Possible parallels are also to be found in Rabbinic references
to Greek proselytes who have accepted Judaism. For example:
"A man's father only brought him into this world; his teacher,
who taught him wisdom, brings him into the life of the world to
come" (*Mishna, Surenhus,* 4. 116). "The stranger who is pro-
selytized is like a child newly born, because he must break away
from his former teachers and principles, as well as from the ties of
kinship" (R. Yose, *Yebamoth,* 22a, 48b, 62a, 97b).[1] But there is
here no idea of a supernatural rebirth, only of a new judicial state
which, by virtue of a legal fiction, changes the former relations
of the proselyte.

[1] Cf. Bernard, *St. John,* p. clxiii.

Nicodemus may have been aware that a convert to Judaism was like a "child newly born", but he could not understand what Jesus meant when he said that none can see the kingdom without being born again. For this "none" included Nicodemus and all other Jews who believed that they were within the covenant. He could not appreciate that it was the purpose of Jesus to create a "New Israel" and that all who would become God's children in the new family of God and enjoy the privileges of the "New Age" must undergo a radical transformation such as is involved in the idea of a supernatural rebirth. The place which the formation of a new community occupies in the Johannine scheme of thought will be discussed in a later chapter. At this point we merely observe that all those who are begotten of God because of their faith in Jesus as the Messiah are constituted members of the New Israel.

This evidence from contemporary literature, showing how widespread were the ideas of rebirth, is all the more interesting when it is recognized that it is not a prominent conception in the New Testament.[1] It occurs in Titus 3. 5, "He saved us through the washing of regeneration" ($\pi\alpha\lambda\iota\gamma\gamma\epsilon\nu\epsilon\sigma\iota\alpha\varsigma$), and in 1 Peter 1. 3, 23, where Christians are described as "begotten again" ($\dot{\alpha}\nu\alpha\gamma\epsilon\nu\nu\dot{\eta}\sigma\alpha\varsigma$). St. Paul comes near to the same conception when he speaks of a man in Christ as being "a new creation" (2 Cor. 1. 17). Dr. W. L. Knox thinks that John 3. 5 ff. is merely a rewriting of Romans 7. 3 ff. in terms of new birth instead of death and resurrection.[2] Dr. E. F. Scott, however, believes that the Johannine doctrine of new birth rests on presuppositions wholly different from those of St. Paul. His reason for thinking this is that in the Fourth Gospel "the birth does not consist in a renewal of the moral nature, but in a transition from the natural state of being to a higher state".[3] He nevertheless admits elsewhere that the Pauline figures of death and resurrection as applied to the Christian suggest the idea, which John works out more fully, of a sudden, mysterious transition from the old life to the new.[4]

---

[1] See Büchsel, *T.W.z.N.T.*, i, p. 687.
[2] *Some Hell. Elements in Prim. Christianity*, p. 62 n.
[3] *The Fourth Gospel*, p. 220.
[4] Ibid., p. 279.

vi. *Children of God*

John's expression in 1. 12, "To them gave he the right to become children of God", suggests a nominal or legal conception of the children of God, like St. Paul's sonship by adoption; but the real sense of fatherhood by begetting is expressed in the same sentence: "which were born, not of blood, nor of the will of the flesh, nor of the will of man, but of God". And in 1 John 3. 1 the privilege of merely nominal sonship is exceeded by the real relation: "Behold what manner of love the Father hath bestowed upon us, that we should be called the children of God—and are".[1] This conception of the real nature of God's parental relation is everywhere prominent in John, and doubtless affected his choice of the word "children" (τέκνα) rather than "sons" (υἱοί) to express likeness of nature rather than a position of privilege.[2] The name Son is reserved for Christ, though 12. 36 may be an exception to this.

We shall be studying later the idea of Jesus as the Son of God; at the moment we shall only draw attention to the fact that John describes the relation of the children to the Father in the same terms as he uses to describe his relation to the Son. The favourite expression which John uses to describe Christ's nature and privilege is that of Son (1. 34; 20. 31; 1 John 2. 22, 23; 5. 23, etc.); and Jesus himself claims no higher title (3. 35, 36; 5. 23; 19. 7). "The only begotten Son" is an expression which John uses (1. 14; 3. 16, 18; 1 John 4. 9) to denote his unique relation of love and privilege.[3] Both terms indicate likeness; and Christ's fitness to reveal God rests upon this unique acquaintance of the only begotten Son with the Father and upon his union with him (1. 18). Yet notwithstanding this uniqueness in position and nature, notwithstanding also the fact that the children are never called sons, there is a very close analogy between the position of the Son and the children. The word children denotes privilege

---

[1] καί ἐσμεν ℵ A B C P 33 424.

[2] "The difference between υἱός and τέκνον appears to be that whereas τέκνον denotes the natural relationship of child to parent, υἱός implies in addition to this the recognized status and legal privileges reserved for sons", Sanday and Headlam, *Romans* (I.C.C.), p. 202.

[3] See below, pp. 62 ff., for a fuller discussion on " the only begotten Son ".

D

(1. 12) and also likeness to God (1 John 3. 2). Still more clearly does the act of begetting imply likeness in the children, as well as in the unique Son: "That which is born of the Spirit is spirit" (3. 6); "If ye know that he is righteous, ye know that every one also that doeth righteousness is begotten of him" (1 John 2. 29); "Every one that loveth is begotten of God" (1 John 4. 7); in 1 John 3. 9 it is expressly the seed of God which works conformity to his likeness, "Whosoever is begotten of God doeth no sin, because his seed abideth in him: and he cannot sin, because he is begotten of God". The analogy is brought out still more clearly in 1 John 5. 1, where both are spoken of under the same term, "Whosoever believeth that Jesus is the Christ is begotten of God: and whosoever loveth him that begat loveth him also that is begotten of him", and in 1 John 5. 18, "We know that whosoever is begotten (γεγεννημένος) of God sinneth not; but he that was begotten (γεννηθείς) of God" (Jesus) "keepeth him".

This conception is founded upon God as the source of all life, and is intimately connected with John's idea of eternal life as the pre-eminent gift of God in Christ. That God is life, is with John an idea co-ordinate with "God is love", "God is light", and the "true God". The idea of the divine Fatherhood is compounded of the two ideas, life and love: the true God is also eternal life (1 John 5. 20). We have to note again that in connexion with God's Fatherhood John is not thinking of life in an earthly sense, but always in the profound significance which he attaches to eternal life. In this sense God alone is the source of life, "the Father hath life in himself, and to the Son he gave to have life in himself" (5. 26). Thus the Son becomes the medium of life for men (6. 57), and he it is in a sense who constitutes the children of God (1. 12). Christ is therefore "the life" (11. 25; 14. 6); he is the "bread of life" (6. 35); and apart from him there is no life possible for men (1 John 5. 11, 12).

When we come to consider the ethical relation involved in the Fatherhood of God, it is not at first sight obvious in what respects John exceeded even the Jewish standpoint. It is true that in the Old Testament some of the rarer spirits in psalmody and prophecy rose to the conception of God as a Father, but it had not become a current name. In contemporary Judaism, however, as the New Testament itself is sufficient to prove, it had already become a familiar designation of God, a common address in prayer, and a boast of Jewish privilege.[1] It is, however, admitted by Montefiore that Jesus spoke more habitually about the Fatherhood of God than did the Rabbis.[2] Furthermore, Jesus in his personal prayers to God avoided the more formal mode of address, "our Father", and used the intimate term *abba*. This was the word used by children when speaking to their fathers in a Jewish home. Jesus thus introduced the idea of an intimate fellowship between God and man. Indeed, as Kittel says, Jesus uses a form of speech in reference to his Father which would have sounded to his listeners irreverent and lacking in respect because it belonged to everyday familiar speech—"the homely language of child and father".[3]

The same intimacy between the heavenly Father and the children is brought out in the Fourth Gospel, but in a widely different way. John, so far from particularizing the relationship, seems to generalize it: his phrase is "the Father", never "our Father", and but once "your Father". This phrase, however, does not denote a Fatherhood of wider range; it is not the Father and mankind, but "the Father and the Son", "the Father" equals "my Father". In the first Epistle especially, "the Father" appears as a set theological designation of God in distinction from "the Son", and the name is used with the same significance even in the speeches of Christ in the Gospel.

This peculiar mode of representation is excellently designed to display Christ's method of bringing home to the disciples the intimacy of God's relation as the Father. For just as the significance of the Father as the begetter of life is seen primarily in relation to the only begotten Son, so too is the Father's ethical relation to the children interpreted in terms of his loving relation to the Son. The constant representation of the Fourth Gospel is to the effect that Jesus did not speak in the terms of popular

---

[1] See Abrahams, *Studies in Pharisaism and the Gospels*, series 1, ch. xix. Rom. 8. 15 might suggest that Saul of Tarsus had not learnt God's Fatherhood in Judaism.
[2] *Hibbert Journal*, xxviii, p. 104.   [3] *T.W.z.N.T.*, i, p. 5.

usage of the Fatherhood of God as a relation common to himself
and his disciples; but he appropriated it peculiarly to himself,
and thereby immeasurably exalted the intimacy and the reality
of the conception.   When he speaks of the Father it is almost
always in relation to himself and in a way which is practically
equivalent to "my Father".   He emphasizes his unique knowledge
of the Father (6. 46), the Father's unique love towards him
(3. 35; 5. 20; 17. 24).   This relationship is so close that he can
say, "I and the Father are one" (10. 30), "I am in the Father,
and the Father in me" (14. 11), and he is in such sense the
medium between the Father and the children, that God's love
is conditioned by the love to Christ (14. 20, 23).

The significance of having thus expressed this deep and
intimate relationship between the Father and the Son is seen
when, at the last hour, Christ transfers to his disciples the fulness
of this intimate relationship in saying, "My Father and your
Father" (20. 17).   In the High Priestly prayer he says: "That
the love wherewith thou hast loved me may be in them" (17. 26).
Having brought his disciples into this relationship of children to
the Father, he establishes a relationship so close that his own
mediatorial position is in a sense superseded; for although the
disciples are instructed to pray in his name (16. 24), he nevertheless adds: "I say not unto you, that I will pray the Father
for you; for the Father himself loveth you" (16. 26, 27).   Though
our union with the Father is mediated by the Son, it is not on that
account less real and close.   Our fellowship with the Father and
our fellowship with his Son are regarded as co-ordinate relations (1 John 1. 3).   We "abide in the Son and in the Father"
(1 John 2. 24).   The same fact is emphasized in the loose employment of personal pronouns (αὐτός, ἐκεῖνος).   Sometimes it is a
real difficulty to know whether the reference is to Christ or to the
Father (1 John 1. 5-10).   The Father has displayed his active
interest in the fact that "he hath sent the Son, the Saviour of the
world" (1 John 4. 14), and he it is who also sends the Spirit of
Truth as "another comforter" (14. 16, 26) who, like the Christ,
abides in us (14. 17).

It is very clear that the more richly the idea of God's Father-

hood is developed, so much the more impossible is it to think of
it in relation to the world in general. As defined by the whole
range of ideas with which Fatherhood is associated in the Johannine
writings, the relation is limited to those whom Christ has chosen
out of the world (15. 19). It is evident that the ideas of begetting,
of the new birth and of eternal life, were not realized in the case
of all men. Even "his own", the nation which boasted that God
was their Father (18. 41), received not Christ (1. 11), thereby
proving that they were not the true children of God (8. 42); but
as many as received him, to them gave he the right to become the
children of God (1. 12). God's Fatherhood is therefore no longer
limited to the nation; his children are scattered abroad and are
brought together into one community by Christ's death (11. 52).

God's love as an attribute of the Father is, in this deeper
sense, limited to the children: "Behold what manner of love the
Father hath bestowed upon us, that we should be called the
children of God" (1 John 3. 1); "Herein was the love of God
manifested in us, that God hath sent his only begotten Son
into the world, that we might live through him" (1 John 4. 9).
From this last verse we see also that God was revealed as love,
not only by Christ's loving service and sacrifice (1 John 3. 16),
but by the very sending of the only begotten Son as a sacrifice
on the part of the Father; and that his love is thereby revealed,
not as complacent affection, but as an active impulse.

This conception of the love of God as an active impulse was
fundamentally different from that which obtained among the
Greeks.[1] The essence of the Platonic idea of love was desire.
Man longs to behold the perfect beauty, and it is love that urges
a man to strive and reach that goal. The pilgrimage of the soul
as it ascends to ever higher forms of beauty has been called the
Heavenly Ladder. It is well described by Plato in the *Symposium*
(211 *b*) as follows: "When anyone having the right kind of love
mounts up and begins to see the beauty present in a beautiful
person, he is not far from the final goal. For the right way of
love, whether one goes alone or is led by another, is to begin with
the beautiful things that are seen here, and ascend ever upwards

---

[1] See Nygren, *Agape and Eros*, pt. i, pp. 118 ff.; Stauffer, *T.W.z.N.T.*, i, pp. 34 ff.

aiming at the beauty that is above, climbing, as it were, on a ladder from one beautiful body to two, and from two to all the others, and from beautiful bodies to beautiful actions, and from the beauty of actions to beautiful forms of knowledge, till at length from these one reaches that knowledge which is the knowledge of nothing other than beauty itself, and so knows at last what beauty really is". Love is therefore the movement of man towards ever higher things; there is no thought of God loving man. The gods have all and need nothing: they can therefore only be the object of love. Love as an active desire belongs exclusively to man, for love is essentially the desire of the lower for the higher.

The same conception is to be found in Aristotle. He, however, extends the idea to the movement of the whole universe. The means by which the world is set in motion is the desire of the lower for the higher, κινεῖ ὡς ἐρώμενον (*Met.* Λ. 7, 1072 *b*). The loved object sets in motion him who loves it by the attraction which it exercises. Thus the whole universe has love for its motive force. Each lower thing strives towards that which is higher, and seeks to become like to it. But, as in Plato, such love cannot be ascribed to God. The object of God's thought must be the best of all possible objects. God cannot, therefore, have an object of thought outside of himself. He is therefore defined by Aristotle as "Thought of Thought" (νόησις νοήσεως, *Met.* Λ. 9, 1074 *b*, 33-35). It is in harmony with this conception that he affirms that God cannot return our love because personal intercourse with him is out of the question (*Magna Moralia*, 1208 *b*, 26-32).

It was therefore a characteristic of pagan thought that God cannot love men; for such love would imply a downward movement, from the level of divine perfection to a lower level. John, no doubt, had this in mind when he stated clearly the essence of Christian love: "Herein is love, not that we loved God, but that he loved us, and sent his Son to be the propitiation for our sins" (1 John 4. 10).

The difference between the pagan and the Christian conceptions of love are summarized by Stauffer as follows [1]: "The

---

[1] *T.W.z.N.T.*, i, p. 37 ; cf. Nygren, *Agape and Eros*, pt. i, p. 165.

word ἔρως is from the beginning an undiscriminating love, which seeks its satisfaction now here, now there. 'Αγάπη is a love which selects its object and cleaves to it. Eros is determined by a more or less undefined impulse towards an object. 'Αγάπη is determined from the side of the subject—it is a free, purposeful act. "Ερως is used, in its highest sense, of the upward striving of humanity, ἀγάπη of love for the divine. 'Αγαπᾶν is chiefly applied to the love of God, the love of the higher which lifts up the lower, and exalts it above others. Eros seeks in another the satisfaction of its own hunger for life, ἀγαπᾶν must often be translated 'to show charity towards'; it is an active, giving love, which seeks the good of its object".

This definition of Christian love is abundantly proved from the conception of love found in the Johannine writings. "God so loved the world that he gave . . ." (3. 16) is the key-note of the Gospel. It is not surprising, therefore, that notwithstanding the special love of God for the children chosen out of the world, John nevertheless regards love and salvation in a universal aspect. God's relation to men as Creator is wider than that of Father, and as Creator he loves his creatures. In 3. 16 we have the most universal expression of God's love towards his rational creation. This naturally follows from the principle that in his very nature, and independent of created object, "God is love" (1 John 4. 9, 16). This attitude of God towards his rational creation will be further discussed under the heading of salvation.

3

THE WORD WITH GOD

(a) THE SELF-WITNESS OF JESUS

i. Relation between Prologue and Gospel

In the previous chapter we discussed the nature of God. In the course of the discussion we saw that the love of God was directed, in the broadest sense, to the whole world; more particularly towards the children chosen out of the world; and in a unique sense towards the only begotten Son. In this chapter and the next we shall discuss more fully the relation of Jesus to the Father. This can best be divided into two parts: Jesus' own witness, as expressed in terms of Sonship, and John's own conception, which is characteristically formulated in connexion with the term Logos.[1]

This is justified because John never attributes the use of the term Logos to Jesus; and also because in his own pronouncements both in the Prologue and in the Epistle he associates with the Son and with the Logos ideas which advance beyond the explicit terms of Jesus' own self-witness.

Harnack argued that the Prologue was not an organic part of the Gospel, and was rather a postscript than a preface. It was the recommendation of the Gospel to those who approached it through metaphysics rather than through history. It was written in order to break the Gospel gently to the Greeks and prepare their minds for the paradox which the Evangelist was about to proclaim.[2] He points out [3] how time has reversed the conditions of the case. To us the Prologue is the difficult part.

[1] The relation of Jesus to the Father is not exhausted by the ideas of Sonship and Logos. It is displayed in many other ways which are discussed elsewhere in this book ; see, e.g., pp. 26 f., 39 ff., 252 ff.

[2] *Über das Verhältniss des Prologs des vierten Evangeliums* in *Zeitschrift für Theologie und Kirche*, ii, pp. 213 f.

[3] *The History of Dogma* (Eng. Trans.), i, p. 329.

But to the first readers of the Gospel the first part of the Prologue would have been familiar ground, while the historical manifestation of the Logos would have been strange and unfamiliar teaching.

In 1898 Baldensperger argued, as against Harnack, that the Prologue is the key to the right understanding of the Gospel. It is a carefully composed rhythmic hymn in which the references to John the Baptist are an integral part.[1] Similarly, Dr. Julius Grill finds throughout the Gospel the same ideas as contained in the Prologue.[2] In the opinion of Loisy: "The theology of the Incarnation is the key to the whole book, and it is that which dominates from the first line to the last".[3] And it appears from this that he means that the Logos doctrine of the Prologue dominates the entire Gospel. Dr. W. L. Knox bases his exposition of the Fourth Gospel on the assumption that the Logos idea is "worked out in the Gospel in a series of episodes, which illustrate the main theme".[4] On the other hand, Dr. A. E. J. Rawlinson says that the Logos "does not in any way dominate or pervade the theology of the Gospel as a whole".[5] He prefers to think that the Christological idea which is really characteristic of the Gospel is the idea of our Lord as the Son of God with whom the Logos is identified. The difference probably arises from the fact "that in the Prologue and the remainder of the Gospel we have the history of the Evangelist's thought in reverse order." [6]

The theory that the Prologue is in the form of a Hebrew poem is a further argument that it has been added to the Gospel. Dr. Rendel Harris believes that behind the Prologue is a hymn in honour of Wisdom,[7] which has been adapted by the Evangelist to suit his own theological ideas. Mr. Cecil Cryer also argues that the Prologue is in the form of a poem in which verses 1-5,

---

[1] *Der Prolog des vierten Evangeliums.*
[2] *Untersuchungen über die Entstehung des vierten Evangeliums,* vol. i.
[3] *Le Quatrième Évangile,* p. 98.
[4] *Some Hell. Elements in Prim. Christianity,* ch. iii.
[5] *The New Testament Doctrine of Christ,* p. 209 ; cf. Lofthouse, *The Father and the Son,* pp. 64 ff.
[6] V. H. Stanton, *The Gospels as Historical Documents,* iii, p. 178.
[7] *The Origin of the Prologue to St. John's Gospel.*

9-14, 16-18 are a series of tristichs and distichs, while verses 6-8 and verse 12 are in prose. He thinks, however, that the poem was written by the author of the Gospel and later added as an introduction to the narrative portion.[1] Dr. F. C. Burney brings forward arguments to show that the Prologue was originally in "the form of a hymn, written in eleven parallel couplets, with comments introduced here and there by the writer".[2] Dr. Burney reconstructs an Aramaic original for the hymn on these lines. Archbishop Bernard suggests another arrangement in Greek, omitting all references to historical personages. He agrees, however, that the model is not Greek but Hebrew.[3]

There is agreement, therefore, as to the literary style of the Prologue, and it is our opinion that it was composed by the author of the Gospel and is an integral part of the whole Gospel. It can readily be seen that John's sense of historical fitness would in itself be sufficient to account for his confining philosophical terms such as λόγος, πλήρωμα, μονογενής θεός, to the Prologue.[4] If we read the Prologue in the light of John 20. 30, 31, we shall see that its leading conceptions occur in the body of the Gospel. We are told in John 20. 30, 31, that the record of Christ's life is to set forth events which are σημεῖα of the nature of his Person. His life was a continual display of these σημεῖα, but such a selection has been made as to throw the real nature of the Person into relief, that men may be persuaded that Jesus who lived on earth was the Jewish Messiah, the Son of God. A belief of this kind is no mere historical certainty nor an intellectual conviction. The full name, the Christ, the Son of God, is a true description of the Person, and if you can believe in the name of Jesus the Christ, the Son of God, you have life. The object of the Gospel, then, is to unfold to men what is signified in these titles. His whole being in all its activity, instinct with the life of the Messiah, the Son of God, is recognized by the believer because it is an expression of divinity. If Jesus is faithfully depicted, belief and life will ensue. The author does not

---

[1] *Expository Times*, xxxii, pp. 440 ff.
[2] *The Aramaic Origin of the Fourth Gospel*, p. 40.
[3] *St. John*, pp. cxliv f.
[4] Cf. Loisy, *Le Quatrième Évangile*, p. 97.

purpose primarily to describe the course of faith and unbelief. These are secondary, though, in the circumstances, inevitable, results. His aim is to show forth the fulness of the life of Christ, to explain its inner meaning, to prove that the God of being and history was revealed in Jesus Christ. Heaven and earth met in him. Of necessity it follows that those who are receptive believe and live. Further, the writer justifies these tremendous assertions from his own experience. He has received life as a result of his acceptance of Jesus as the Messiah, the Son of God. His discovery of the meaning of that life brought him life, and he believes that by recording the facts as he has come to see them, others will have the same blessed experience.

These thoughts are found in the Prologue. Prominent in it is the witness of personal testimony. "The Word became flesh, and dwelt among us, and we beheld his glory . . . of his fulness we all received." We recognize the divine attributes of grace and truth because their completeness brought grace and truth into our own souls. Now for the first time we have had a full revelation of the nature of God. Not that it came to us entirely as a surprise, for we had been long looking for such a theophany. The Old Testament had spoken of man as made in the image of God and of the coming of a Messiah. We who knew the highest that the Old Testament could give have now found a higher. It is because we read the past aright that we understand the present revelation.

ii. *The Son of God*

It is significant that the Prologue develops in accordance with 20. 31, through three manifestations of the same person —the Son of God, the Messiah, Jesus. It is to be observed that the order of progress in the Prologue is the reverse of that in 20. 31, the reason for which is obvious. If the Prologue enunciates the principles of history, there the author naturally proceeds from the more general statements and the eternal conditions to the concrete realization; while in the Gospel, which is history, the process of the life of Jesus makes manifest a character so full of grace and truth that he must be the Christ, and therefore the

Son of God. We may therefore assume that the teaching contained in the body of the Gospel about the relationship of the Father and the Son is in substantial agreement with that contained in the Prologue.

It is generally said that John does not note, as do the Synoptists, a progression in the self-witness of Jesus. This opinion is no doubt due to the fact that, when John wrote, Christian reflexion and Christian experience had reached a doctrine of Christ's Person which had not been clearly thought out by Christians in the early days of Christianity. Nevertheless there are two things to be said on this point.

(a) The difference between the Synoptists and John is not a difference between a human Jesus and a divine Christ. We can discern in Mark and the document called Q a Christology as profound as that found in John. The general representation of the Synoptic Gospels is that Jesus is not just one teacher among many. He is the teacher who speaks with authority (Matt. 7. 29). His revelation is final. We are not to "look for another" (Matt. 11. 3). God has "visited and redeemed his people" (Luke 1. 68). The old clear-cut distinction between history and interpretation can no longer be recognized.[1] As Dr. W. Manson remarks, there is no smallest unit of the Synoptic tradition which is not instinct with Christological significance. And this is because the motive which from the start led to the preservation of historical material in the Tradition was a Christological motive.[2]

When we turn to the rest of the New Testament the Christological pattern is seen to be the same. In point of time the Pauline Epistles are earlier than the Gospels. As Karl Ludwig Schmidt remarks,[3] the Gospels can only be explained in the light of the early Christian kerygma as it is found in the speeches of Acts and the Pauline letters. It is significant that there is no evidence of any dispute between the original leaders of the Church and St. Paul on the question of the Person of Christ. The

---

[1] See R. H. Lightfoot, *History and Interpretation in the Gospels*, pp. 208-225.
[2] *Jesus the Messiah*, p. 94.
[3] *Theologische Blätter*, May 1931.

substance of St. Paul's theology was apparently approved by the Church at Jerusalem (Gal. 2. 2-10). We may therefore assume that his Christology was in accordance with the belief of the Church in the earliest days. As we shall see later, there is to be found in St. Paul a Logos doctrine as profound as that found in the Fourth Gospel. Jesus was the Lord whom he had seen manifested in glory (Acts 9. 3; 22. 6; 26. 13), he is the "Man" from heaven (1 Cor. 15. 47), God's "own Son" (Rom. 8. 3), the true "image" of God (2 Cor. 4. 4; Col. 1. 15), the "firstborn of all creation" (Col. 1. 15), one who in the "form" of God existed from all eternity (Phil. 2. 6).

Similarly for the writer of Hebrews, Christ is the "express image" of God's "being" and the "effulgence" of his "glory" (Heb. 1. 3). He is the Son of God who was made "lower than the angels" (Heb. 2. 6 ff.), but who has now been "crowned with glory and honour" (Heb. 2. 9). The Apocalypse, which has many affinities with the Fourth Gospel, was probably the first Christian writing to identify Christ with the Divine Word (Rev. 19. 13). It is clear, therefore, that there is a deep underlying unity in the New Testament conception of Christ. There are differences of expression, but every stage in the formation of the Tradition bears witness to the belief that Jesus is the Messiah, Saviour, and Lord. If the Fourth Gospel displays a more mature reflexion on the Person of Christ, the author only makes explicit what is implicit in the earlier records. As has already been pointed out, the clearer statements in the Fourth Gospel are due to the different circumstances in which the Gospel was written. They were evoked by the growth of a false *gnosis* and by the intellectual needs of a Greek-speaking society.

(*b*) If we pay close attention to this question of progress we shall observe that there is a progress, though of a kind different from that found in the Synoptists. John marks clearly the progress of the disciples' appreciation of the significance of Jesus' claim. "All is so arranged as to give the effect of an ascending series of confessions of belief or recognition of Jesus as the Son of God." [1] The claim to divine Sonship remains constant; there

---

[1] W. F. Lofthouse, *The Father and the Son*, p. 38.

is no indication that Jesus gradually realized his vocation and the significance of his Person. But the Evangelist records how those who believed on Jesus arrived at an ever deeper appreciation of his divine nature. He shows how the disciples passed through every stage of belief from the expression of a relation which every Israelite might claim (1. 49) to the confession of Thomas (20. 28), "My Lord and my God". Human faith thus perceives the truth that was recorded in the Prologue and the point of view from which the whole Gospel was written.

In the name "Son of God" there was nothing peculiar. In the Old Testament it had been used of angels (Gen. 6. 1-4); of magistrates (Ps. 82); of individual Israelites (Deut. 14. 1, 2); the theocratic king (2 Sam. 7. 14; Ps. 39. 27); and of the nation of Israel (Ex. 4. 22; Deut. 32. 6-10). These examples show that in the Old Testament the idea of Sonship to God indicated special nearness to him. The title is not used as a specific designation for the Messiah, although the passages cited in which the ideal theocratic king is called God's Son and "firstborn" point to the appropriateness with which the Messiah might be called the unique son. We find a development along these lines in the extra-canonical Jewish writings. In 4 Esdras 7. 28, for example, we find: "For my son, Messias, shall be revealed with those that are with him". "And it shall come to pass after these years that my son, Messias, shall die, etc." (4 Esdras 7. 29). This relation between the Son and the Messiah is found in New Testament usage. In Mark 14. 61 the High Priest asks: "Art thou the Christ, the Son of the Blessed?" The exact relation between the two terms is a matter of dispute among New Testament scholars. It is argued by Montefiore that the claim to be the Messiah was the basis of the claim to be the Son of God.[1] But the sense of sonship was almost certainly prior to the consciousness of Messiahship.[2] And it would appear that Jesus avoided the Messianic significance of the term Son of God and used it

[1] *Synoptic Gospels*, i, pp. lxvi, 19, 85-87.
[2] Wendt, *The Teaching of Jesus*, i, pp. 180 f., 191, 393 f. ; W. Manson, *Jesus the Messiah*, p. 109. In the opinion of Dr. Major, "This theocentric egoism is the very core of the Messianic consciousness of Jesus" (*Message and Mission of Jesus*, p. 112).

rather to denote a personal relation of fellowship and intimacy with God. As Kittel says, the Father-Son relationship of Jesus "far and away surpasses in intimacy all the potentialities inherent in Judaism, replacing them rather by something new".[1] But in a strictly Jewish context the title would not in itself signify more than enthronement as the divinely upheld Monarch and Ruler of the people of God.[2]

In view of the Jewish antecedents of the title it would be natural if John had been influenced by them in his choice of the term, especially as it had been used by the Synoptists and by our Lord himself (Matt. 11. 27). This Q saying implies a uniquely close intimacy between Jesus and the Father, and in a typically Johannine form.[3] In these verses Jesus claims such an exclusive knowledge of the Father that nothing less than an absolutely unique self-consciousness, on an equality with that of the Father, is involved. There is, however, a passage in Origen's *Contra Celsum* which leads us to another possible source of influence. Celsus says: "It is both easy and useful for such persons to say, 'I am God, or a son of God, or a divine spirit. I have come. Already the world is at the point of destruction, and you, O men, are lost through your unrighteousness, but I am willing to save you; and you shall see me again coming unto you with heavenly power; blessed is he who now worships me; upon all others I will cast fire eternal, upon both cities and country estates; and men, except they acknowledge their deserts, shall groan for it and repent in vain; but those who obey me I will preserve for ever'".[4] The reference is, of course, to the ideas popularly conveyed in the Hellenistic world by such titles as "son of God", and θεῖος ἄνθρωπος.[5] It would appear that the phrase υἱὸς θεοῦ came to mean among Hellenized Semitic populations "a divine being", "a god", "a supernatural person". The supernatural power might be proclaimed in many ways—in miracles

---

[1] *T.W.z.N.T.*, i, p. 6 ; see also p. 51 above.
[2] See Stevens, *The Theology of the New Testament*, pp. 56 ff., and *H.D.B.*, iv, pp. 570 ff.
[3] See Dodd, *Mysterium Christi*, p. 63, and T. W. Manson, *The Teaching of Jesus*, pp. 109 ff.   [4] Origen, *Contra Celsum*, 7. 9.
[5] See Angus, *The Mystery Religions and Christianity*, pp. 106-112.

and wonders, in ecstasies and visions. On account of any of these a man might establish a claim to be θεῖος ἄνθρωπος or a "son of God".[1]

John would be aware of these many claims to divine honours, and our Lord's claim to be a "Son of God" falls naturally into such a context, though, as we shall see, John regards Jesus as the Son of God in a unique way that differentiates him in kind from all other "sons of God". It should be noticed also that the Fourth Gospel contains elements of primitive Judaeo-Christian ideas about Christ. "Rabbi," says Nathanael to Jesus, "thou art the Son of God, thou art the king of Israel". This passage betrays the fact that John is "well aware that originally, and in a purely Jewish as distinct from a specifically Christian context of thought, the title 'Son of God' was synonymous with that of Messiah, and denoted simply the theocratic King of the people of God".[2]

In the Old Testament the term "begotten" is used as a metaphor in connexion with divine sonship (Ps. 2. 7). There is, however, no question of physical action being implied by such a statement. In all other religions, and particularly among the Greeks, divine paternity suggests little else. But such a thought would have appeared blasphemous to a Jew. It was one of the outstanding characteristics of the Jewish religion that, unlike the mass of Semitic deities, Jahweh was associated with no consort. This explains the rarity of the conception in the Old Testament. The term appears frequently in Greek literature. For example, in the Liturgy of Mithra we read: "I am a man . . . born of mortal womb . . . having been this day begotten again by Thee, out of so many myriads rendered immortal in this hour by the good will of God in his abounding goodness".[3]

---

[1] Rawlinson, *The New Testament Doctrine of Christ*, p. 70. Compare Mark 15. 37-39, ἀληθῶς ὁ ἄνθρωπος οὗτος υἱὸς ἦν θεοῦ, with the following passage from Plutarch, *Cleomenes*, 39, 823 c : " When Cleomenes was impaled the report of a portent at the time of his death gave rise to the popular rumour that he was a hero and a son of the gods (ἥρωα τὸν Κλεομένη καὶ θεῶν παῖδα προσαγορεύοντες) ", quoted by W. Manson in *Jesus the Messiah*, p. 105.

[2] Ibid., pp. 212, 213. Abbott suggests that " Son of God " here means no more than " Son of the Supreme Angel " (*Son of Man*, par. 3377, p. 419).

[3] *The Vision of God*, by Kirk, p. 473.

But according to John the begetting of Jesus as the Son of God was something quite different from both Hebrew and Hellenistic usage. For him the term has a value absolutely *sui generis*; Jesus is the "only begotten Son of God" (1. 14). Only John in the New Testament applies the word μονογενής to Jesus, and he does this four times in the Gospel and once in the Epistle (1. 14; 1. 18; 3. 16; 3. 18; 1 John 4. 19). The word is used primarily of an only child who is specially dear to its parents (Judges 11. 34; Tob. 3. 15; Luke 7. 12; 8. 42; 19. 38). Conversely, as Dr. Turner points out, ἀγαπητός is used for an only son in the LXX (Gen. 22. 2, 12, 17; Amos 8. 10; Jer. 6. 26; Zech. 12. 10 ; Ps. 2. 7).[1] The term therefore represents a relation of tender love. But it can hardly fail to have also the significance of real derivation from the divine nature. In 1 John 5. 1, the children are also begotten; but, if the relation of the Son to the Father were upon the same plane as that of the children, we should expect him to be called, as by St. Paul, "the first begotten among many brethren" (Rom. 8. 29). Instead of that, he occupies in John's thought an absolutely singular relation to God as the only begotten Son. The true significance of the term is brought out by the Old Latin texts *a, e, q,* which have *unicus* instead of *unigenitus.* In the Greek the emphasis is upon μονο- rather than upon γενής. The word is thus used by Parmenides in the poem *On Nature* where he describes the "Existent" as wholly μονογενής, not "only begotten", but an "only one", entirely unique.[2] Similarly, Clement of Rome speaks of the Phoenix, a legendary bird, as only begotten.[3] When, therefore, the Evangelist applies the term to Christ he means that Jesus is the "Son of God" in a unique sense; the other sons of God are different not only in degree but in kind. The use of the term prevents us from thinking of the Logos as a diffused, impersonal force working in nature and history. The Logos does not dwell

[1] *New Commentary* (S.P.C.K.), iii, p. 52.
[2] Quoted by Carpenter, *The Johannine Writings*, pp. 331 f.
[3] *Ad Cor.* 1. 25. Schmiedel is of the opinion that both parts of the word should be emphasized (*Johannine Writings*, p. 153). Schlatter observes that the sacrifice of Abraham's son, the only begotten, may have influenced John in applying the word to Jesus (*Der Evangelist Johannes*, 25, 26).

E

in Christ as in men; the Logos is "only begotten", is Jesus Christ. The Logos and the only begotten Son refer to the same person and are explanatory of one another. The distinction between Jesus as the Son of God and other men as sons of God is emphasized by the way in which John refrains from the use of the expression sons (υἱοί) of God in relation to men, and substitutes for it the word children (τέκνα).

It would seem, therefore, reasonable to say that the ethical relation which is everywhere prominent in the expression we are studying rather suggests than excludes a substantial relation. We must, however, be careful when using non-Scriptural terms to express Biblical ideas. Such terms may have arisen from certain Biblical texts, but they have associations and presuppositions that draw the mind away from the Biblical conceptions. The use of them also implies a knowledge of their exact meaning within the framework of ancient philosophy. Nevertheless we may affirm that when Jesus claimed to be the Son of God, John understood by this that a definite, far-reaching, and unique relationship existed between the Father and Jesus as the Son. There is no doubt, as has already been remarked, that in the Epistles "the Son" denotes a nature more closely allied to God than to men. The constant conjunction of the Son and the Father is of itself sufficient to establish John's doctrine on this subject. The believer's relation to the Father and to the Son is expressed in the same terms (1 John 2. 22-24), and the last verse but one of the Epistle includes both "him that is true, and his Son Jesus Christ" in the affirmation, "this is the true God and everlasting life".

There is, therefore, no contradiction between the teaching of the Prologue and the body of the Gospel on this matter. The phrase "the only begotten Son" is substantially equivalent to the Logos, and as such shares the divine glory. "The glory of the Incarnate Word was such glory as the only begotten Son of the eternal Father would derive from him and so could exhibit it to the faithful." [1] Jesus' self-witness could hardly be said to fall short of this, though it may perhaps be more justly said to lead

---

[1] Bernard, St. John, p. 24.

up to it. The "comfortable word" of 3. 16 is a comment by John on the words he has already ascribed to Jesus in his discourse with Nicodemus. Both the style and the grammar suggest that the writer is meditating on the great events of the past.

When Jesus said "my Father worketh even until now, and I work", he prompted the Jews to say that he was "making himself equal with God" (5. 17, 18). Dr. Odeberg has shown that the phrase ἴσον ποιεῖ ἑαυτὸν τῷ θεῷ corresponds exactly to the Rabbinic expression which suggested to anyone trained in that mode of speech "to make himself independent of God". Dr. Odeberg paraphrases verses 19 ff. as follows: "The Son does not 'make himself equal with' the Father, he does not presume upon an independent authority. On the contrary, all his authority is derived from his Father. He is not a rebellious son, a blasphemer of the divine Father; on the contrary, his peculiar opposition is justified by his being and acting in absolute unity of intention and thought with his Father. His continual activity is not independent of the Father's activity; on the contrary, he does the Father's works, he executes what the Father shows him, and commands him to do".[1] This is an illustration of the claim that the Fourth Gospel contains a genuine tradition of Jesus' teaching, reflecting the actual circumstances in which these words were spoken.

The intimate relation between the Father and the Son is illustrated by the fact that in the Fourth Gospel Jesus never refers to God as "our Father". He speaks of "the Father", or "my Father", or sometimes "the Father who sent me". In prayer, Jesus always uses the simple vocative, "Father", not "my Father", as in the Synoptists; once in the High Priestly prayer, "holy Father". In 8. 54 he distinguishes his own position sharply from that of the Jews in the contrast, "my Father—your God". He claims that "all things which the Father hath are mine" (16. 15). A perfect fellowship of life, purpose, and work exists between them. "The Son doeth nothing from (ἀπό) himself; for the Father loveth the Son, and showeth him all things that himself doeth" (5. 20). It is because the Son perfectly reveals

---

[1] *The Fourth Gospel* etc., p. 203 ; cf. Schlatter, *Der Evangelist Johannes*, p. 147.

and embodies the Father's will that he is able to say, "He that hath seen me hath seen the Father" (14. 19). "Believe in God, believe also in me" (14. 1). This simultaneous injunction of faith in God and in Christ under the same conditions and expressed in the same way (πιστεύετε εἰς) is very striking.[1] To this we add the remarkable claim, "we will come unto him and make our abode with him" (14. 23). It is in the light of such testimony that we must read the claim, "I and the Father are one" (10. 30) and "I am in the Father, and the Father in me" (14. 11). The neuter pronoun suggests the abstract term, unity. But the unity that is represented here is not that of metaphysics. It is a unity of action and purpose. The Son loves, wills, and acts, as the Father loves, wills, and acts. Concerning this union of the Father and the Son, Dr. Lock quotes Dr. Sanday as follows : "Unclouded openness of mind of the Son to the mind of the Father, that was the essence of his being . . . a profound inner sense of harmony and indeed unity of will".[2]

If we attempt to sum up the details of Jesus' testimony about himself, the total impression can hardly be other than this : that he had the consciousness and made the claim of being in intimate and unique fellowship with the Father. This must mean more than mere moral unity or agreement of character. The Jews would not have regarded as blasphemy a claim to regulate his actions according to the will of God. His union with the Father was such that he represented himself as an object of faith, and honour paid to him was honour paid to the Father. The Evangelist grounds the perfection and saving power of Christ upon his claim to eternal and essential oneness with God.

iii. *The Pre-existence of Jesus*

Another question arises : Did Jesus express the fact of his pre-existence in so many words, or did he leave it to be inferred

---

[1] Cf. Moulton, *Grammar of New Testament Greek*, i, p. 68 : "The really important matter is the recognition of a clear distinction between believe on or believe in with the dative simply " ; and Oepke, *T.W.z.N.T.*, article "εἰς ", ii, p. 430.

[2] *New Commentary*, iii, p. 260. For the Filial Consciousness of Jesus see Rawlinson, *The New Testament Doctrine of Christ*, pp. 251 ff. ; Bartlet in *D.C.G.*, ii, pp. 700, 704.

from his claim to be perfectly at one with the Father? The fact is that Jesus' consciousness of pre-existence is so clearly expressed that one wonders how it could be called in question. It is only by ascribing to John an extremely subtle and philosophical mind that otherwise clear statements are made to bear a meaning alien to the natural use of language. It is not proved by the frequent expressions which represent him as "sent" or even "sent into the world", for such expressions are used of John the Baptist and others. Nor is it indubitably expressed in the claim of learning from the Father, of doing and saying what he has seen and heard from him; for this might conceivably be the result of inspiration and inspired vision. There are other expressions that denote derivation from God, but not pre-existence: "I am come forth and am come from God" (8. 42). Wendt says [1] that this is to be understood in the same sense as when the disciples are spoken of as being not "from the world" (15. 19), or as when the Jews are described as being "from the Devil" (8. 44). Believers also are described as being from God (1 John 4. 4).[2]

We may, however, with more confidence point to those expressions which represent Jesus as coming down from heaven (3. 31; 6. 33, 38, 41, 42, 51). Among the Jews it was taught that the soul of man came from heaven, whereas his body was of the earth. In the Fourth Gospel no such distinction is made between soul and body. It is the Christ who is from heaven.[3] There are also other statements which would seem to admit of no misunderstanding. For example, he speaks of the "Son of Man ascending where he was before" (6. 62). Such would be the climax of the historical revelation of the Son of God, the other elements being the Incarnation, the ministry, the death and resurrection. The same idea is repeated in 16. 28, where he says: "I came out from the Father, and am come into the world, and go

[1] *The Teaching of Jesus*, ii, p. 168.

[2] The question whether the title Son of Man includes in itself the idea of pre-existence is discussed later in this book. As a negative answer is there given, nothing further need be said at this point.

[3] Cf. Schlatter's comment in *Der Evangelist Johannes*, p. 22 and p. 110 : "John does not share the dualist psychology. Who ever separated body and soul could never say that the Word became flesh".

unto the Father". In the High Priestly prayer he says: "for thou lovedst me before the foundation of the world" (17. 24); and he speaks of the "glory which I had with thee before the world was" (17. 5). Glory was the term which designated the radiant being of the Deity on whom Moses had longed to gaze (Ex. 33. 18, 22), and it supplied the name for God as the Lord of Glory or Great Glory.[1] Christ, therefore, claims to have shared from all eternity the divine nature of God. It is that divine nature that he now manifests to the world. Glory in the Old Testament means the revealed purposes of God. God's intention for the ultimate salvation of men was expressed in the crossing of the Red Sea and the deliverance from Captivity. God's glory was manifested in these acts. From this point of view, Jesus is here claiming to have shared in the divine counsels from before the foundation of the world. As the Passion draws near he prays that his great act of sacrifice may be fully in accordance with the will of God. The purposes of God are most fully manifested in the lifting up on the cross. There upon the cross the glory of God is displayed. When Jesus prays that God would glorify him with the glory which he had with the Father before the world was, he is asking that God's will may be accomplished in him (cf. Mark 14. 36). The glory of God is displayed in an act of loving sacrifice. Love is therefore God's peculiar glory, and the very character of his nature as light (1 John 1. 5). It is this love which is given to the disciples because of their union with him, the love which Jesus shared with the Father before the foundation of the world, and which is the bond of union in the new *koinonia*.

But Jesus' testimony does not end with a claim for relative pre-existence. He demands belief in his absolute pre-existence. "Believe that I am", "before Abraham was, I am" (7. 24; 8. 58). According to Wendt, this indicates an ideal pre-existence only.[2]

---

[1] See Strachan, *The Fourth Gospel*, pp. 103-106. Kittel in *T.W.z.N.T.*, ii, p. 255, quotes as a parallel to John 17. 5 the following words from a Greek papyrus: δόξασόν μοι, ὡς ἐδόξασα τὸ ὄνομα τοῦ υἱοῦ σου ᾽Ωρου. This might suggest that the Johannine conception of δόξα is of Hellenistic origin. But the source of the quotation is a Greek magical papyrus of the 3rd century A.D. (P. Lond. 121, 502 ff., 1. p. 100). See also Schlatter, *Der Evangelist Johannes*, pp. 24 f., who shows that the idea was well known in Jewish circles.

[2] *The Teaching of Jesus*, ii, p. 169.

As Abraham's vision of Messiah's day was only an ideal, so the existence of the Messiah at the time was only in the plan and purpose of God. But such an interpretation does not suit the context in which the words stand. To the assertion of Jesus that Abraham saw his day (8. 56) in prophetic vision the Jews reply that Jesus was not yet fifty years old (8. 57) and had not reached the age of responsibility. He could not therefore have been the subject of prophetic vision on the part of Abraham.[1] Jesus meets this objection by asserting not only that Abraham had seen him as the Messiah of the future, but that he existed before Abraham was born. His own timeless being embraced all history. Nothing but a reference to real personal existence in the answer of Jesus fits the meaning of the objection which it called forth.

Canon W. L. Knox [2] sees in this sentence a conflation of the words in which Jahweh proclaims himself to Moses at the bush with the phrase ἐγώ εἰμι which frequently appears in Hellenistic literature.[3] He points out that the language of Exodus 3. 14 was often used by Jewish controversialists to prove that the God of Israel was really the God of philosophy. "Thus Jesus here practically proclaims himself as the Logos of the God of pure being who appeared to Moses at the bush; and it is scarcely surprising that the Jews should seek to stone him." Such an interpretation necessarily involves the idea of pre-existence.[4]

Dr. C. J. Wright [5] would dispose of the matter another way. He says that Jesus is here speaking of a "pre-temporal life". It was a life not of time, but of eternity. The whole emphasis of the Gospel, he says, is on life in its eternal and essential quality. Eternal life is not a life of never-ending duration; it is a life of perduring essence. "What he said to them was that the life

---

[1] See Dodd, *Bulletin of John Rylands Library*, xix, p. 334. The Rabbis interpreted Gen. 24. 1 as meaning that Abraham entered by prophetic vision into all the coming days, including the days of the Messiah.

[2] *Some Hell. Elements in Prim. Christianity*, pp. 70 ff.

[3] For instances see Bernard, *St. John*, p. cxix ; E. Norden, *Agnostos Theos*, pp. 177 ff. ; and Stauffer's article on " ἐγώ " in *T.W.z.N.T.*, ii, p. 343.

[4] Cf. Bernard, *St. John*, p. 332 : " It is clear that J. means to represent Jesus as thus claiming for himself the timeless being of Deity, as distinct from the temporal existence of man ".

[5] *The Message and Mission of Jesus*, p. 684 f. Cf. Bernard, note above.

he knew was qualitatively different from all existence which is measured in years." Similarly, Baron von Hügel speaks of mystical experience as rising above successiveness to a "simultaneity" which is akin to the Divine Thought.[1]

With this we may agree, but such a view of eternal life does not necessarily exclude the idea of time, or we may deny pre-existence to God himself. The relation between time and eternity is an abstruse problem into which we cannot enter here.[2] But this at least may be said: if God were absolutely timeless, the conception of the divine will and purpose would be meaningless. Furthermore, the thought of eternal life without some conception of time would be foreign to the mind of John, brought up in a Hebrew atmosphere of thought. It is true, as Dr. Wright says, that the life of Jesus "in its essential nature was grounded in the eternal nature of God himself. It partook of the very 'Being' of him who was 'I am that I am'". That is the claim of Jesus in the Fourth Gospel, and it is a unique claim. But we may go on to say that such a claim to share the eternal life of God himself does not exclude the idea of pre-existence, but pre-supposes it, unless we are also to deny pre-existence to God himself. There is nothing inconsistent in introducing the conception of time when comparing the eternal life of Jesus in fellowship with God and the earthly life of men. As we have seen, Jesus himself introduces the idea of time in his comparison with Abraham, πρὶν Ἀβραὰμ γενέσθαι ἐγώ εἰμι. That the Fourth Gospel represented Christ as claiming to have existed personally from all eternity is a reasonable conclusion from the evidence before us.

The phrase "before Abraham was, I am" signifies even more than pre-existence.[3] By it Jesus claims to be the ever-existent

---

[1] *Mystical Element in Religion*, ii, pp. 246 ff.

[2] See Temple, *Nature, Man, and God*, Lecture xvii, and Matthews, *God in Christian Thought and Experience*, ch. xii.

[3] Cf. Stauffer, *T.W.z.N.T.*, ii, p. 352 : "In the 1st-person speeches of the Gospel of St. John Jesus contends with the pseudo-saviours and pseudo-gods of the polytheistic world for the claim to soteriological 1st-person predication. He excels them all, and reveals himself as the only valid representative of God in the absolute divine formula ἐγώ εἰμι, the purest expression of his unique and still utterly inconceivable significance ".

and ever-central Son, to whom everything and every being of the spiritual world are constitutively and essentially related; their very existence in the spiritual world is bound up with him as truly and essentially as they are bound up with the Father. The essential claim of Jesus could not be better expressed than in applying to himself the divine name *'ehyeh 'aher 'ehyeh* (Ex. 3.14) of the Hebrew Scriptures. There can be no better summary of the claim of Jesus to enjoy a unique Sonship to God—an incomparable fellowship with the Father.

4

THE WORD WITH GOD

(b) The Prologue

i. *The Logos*

The discussion in the previous chapter was limited to two propositions: the self-witness of Jesus and his consciousness of pre-existence. The historical manifestation of Jesus as interpreted by himself in word and work not only was the foundation and starting-point of John's own belief, but in the main covers it and coincides with it, even in the form of expression. But John does advance beyond this historical witness. By sinking himself ever more deeply in the contemplation of the eternal pre-existence of the Son he reaches a standpoint possible only in the light of Christ's resurrection. This developed point of view he represents not at the end of the Gospel, like the confession of Thomas, "My Lord and my God", which was the culminating expression of the disciples' faith after the resurrection, but at the very beginning, and as the standpoint from which the earthly history should be regarded.

Bishop Westcott points out that John's teaching on the Logos is properly a question of doctrine and not of nomenclature.[1] We have already quoted Dr. B. W. Bacon to the effect that the whole of the Logos doctrine is to be found in St. Paul.[2]

In relation to God the Father, Christ is described by St. Paul as the image ($\epsilon i\kappa\omega\nu$) of God (2 Cor. 4. 4). In the Epistle to the Colossians (1. 15) we have a much more elaborate statement— "the image of the invisible God" ($\epsilon i\kappa\omega\nu$ $\tau o\hat{u}$ $\theta\epsilon o\hat{u}$ $\tau o\hat{u}$ $\dot{a}o\rho\dot{a}\tau ov$). The $\epsilon i\kappa\omega\nu$ suggests a fairly definite idea, and was much used by Philo; it has the sense not merely of a copy from an original, but of a representation or manifestation of its original. The thought may

---

[1] *The Gospel of St. John*, p. xv.
[2] P. 13.

74

be compared with that of the last verse of the Prologue to the Gospel (1. 18). Christ is further described as possessing the *pleroma* of God, the fulness or totality of the divine attributes, as in Colossians 2. 9: "In him dwelleth all the fulness of the Godhead bodily". The force of this expression is to show that the Father needs no subordinate "thrones, dominions or powers" to mediate between him and the finite universe.

In his relation to the world, Christ is represented as the Agent in creation. He is "the firstborn of all creation (πρωτότοκος πάσης κτίσεως); for in him were all things created ... all things have been created through (διά) him and unto (εἰς) him: he is before all things (ἐστι πρὸ πάντων), and in him all things consist (συνέστηκε)" (Col. 1. 15-17). To the same effect is 1 Corinthians 8. 6. Again, Christ is described in Philippians 2. 6 as having a pre-temporal existence: "Being originally (ὑπάρχων) in the form of God (ἐν μορφῇ θεοῦ)". God's eternal purpose is "to sum up (ἀνακεφαλαιώσασθαι) all things in Christ" (Eph. 1. 10). "Christ is all in all" (πάντα καὶ ἐν πᾶσιν, Col. 3. 11).

In his relation to the human soul, Christ, "the last Adam", is a "life-giving Spirit" (πνεῦμα ζωοποιοῦν, 1 Cor. 15. 45). He dwells in all believers, "forming himself" in them (μορφωθῇ Χριστὸς ἐν ὑμῖν, Gal. 4. 19). He transforms believers into his own image (2 Cor. 3. 18). Christ has an almost hypostatic union with the soul of the believer—"I live, and yet no longer I, but Christ liveth in me" (Gal. 2. 20).

These passages, selected from a much larger number which are to be found in the Pauline Epistles, are sufficient to show the existence of a well-developed Logos-doctrine in St. Paul. It is surprising, therefore, that St. Paul does not use the term Logos, for it must have been known in Ephesus. He had furthermore come into close contact with the Alexandrian Apollos. Canon W. L. Knox thinks that St. Paul was unacquainted with the word. He says [1]: "It is interesting to observe as showing the gradual diffusion of the language of the Synagogues of the Dispersion that Paul is not acquainted with Philo's far more convenient word, while the author of the Fourth Gospel is. The latter writer has

[1] *St. Paul and the Church of the Gentiles*, p. 114 n.

even less contact with Philo's outlook than Paul himself, but Philo's word has become by this time a commonplace of the Synagogues".

It is difficult to believe that St. Paul was unaware of the term Logos, and there was probably some reason why he avoided the use of it. It is to be noticed that St. Paul does not use the closely related term "wisdom" in his later Epistles. He uses it in First Corinthians (1. 30), but in Colossians, where his language is very like that of the Wisdom books, he avoids the term (Col. 1. 15). The same characteristic is to be found in the Epistle to the Hebrews. It may be, therefore, that early Christian writers shunned the use of a term which was current in the pagan world lest there should be confusion and misunderstanding. But no such inhibition troubled John, and he boldly adopted a term well known at Ephesus and filled it with a Christian content.[1]

It may seem strange at first sight that he should adopt a word which had been avoided by earlier Christian writers. We have seen what an exalted significance John attaches to the title Son of God. His affirmation in regard to the Son rises to full height when at the conclusion of the Epistle he says: "This is the true God and everlasting life". Still more significant would be the assertion of 1. 18 if we accepted the strongly supported reading, "The only begotten God".[2] This expression retains the idea of begetting, and at the same time affirms absolute identity of nature. John was, however, faced with two problems for which he was seeking not so much an explanation as a name. The name he found in the term Logos, and the problems were as follows:

ii. *The Logos in Greek Philosophy*

(*a*) There was the problem which had worried all religious philosophers from time immemorial: How can God reveal

---

[1] It should be noticed, however, that John avoids such gnostic words as γνῶσις, πίστις, and σοφία.

[2] See discussion on various readings in Westcott, *The Gospel of St. John*, pp. 32 ff. ; cf. Burney's interesting suggestion that the Aramaic has been misunderstood for the Absolute for Construct State and so rendered "The only begotten God"; see *The Aramaic Origin of the Fourth Gospel*, pp. 39, 40.

himself to man? For the Jew the question was: How can "God who inhabiteth eternity" also "dwell with him that is of a contrite and humble spirit"? For the Greek the problem was: How can God who is Pure Being, Essential Essence, τὸ ὄντως ὄν, and can therefore have no contact with the finite and weak elements of our nature, have any dealings with the affairs of daily life? Israel's problem was religious as the Greek's was metaphysical. The former seeks to bring two persons together, the latter to achieve a synthesis of pure thought. The answers which had been given to these problems and which were the subjects of discussion among the religious people at Ephesus will be considered in a moment.

(b) The second problem was a peculiarly Christian one. John, with the other Christians, was convinced that Jesus was God. The whole of the Fourth Gospel was written in the conviction that "the Word was God". This stupendous fact had been forced upon the disciples when, in the light of the resurrection, they considered the teaching and works of Jesus. This belief seemed to be set in irreconcilable contradiction to the fundamental monotheism of the Jewish religion from which Christianity had sprung. To a Hebrew who believed that Jesus was God in a real sense, this was the supreme problem of his faith. The name Son was unsuited to meet this precise difficulty, because its chief stress lay upon the idea of personality, and so upon distinction in the Godhead. What was wanted was a name which would designate Jesus according to his nature, and in eternal communion, not only with God in the abstract but with the God of the Old Testament.

It so happens that the term Logos had been used in such a way that it could be adapted to provide a solution to both these problems. Dr. E. Krebs suggests that the term may have been selected deliberately in opposition to the various Logos doctrines of heathenism.[1] It would certainly appear that John was offering to the pagan world a reasoned answer to a problem that had exercised the best minds in Greek philosophy and Jewish religion. John crowns and completes the Pauline doctrine

[1] *Der Logos als Heiland im ersten Jahrhundert*, pp. 98 ff.

by his definite and absolute identification of Jesus with the Logos. He thus shows that in Jesus Christ, God and man, time and eternity, were brought together; he also showed that the belief in Jesus as the Logos was a reasonable deduction from the Jews' own teaching about God's relation with the world. It must be observed, however, that the primary purpose of John was not to set forth either a metaphysic of the divine nature or a philosophy of the Incarnation. His primary purpose was rather to proclaim the Gospel of God's redeeming purpose through the Son of God. Nevertheless we may be grateful that the Christian Church had in those days a thinker who could present the Gospel in terms which could be appreciated by the leaders of pagan thought. In the words of Schmiedel, "he did great service to his age by showing that one could be a thinker, appreciate knowledge, stand in the midst of a stream of thoroughly intellectual movements, and yet remain a faithful son of the Church".[1] In order to appreciate the Johannine contribution to religious thought by his identification of Jesus with the Logos we shall consider the place which this term occupied in contemporary thought.

The doctrine of the Logos is found in many religions and philosophical systems, in India, in Persia, in Egypt, and in Greece.[2] Our interest in this section lies mainly with the Greek philosophers, for it was in the intellectual atmosphere created by their writings that Christianity was moulded. The Greek philosophers regarded the world as an ordered whole and as the product of reason. Consequently, the idea of the Logos occupies a prominent place in one form or another in most Greek systems of thought.

It acquires its first importance in the theories of Heraclitus

---

[1] *The Johannine Writings*, p. 236.

[2] For a full discussion see *Der Logos als Heiland im ersten Jahrhundert* by Engelbert Krebs. Dr. Krebs shows that the attempt to find in Indian religion and philosophy a relationship with the Logos conception of the first century has been generally abandoned. He also argues that neither in Persian nor in Egyptian religious ideas can any direct source for the Biblical conceptions be found. He thinks, however, that the Persian doctrine of Ameshas Spentas and the Egyptian conception of creation by the word of the gods exercised some indirect influence upon the Christian doctrine of the Logos.

(*c.* 535-475 B.C.). About one hundred and thirty fragments of the writings of Heraclitus remain, and of these there are only six fragments in which the term Logos is used, and in two of these the word is used in an untechnical sense.[1] From this small amount of material we can determine the main lines of the Heraclitean conception of the Logos. The Logos is eternal, for it "is always existent" (*fr.* 2); it is omnipresent, for, according to fragment 2, "all things happen by way of the Logos"; it is rational; it is embodied in fire; it is divine; it is the principle of harmony between opposing forces; the Logos is rejected by men: "Though the Logos is always existent, yet men are unable to understand it when they hear it" (*fr.* 2). This is all we know about the Logos teaching of Heraclitus, yet it has had great influence upon subsequent thinkers.[2] Dr. W. R. Inge thinks that the author of the Fourth Gospel deliberately refers to the "lofty doctrine of the great Ephesian idealist".[3]

After Heraclitus the doctrine of the Logos was submerged for a time in that of a kindred conception, the νοῦς or mind. It was Anaxagoras who introduced the idea of a supreme intellectual principle active in the world and yet above it. This was a most important step in the history of human speculation, for in conceiving of a ruling principle of the universe he clearly added the idea of transcendence to that of immanence.[4] Both Plato and Aristotle built their philosophical systems upon the assumption of Anaxagoras that God is a creative intelligence who brought order out of chaos. They both sought to overcome this dualism by subjecting matter to the operations of the mind. Though Aristotle protested against the Platonic theory of ideas on the ground that it left an unbridged chasm between material

---

[1] These fragments have been edited by Mr. I. Bywater in *Heracliti Reliquiae* (1877). They are translated by Dr. J. Burnet in *Early Greek Philosophy*, and by Dr. J. Adam in *The Religious Teachers of Greece*. Dr. Adam discusses fully the Logos conception of Heraclitus in *The Vitality of Platonism*, pp. 77 ff.

[2] Cf. Diels, *E.R.E.*, vi, p. 591 : "Heraclitus is the profoundest thinker before Plato, and is the joint founder with him of the idealism which under the influence of Plato and Christianity has prevailed over other systems".

[3] *Christian Mysticism*, p. 147 n.

[4] Cf. Hegel, *History of Philosophy*, i, p. 319 : "With Anaxagoras a light, if still a weak one, begins to dawn, because the understanding is now the principle".

objects and the ideas, he did not himself succeed in resolving the dualism. He conceived nature as an hierarchy of species in each of which the essence tends towards its full actualization in a series of phenomena drawn towards its ultimate perfection by the final causality of the supreme Unmoved Mover. It still remains the case, however, that God as pure intelligence cannot have any dealings with the material world.

This accentuation of the divine transcendence obviously favoured the development of Logoi, Spirits, and Powers, forming an hierarchy between God and the world. Both Plato and Aristotle realized the need of linking the two together, for man could never rest content with being separated absolutely from God. But it is clear that such Logoi, Spirits, and Powers must be less divine than the Supreme Spirit, whose character is such that it can never be defiled by contact with the material world.

The monistic philosophy of the Stoics was developed in opposition to the dualism which had been characteristic of Greek philosophy from the time of Anaxagoras. The Stoics refused to distinguish between mind and matter. In their view the material and the spiritual have a common nature and origin, and both may be regarded as different aspects of the same thing. Though they borrowed some ideas from Plato and Aristotle they made the teaching of Heraclitus the metaphysical basis for their philosophy. The very term Logos came back into the literature of the period. The Logos is the Stoic God and is represented as dwelling both in the physical world and in the souls of men.

One of the firmest convictions of the Stoics was that the world was rational. Writer after writer employ almost every argument possible to establish the action of reason in the world. The whole of the second book of Cicero's *De Natura Deorum* might be quoted as evidence of the belief that nature exhibits a rational design. The significance of this organic unity of the whole, or, as the Stoics called it, this sympathy of all the parts with one another, is that it is the achievement of the Logos or Universal Reason. The Logos pervades the whole world "as honey fills the cells of the honey comb". The past, present, and future are linked together by the Logos as a chain which unrolls itself throughout the centuries in a destined series of events.[1]

In inorganic objects the Logos acts as the principle of cohesion (ἕξις), in plants it rises to the rank of φύσις or growth-power, in animals which possess a soul (ψυχή) it manifests itself in the powers of observation and independent movement, in men and gods it appears as reason (λόγος). This reason is a ray of celestial fire, "that particle of Zeus, which Zeus gives to man for his controller and governor".[2] Because of this indwelling of the divine Logos, man himself partakes of the divine nature. "From him (i.e. Zeus) have descended seeds, not only to my father and my grandfather, but to all things that have been begotten and are nourished on the earth, but chiefly to those that possess reason, for these alone are privileged to hold communion with God, being united with him in intercourse through reason: why may not a man then call himself a citizen of the world? Why not a son of God?"[3] This reason is the ruling faculty in man, and to it are subordinated the other seven parts of the soul, namely, the five senses, speech, and reproduction. But the chief division to be noted for our purpose is the distinction between the Logos as thought (ἐνδιάθετος) and as speech (προφορικός). The former enables a man to participate in the Soul of the world, and through the latter he is able to communicate with the gods and men. Later, Speech came to be identified with Hermes, and the Logos reduced to an intermediate being between the Supreme God and the world. But at first no essential distinction was made between Zeus and the Logos.

We find an important development in the writings of Cornutus, a contemporary of the Fourth Evangelist. He identifies the Logos of Stoic speculation with many of the old gods such as Pan, Eros, and Atlas. But he also finds the personification of the human Logos in Hermes, and Hermes, according to him, is the god of speech rather than reason.[4] Because of this the tongues

[1] Cicero, De Div. 1, 36, 127.
[2] Marcus Aurelius, Meditations, 5. 27.
[3] Epictetus, Discourses, 1. 9.
[4] Cornutus, Theologia Graeca, ch. 16, p. 20, in Bibliotheca Scriptorum Graecorum et Romanorum Teubneriana, ed. C. Lang (1881).

F

of men, as the organ of speech, are dedicated to Hermes.[1] He says that Hermes was born of Zeus and Maia, because speech is the daughter of study and research.[2] Cornutus thus introduces two Logoi into his scheme of thought. There is the Logos which is identified with such divinities as Pan, Eros, and Atlas, and which retains the original meaning of Universal Reason. There is also the Logos which is identified with Hermes, that is, the Logos of human speech. Thus Hermes as the Logos immanent in men is distinguished from the Logos of Universal Reason, which in popular thought received the honour of apotheosis and may be regarded as transcendent.

A further step was taken when Heraclitus, the author of *Quaestiones Homericae*, regarded Hermes as the only God which could be identified with the Logos. No distinction is recognized between human speech and reason. They are merely two manifestations of the activity of the god Hermes. Hermes is called Ἀργειφόντης not because he was the slayer of Argus, which was the usual meaning of the word, but because speech is that which manifests thought.[3] A distinction is, however, made between λόγος ἐνδιάθετος and λόγος προφορικός. The former represents Hermes as dwelling in the human heart, and the latter as Hermes who dwells in heaven and only manifests himself from a distance.[4] One of the results of uniting in the person of Hermes both speech and reason and the recognition that in one aspect Hermes transcended the human heart was that he came to be regarded as an intermediary between the Supreme God and men. He was the messenger of the gods and the divine word which dwells in men and reveals to them the will of the gods. This was the position occupied by the Logos in Alexandrian philosophy, and it is possible that the identification of the Logos with Hermes influenced philosophical speculation in this direction.

This brief survey of the Logos-conception in Greek thought will have made it apparent that it was a dominant conception

---

[1] Cornutus, *Theologia Graeca*, ch. 16, p. 21.

[2] Ibid., p. 23.

[3] Heraclitus, *Quaestiones Homericae* in Bibliotheca Scriptorum Graecorum et Romanorum Teubneriana, ch. 72, p. 95.

[4] Ibid., ch. 72, pp. 95, 96.

among the Greek philosophers. It was, as Harnack remarked, "Greek philosophy *in nuce*". The history of the Logos idea summarizes substantially what the Greek mind could contribute to the explanation of the world and God's relation with it. In its different stages it was the first and last word of the most serious pagan thinkers on the relationship between God, who is of purer eyes than to behold iniquity, and the material creation. At first it was thought that there could be no contact between God, who is Pure Being, and the finite elements of human nature. But there was a certain amount of uneasiness about this position and attempts were made to bridge the gulf between God and the created world. The gap was completely closed when the Stoics taught that God and the world were one. For the Stoics the Logos as Reason was God. This may have satisfied the speculative mind, but the religious man needs a god who is transcendent, to whom prayers may be made and worship offered. We find, therefore, among some of the Stoics concessions made to the religious needs of men. The Logos comes to occupy the position of an intermediary between the Supreme God and the created world. Among some thinkers he was regarded both as dwelling in man and as being identified with a god who was transcendent. But it is to be noticed that such a god was always regarded as a lesser god: the Supreme God remained far removed from the created world. The implication is that the sovereign and unoriginate God is debarred by his own nature from performing functions which were delegated to this lesser god with whom the Logos was identified.

The Johannine proclamation is in complete contrast to such a conception. According to the Fourth Gospel there is no metaphysical dualism between spirit and matter; there is no insuperable barrier to the incarnation of the Word. The divine Word is represented as performing a task in union with God. The Word is not an inferior and subordinate agent. His Father is associated with all he does: "My Father worketh hitherto and I work"; "I and the Father are one". Thus God is not isolated from the world with which he makes contact in and through the Son. The Father and the Son do not stand over against each other as a principal and a secondary god, the former remaining apart from the world while the latter creates, organizes, and sustains. But they are related to one another in terms of absolute harmony and identity of purpose.

The popularity of the term Logos is further illustrated by the use of it in the Hermetic literature. The doctrine of the divine Word as the agent of creation was familiar in these circles. Even before Hermes came to be identified with Thoth, there was a legend that the god of Hermopolis had produced the world by the power of his Word. "Creation was not for him the muscular effort to which the other gods owed their birth; he had accomplished the task by formula, or by his voice alone at the first moment of his awakening in the Nu".[1] There were other and more fantastic legends to the effect that the Logos was worshipped by Osiris, the Father of Horus, in the weasel and the crocodile.[2] It is not surprising, therefore, to find in the cosmogony of the *Poimandres* a prominent place assigned to the Logos. As the author of the *Poimandres* was also dependent upon the Genesis account of creation, it is possible that he was influenced by the Jewish doctrine of creation by the Word of God. Scott thinks the author is also indebted to a school of thinkers who brought to bear upon the study of their sacred books a knowledge of Greek philosophy such as is exhibited in the writings of Philo.[3] It does not appear, however, that the Hermetist was indebted to Philo's conception of the divine Word. As Dr. C. H. Dodd points out, the Logos of Philo is $\kappa \acute{o} \sigma \mu o s \ \nu o \eta \tau \acute{o} s$. The Logos of the *Poimandres* is the spoken word of God, the Voice of the Light. He is therefore much nearer to the thought of Genesis 1 than to Philo in this respect.[4]

The doctrine of the Logos in the *Poimandres* is as follows: There is one supreme God, the Mind of Sovereignty, who is Life and Light. This supreme God gives birth to two sons, to the Logos, who is described as being the Son of God, and to another

---

[1] Maspero, *The Dawn of Civilization*, pp. 146 f.
[2] Other examples may be found in Reitzenstein, *Poimandres*, pp. 59 ff.
[3] *Hermetica*, i, p. 7.
[4] *The Bible and the Greeks*, p. 120.

Mind, a Maker of things. The Logos who comes forth from the Light is called a Holy Word in contrast to the speechless chaos which it assails and reduces to order. "The watery substance, having received the Word, was fashioned into an ordered world; the elements being separated from it; and from the elements came forth the brood of living creatures." [1] The Logos thus has the task of separating the elements; the function of making living things is reserved for the Second Mind. The two, however, are really one, for when the Logos had completed his task he returned to the highest sphere of heaven and "was united with the Second Mind; for he was of one substance with him". From this point onward they are considered as one.

The Logos is called the Son of God, and when the Seer asks how this can be, the reply is made that if he looks into the constitution of his own nature he will learn by analogy what is meant by this title.[2] The argument is that "your Logos (speech) may be called the son of your mind or thought, because it issues from your νοῦς, and is inseparably connected with it, and in the same sense the divine λόγος may be called the son of the divine νοῦς".[3]

A different conception of the Logos is to be found in *Libellus* 13. This tractate discusses the manner in which rebirth may be accomplished. When the powers of evil are driven out of a man "then is the Word (of God) built up in him".[4] Thus when the rebirth is accomplished Hermes can say: "Rejoice now, my son; you are being cleansed by the Powers of God; for they have come to build up in you the body of the Word (of God)".[5] According to Mr. W. Scott, the Logos in this *Libellus* signifies "an organism of which the several powers of God are the constituent parts; and the organism is built up in the reborn man, as the body is built up out of the several members".[6] He thinks that it corresponds more or less to what Plato called τὸ λογιστικόν and Aristotle τὸ λόγον ἔχον. It does not, therefore, possess the distinct personality of the Logos in the *Poimandres*. It is in fact

---

[1] *Libellus* 1. 8 b.   [2] Ibid., 1. 6.
[3] Scott, *Hermetica*, ii, p. 26 ; cf. Dodd, *The Bible and the Greeks*, pp. 117 ff.
[4] *Libellus* 13. 7 b.   [5] Ibid., 13. 8 b.   [6] *Hermetica*, i, p. 245 n.

only in the *Poimandres* and a few sentences quoted by Cyril of Alexandria that the conception of the hypostatized Logos appears in the Hermetic writings.

Reitzenstein in *Zwei religionsgeschichtliche Fragen* (1901) and the *Poimandres* (1904) argued that the Logos doctrine of the Fourth Gospel was derived from a synthesis of the Stoic doctrine of Hermes as the Logos and the Egyptian God Thoth. As the identification of these two ideas had taken place in the time of the Ptolemies, Reitzenstein thought that there must have existed at that time a Hermes religion with theological writings similar to the extant Hermetic literature. On this supposition he asserted that the most important thoughts which appear in the Hermetic literature of post-Christian times actually existed in the first century before Christ. From this he reaches the conclusion that the religious conception of the Word as possessing a distinct personality in the Fourth Gospel is to be explained by the union of the Stoic and Egyptian theories.[1]

It is agreed that there are some striking parallels between the Fourth Gospel and the Hermetic writings, some of which have been quoted. But the ethical interest of John differs completely from the magical point of view of the *Poimandres*. It has been strongly argued by Dr. E. Krebs that the Biblical conceptions have rather influenced the Hermetic literature.[2] On the whole, modern scholarship has inclined to the position that there has been very little literary dependence on the one side or the other. Prof. C. H. Dodd says that whatever likeness there is between the different documents may best be explained "as the result of minds working under the same general influence".[3] Dr. Carpenter comes to the same conclusion : "With some common religious terminology . . . the Hermetica and the Fourth Gospel

---

[1] Cf. Grill, *Untersuchungen über die Entstehung des vierten Evangeliums*, i, pp. xi ff. : " At all events it would be natural to suppose that the Logos—in the form in which, according to the theology, and particularly the cosmogony of Stoic Egyptian Hellenism, it is associated with Hermes-Thoth, the creative god of the Word (speech), and is conceived as a personal principle of revelation—furnished in a certain sense a helpful model and a positive starting-point for the Logos idea of the Evangelist."

[2] See the appendix to *Der Logos als Heiland im ersten Jahrhundert* ; cf. F. Granger, 'The Poimandres of Hermes Trismegistos " in *J.T.S.*, 1904, pp. 395 ff.

[3] *The Bible and the Greeks*, p. 247 ; cf. pp. 17 ff.

appear wholly independent. Each makes its contribution to
the spiritual life of its age in its own form".[1]

iii. The Logos in Philo

The writings of Philo represent a link between the philosophers of Greece and the Christian theologians. Philo attempted
a synthesis between the Jewish Scriptures and Greek philosophy
in which the idea of the Logos occupies a prominent place. He
is not, however, the solitary figure that Bousset thought him to be.
The very fact that he spent the whole of his life at Alexandria
makes it almost certain that the kind of religious speculation we
find in his writings was a characteristic feature of his contemporaries. "Even though the writings of his predecessors have
disappeared to the last fragment, one has only to go through his
works to see how numerous were these predecessors who loved to
discover in the Bible the whole philosophical teaching of Greece,
her physics, her psychology, and her ethics." [2] He is, however,
the sole remaining exponent of this "new learning" which had
so great an influence upon the Jews of the Diaspora, and upon
Christian theology in the early days of the Church.

As Philo was born not later than 20 B.C. and died some time
after A.D. 41, he was a contemporary of both Jesus and St. Paul.
Incorporated in his writings are examples of the kind of speculations that were current in the Schools and Synagogues of
Alexandria. And it is not unlikely that similar methods of exposition were to be found in the Rabbinical Schools at Jerusalem
and among the Jews of the Dispersion in the great cities of the
West. It is possible, therefore, that John was aware of the kind of
speculation about the Logos which appears in the writings of
Philo. "In the Fourth Gospel", says Canon Knox, "Jesus as
the Logos fulfilled the same function as the Logos of Philo, and
a large part of the Gospel is devoted to an exposition of his life and
work in terms of the same allegorical symbolism as that which
Philo habitually employs, and reads into that symbolism the
same conventional conceptions of theistic philosophy." [3] If this

---

[1] The Johannine Writings, p. 312.
[2] Lebreton, The History of the Dogma of the Trinity (Eng. Trans., 1939), p. 135.
[3] Some Hell. Elements in Prim. Christianity, p. 43.

statement had stood by itself it would do less than justice to
the different conceptions of the Logos and give a completely
wrong impression of the originality and religious insight of the
Fourth Gospel. But Canon Knox goes on to say: "On the
other hand, nothing could be more fantastic than to suppose
that the writer had read Philo's works and deliberately substituted the figure of Jesus for the Philonic Logos. It would
be inconceivable that the freshness and spontaneity of the Gospel
were derived from the laborious pedantry of Philo". It is
reasonable to suppose that John was aware of the kind of
Midrashic tradition upon which Philo exercised his ingenuity.
They were both seeking to interpret their faith to the
Gentile world, and both the similarities and the differences
between the two conceptions are significant.[1]

Philo uses the term Logos no less than thirteen hundred
times, and he uses the word to "express the conception of a
mediator between the transcendent God and the universe, an
immanent power active in creation and revelation".[2] Typical
utterances of Philo are as follows: "The primal existence is God,
and next to him is the Logos of God" (*Leg. Alleg.* 2. 86). "The
image of God is the Logos, through whom the whole universe
was framed" (*De Spec. Leg.* 1. 81; cf. *De Somn.* 2. 6). "If the
whole creation . . . is a copy of the divine image, it is manifest
that the archetypal seal also, which we aver to be the world
descried by mind, would be the very Logos of God" (*De Mund. Op.*
25). The Logos is eternal: "It is signed and impressed by the
seal of God, the stamp of which is the Eternal Word" (ἀΐδιος
λόγος, *De Plant.* 18). Similarly, the attribute of eternity is applied
to the Logos in the following passage: "If we have not yet
become fit to be thought sons of God, yet we may be sons of his
eternal image, the most holy Word. For the Word is the eldest
born image of God" (*De Conf. Ling.* 147). "Being the Word of
God the Eternal must needs himself be imperishable" (*De Conf.*

---

[1] For the Philonic conception of the Logos see Siegfried, *Philo von Alexandria*,
pp. 219 ff.; Drummond, *Philo Judaeus*, ii, pp. 185 ff.; Bréhier, *Les Idées philosophiques
et religieuses de Philon d'Alexandrie*, pp. 83 ff.; Lebreton, *The History of the Dogma of the
Trinity* (Eng. Trans., 1939), pp. 133 ff.

[2] W. F. Howard, *Christianity according to St. John*, pp. 152 ff.

Ling. 41). There are two passages in which Philo refers to the Logos as God (*De Somn.* 1. 39-41 and *Leg. Alleg.* 3. 73), but in both cases Philo is only making a concession because men are unable to comprehend the supreme God. In one passage the Logos is referred to as a Second God (*Q. in Gen.* 4. 180). This was probably due to the influence of Stoicism. The Logos as the immanent cosmic principle of the material universe was divine, but only because it was an expression of the energy of the transcendent God.

The link, therefore, between the timeless and immutable God and the material world was the Logos. This was the answer given by Philo to John's first problem. But the answer given by John was much fuller and more satisfying. Philo was prevented by his own principles from arriving at the Christian solution of the problem. "There are", he said, "three kinds of life: one which is πρὸς θεόν, another πρὸς γένεσιν, and a third which is a mixture of both. But the ζωὴ πρὸς θεόν has not descended to us, nor has it come as far as the necessities of the body" (*Quis rer. div. haer.* 9). The Logos of John accomplished what Philo's Logos could not do: "The Word became flesh and dwelt among us". John was able to bridge by the Incarnation the gulf which Philo, by speculation, thought impassable.

These religious speculations and the use of the term Logos to provide the link between God and the world were bound to influence John's mind as he thought upon the first problem and how it fitted in with his belief about Jesus. He would be further strengthened in his choice of the word Logos, for when looking back upon the literature of the Old Testament he found suggestions that not only provided material for the solution of the first problem but also provided a scheme of thought in which the Person of Jesus could find a place without too violent a break with the rigid monotheism of the Hebrews.

iv. *The Word in the Old Testament*

The idea of the divine Word as possessing a quasi-independence was well known among the Sumerians. The importance of the word was such that when something did not exist it was not regarded as having a name.[1]   The power of the word is illustrated by the use made of it by the magician.   It was by the spoken word that he gained power over other people's lives, over disease and death.   It was in this way that a number of words developed into a fixed incantation, or ritual formula, which could bring a blessing or a curse to men.   Reference is made to the "Word of Marduk", "whose thoughts are unsearchable, whose word is true, against whose command there is no turning back, whose utterance is unalterable".   The divine Word thus carried with it the idea of power, of a divine activity ordering and disposing the activities of men and nature.   The spoken word is not regarded as an accomplished work (ἔργον), but a creative activity (ἐνέργεια).   Such a view of the word as dynamic and energetic is a special characteristic of Hebrew thought.   Even the word in Hebrew which means "to say a man is such and such" also means "to make a man such and such".[2]   In this it differs from the Greek idea of the spoken word, which was conceptual and persuasive.   "Man as a thinker speaks the language in which logicians and philosophers are interested; man as a rational and a feeling being is struck and persuaded by rhetoric and poetry." [3]   But the Hebrews refused to make such an artificial distinction.   The spoken word was the expression of the whole man.   Thus God's word was not merely the abstract revelation of his mind; it was the expression of God's will in nature, in men, and in history.

In the creation epic recorded on the clay tablets discovered among the ruins of Asshurbanipal's library in Nineveh in 1873 there appears a reference to Mammu, which is an epithet for Tiamat, and a name for the son of Apsu.   It has been thought that we have here a reference to the Word of the Creator.[4] As the Genesis account of creation was almost certainly based on the cosmological ideas current in Babylon, it may be that this is the origin of the idea of creation by the divine Word.   Egyptian

---

[1] See Guillaume, *Prophecy and Divination*, pp. 19 ff.

[2] Pedersen, *Israel*, p. 167, and A. H. F. Thornton in *Hibbert Journal*, Jan. 1946, p. 132, "The Hebrew Conception of Speech as Creative Energy".

[3] A. H. F. Thornton, ibid., p. 132.

[4] See *Primitive Christianity and its Non-Jewish Sources*, by C. Clemen, p. 82.

influences, however, must not be overlooked. The long sojourn of the tribes of Israel in Egypt, and the close relationship which always existed between the peoples of Palestine and Egypt, provided every opportunity for Egyptian ideas to influence Hebrew thought. The Hebrews, however, did not come to believe in the Word of God as the agent in creation until comparatively late in their history. They were always firmly convinced that the Word of God was the agent in revelation; and it is to this belief that we owe the revelation of the will of God as it was made known by the Hebrew prophets.[1]

Whatever may have been the origin of the conception, it is clear that the idea of the Word possessing power to create and to destroy assumed great importance among the Hebrews. In the Genesis account of creation the Word of God is represented as a force locked up in the being of God. The Word of God proceeding from him, in accordance with his will, produces the forms of the world. In other words, God's inner world of thought becomes, through his will, the source of life outside of himself. "God said, Let there be light, and there was light." The same idea is expressed again and again in the Psalms and elsewhere in the Old Testament. "By the word of the Lord were the heavens made, and by the breath of his mouth all their host. . . . He commanded and it stood still." We shall consider the parallelism between the Prologue of the Fourth Gospel and Genesis later. But we must point out here that the words Ἐν ἀρχῇ, ὁ θεός, ἐγένετο, σκοτία, κόσμος, φῶς, and ζωή all suggest that the first chapter of Genesis was in the mind of John when he wrote the Prologue.

In the Old Testament the Word of God is regarded as being effective not only at the initial moment of creation, but in accomplishing his will in the world at all times. "For as the rain cometh down and the snow from heaven, and returneth not thither, but watereth the earth, and maketh it bring forth and bud, and giveth seed to the sower and bread to the eater; so shall my word be that goeth forth out of my mouth: it shall not return unto me void, but it shall accomplish that which

[1] Cf. Guillaume, op. cit., p. 25.

I please, and it shall prosper in the thing whereto I sent it" (Is. 55. 10 ff.).

But the Word of the Lord is specially regarded as the means of revelation. He is a messenger who reveals the will of God, and when the Psalmist says that God's word runneth very swiftly (Ps. 147. 15) he understands this almost in a literal sense. Similarly, "The Lord sent a word into Jacob, and it hath lighted upon Israel" (Is. 9. 8). The Word of the Lord may take possession of a man and use him as an instrument to accomplish his purposes: "The Lord God hath spoken; who can but prophesy?" (Amos 3. 8); "I restrained myself, but thy word was like a fire in my bones" (Jer. 20. 9).

The prophet encountered the Lord in different ways, through the events of history, in dreams, auditions, and visions. But the meaning of these experiences must first be thought out in the mind of the prophet and then declared by him through a *dabar*. The prophet was one who was able to identify himself with both man and God. He was the representative of Israel standing before God, and he was the mouth of God proclaiming his will to men. It is this relation with both God and Israel that makes the prophet the focus of revelation. The prophet is a man who has stood in the council of God, has heard his Word, and delivers what he has heard. The "Word" is the actual medium of revelation. When the "Word" is proclaimed the eternal order breaks through into this world of time and space. When we remember that in the Fourth Gospel the Word of God is represented as sharing the counsels of God from all eternity and that at a certain point in time the Word became flesh in order to declare and accomplish the will of God, the significance of the prophetic conception of the Word of God will be apparent.

The semi-independence of the word is seen even more clearly in the giving of a blessing or a curse. The word is not merely the expression of the speaker's mind; it contains within itself the actual blessing or curse. Hence, once it has been spoken it is impossible to revoke it. When Isaac gave Jacob a blessing which he had reserved for Esau, he could not withdraw the word that had been spoken (Gen. 27. 33). All he could do was to give Esau another blessing. Similarly, when Micah learns of the curse his mother pronounced upon the unknown person who had stolen the eleven hundred pieces of silver from her, he is afraid and confesses to the theft himself. But his mother cannot remove the curse; she can only try to divert the consequences by making the pieces into a graven image and thus dedicating the silver to the Lord (Judges 17. 1-4). When the Lord pronounces a judgement on a nation, it is the word which possesses the power to destroy. "Then the Lord put forth his hand, and touched my mouth: and the Lord said unto me, Behold, I have put my words into thy mouth: see, I have this day set thee over nations and over kingdoms, to pluck and to break down, and to destroy and to overthrow, to build and to plant" (Jer. 1. 9-10; cf. Zech. 5. 1-4).

In all this we are not to see a complete hypostasis distinct from God. It was a characteristic of Jewish thought to express abstract and spiritual conceptions in a concrete form. In the words of Dr. Purves, "Hebrew thought tended to represent God's self-manifestation as mediated by an agent, more or less conceived as personal and yet blending with the divine personality itself ".[1] It is clear that such a conception of the word as possessing an almost independent existence could be developed in such a way as to suggest the possibility of a Divine Logos who should fully reveal the mind and will of God in a person.

We see in the Wisdom literature such a development in process. In Ecclesiasticus we have, according to the Syrian and Aethiopic gloss, "By his word his works were created" (Eccles. 42. 15), and "by his word all things consist" (Eccles. 43. 26). The same thought appears in 4 Esdras, "Lord, Thou spakest on the first day of creation: Let there be heaven and earth, and Thy word hath accomplished the work" (4 Esdras 6. 38). In this there is a clear suggestion that the word possesses a power that is almost independent of God who utters the word.

But it is especially in the Book of Wisdom that the word is referred to in terms that suggest a distinct personality. The author is probably a Hellenistic Greek whose philosophical outlook points to Alexandria or, at least, Egypt as his home. He

---

[1] G. T. Purves, *H.D.B.*, iii, p. 134.

reveals a first-hand knowledge of Plato's *Phaedo* and *Republic* and of Xenophon's *Memorabilia Socratis* (2. 12-20 ; 9. 15; 11. 17). It is possible that he was also acquainted with the philosophy of Heraclitus, which may have influenced his conception of the word. The important difference is that the Biblical writer thought of God and his Word as transcending the universe, whereas Heraclitus regarded the Logos or God as identical with the universe. The actual term Logos does not occupy a prominent place in the Book of Wisdom. It is Wisdom, rather than the Word, that fulfils the function of the Logos. This suggests that though there are many affinities with the Alexandrian conception of the Logos, the book is earlier than Philo. It is indeed probably the first important attempt to achieve a synthesis between the Hebrew and the Greek approach to religion.

In Solomon's Prayer for Wisdom appeal is made to the "God of the fathers, and Lord who keepest mercy, who madest all things by thy word, and by thy wisdom thou formedst man" (Wisd. Sol. 9. 1-2). At first sight there appears to be no more in the use of the "word" here than in the earlier passages in the Bible. But it is parallel to "wisdom", and in a book where wisdom is personified in a remarkable degree it is difficult not to ascribe the same degree of individuality to the "word". This impression is confirmed by 18. 14: "For while peaceful silence enwrapped all things, and night in her own swiftness was in mid-course, thine all-powerful word leaped into the midst of the doomed land, bearing as a sharp sword thine unfeigned commandment; and standing it filleth all things with death". Dr. Charles Harris commenting on this passage says: "The personification of 'thine all-powerful word' (Logos) in this passage is so vivid that there is much to be said for the supposition of Eichhorn, Gfrörer, Burton, and Fairweather, that the Logos is here hypostatized as in Philo and St. John". Dr. Harris's own feeling is that the meaning is similar to that of such Old Testament passages as Hosea 6. 5-11, Jeremiah 23. 29, and Psalm 147. 15 ff.[1]

In deciding which of these two views should be adopted, two points must be taken into consideration. First, the general

---

[1] *New Commentary* (S.P.C.K.), ii, p. 78.

theology of the book. This teaches that both creation and salvation, though acts of God, are mediated through a personal, or
quasi-personal, agent or mediator. This mediator is chiefly
spoken of as Wisdom. But in this passage Logos and Wisdom are
to be identified and fulfil the same functions. In the second
place, the environment in which the author lived encourages us
to accept the Alexandrian interpretation of the Word. Although
the Book of Wisdom was probably written before Philo was born,
the Hellenists long before Philo had introduced the idea of the
Logos into their speculations on the Bible. Ezekiel the Tragic,
who wrote in the second century B.C., asserted that it was the
λόγος θεῖος who appeared to Moses in the burning bush.[1]
And Philo himself witnesses to earlier speculations on the subject
of the Logos.[2] It seems likely, therefore, that the author of the
Book of Wisdom was influenced by these earlier speculations
in his references to the Word. He personifies the Word to a
greater degree than had yet appeared in the pages of the
Old Testament. Nevertheless he does not adopt the general
Alexandrian idea of the Word as metaphysically distinct from
God. The functions of the Word do not exclude God's intimate
contact with the world; it is rather the means by which God
approaches men and exercises his will in the world. In this the
Book of Wisdom remains faithful to the Hebrew use of the Word.

The Old Testament conception of God as One who, though
he dwells in the high and holy place, is also with him that is of
a contrite and humble spirit, made it unnecessary to interpose
an intermediary between the transcendent God and the created
world in the same way as the Greeks. The Greek conception
of God as static being was quite foreign to the Hebrew mind:
God was essentially one who does things. He was the living
God. Nevertheless we believe that in the Hebrew conception
of the Word we have in the Old Testament the pregnant thought
that the inner, conscious life of the divine will, proceeding from
God to accomplish some purpose, may possess an activity of
its own. The divine Word was, however, never reduced to a
δεύτερος θεός and was never regarded as a substitute for God.

---

[1] Eusebius, *Praep. Evang.* 9. 29.   [2] *De Somn.* I. 118 ff.

When, therefore, John proclaimed that Jesus was the Logos and that he was one with the Father, it is difficult to avoid the conclusion that he had in mind the kind of relationship that existed between God and the Word in the Old Testament. The Johannine doctrine of the Word is in the natural line of development of the Old Testament conception of the Word which implied that in certain circumstances the divine will could be represented as an "activity" in some sense distinct from God.

v.   *The Memra in Rabbinic Literature*

The Word or *Memra* is frequently used in the later Rabbinical writings, and some have seen in this use one of the sources of the Johannine conception. Sometimes the *Memra* is represented as an Intercessor before God. For example, in the Targum of Jonathan to the Prophets, written in the early part of the first century, the *Memra* is spoken of as the Intercessor who pleads to God on behalf of Israel (*Targ. Jon. to Jer.* 29. 14). In the Targum of Onkelos to the Pentateuch, written almost within the lifetime of Jesus, the *Memra* is frequently referred to as the Helper of the righteous in Israel. In the Palestinian Targum to the Pentateuch the *Memra* is referred to as the means whereby God turns again to his people (*Targ. to Lev.* 26. 9). In the same Targum to Deut. 4. 7 it is said that "the *Memra* brings Israel nigh unto God, and sits on his throne receiving the prayers of Israel".

Such quotations might be multiplied almost without end. But there would not be much point in doing so, for it is now generally agreed that the *Memra* does not indicate an intermediary between God and the world, but is merely a circumlocution for the divine name. The reasons for arriving at this conclusion are clearly set forth by Dr. G. F. Moore in *Intermediaries in Jewish Theology*.[1] He points out that the term *Memra* is not employed in the Targums to render such phrases as "the word (*dabar*) of the Lord", the "word of God", and "my word". The word *pitgama*, or rarely *milla*, is used to translate such phrases. In other words, "where the 'word of God' in the Hebrew

---

[1] Reprint from *Harvard Theological Review*, xv (1922).

Scriptures is the medium or instrumentality of revelation or of communication with men, it is not in the Targums his *Memra*; nor is the creative word of God his *Memra*".[1]

On those occasions when the word *Memra* is employed it has, according to Dr. Moore, "sometimes the connotation of command —we might in imitation of the etymology say 'edict'—the expression of his will which is an effective force in nature and providence; sometimes it might best be translated 'oracle', the revelation of his will or purpose (not, however, a specific word of prophecy); sometimes it is the resolution of a metaphor for God's power, his protection, and the like. In many instances it is merely a verbal buffer—one of many such in the Targums— to keep God from seeming to come to too close quarters with men and things; but it is always a buffer *word*, not a buffer idea, still less a buffer person".[2]

Dr. Moore concludes his investigation by saying: "the sum of the whole matter is that nowhere in these Targums is *Memra* a 'being' of any kind or in any sense, whether conceived personally as an angel employed in communication with men, or as a philosophically impersonal created potency".[3] There is nothing, therefore, between the Logos of the Prologue and the *Memra* of the Targums except verbal analogy. The contents of the two words are quite different. The *Memra* is an abstract paraphrase of the divine name. The Logos in the Prologue refers to a living active person who at a certain point in history was incarnate. As the *Memra* was only a peculiarity of translation it is doubtful whether even the word, apart from the meaning, had any influence upon John when he adopted the term Logos.[4]

vi. *Wisdom in Jewish Literature*

We have seen that in the Old Testament the term Word is used to express God's power and the means by which he re-

---

[1] *Judaism*, i, pp. 417 f.
[2] *Intermediaries*, p. 53.
[3] Ibid., p. 54.
[4] It is possible, however, that the *Memra* played a larger part in Jewish speculation in the first century than the extant Jewish literature suggests : see Knox, *Some Hell. Elements in Prim. Christianity*, p. 43.

vealed his will to men. As John interpreted salvation in the terms
of revelation, the Life of God becoming the Light of men and
producing life in them, the term Word must have appeared most
appropriate for his purpose. And as revelation reached its full
climax in the Person of Jesus, the identification of Jesus with the
Word of revelation, the union of the Old Testament with the
New Testament conception, must have been attractive. There
are, however, other converging lines of thought in the Old
Testament which, if John had thought of them, must have
influenced his choice of the term Logos. In addition to the use
of the "Word of the Lord" to avoid involving God in too close
a contact with the material world, we can see in the development
of the term Wisdom a similar desire.

In the course of time Wisdom gradually acquired a half-
defined personality. For example, in the Book of Proverbs,
Wisdom is represented as being with God before the world was;
she was brought forth by him as the first of his works, that is, as
the first objective expression of his being and will. She is the
partner of his throne and his associate (Prov. 8. 30). By her he
created the world (Prov. 3. 19 ff.; 8. 22 ff., 27 ff., 30); by her
he guides it (Prov. 8. 14 ff.). She sports before God on his habit-
able earth; and her delight is with the children of men (Prov. 8.
31). She then comes to men, addresses them as their best friend,
recommends to them the path by which life is to be found, and
invites them to the marriage feast (Prov. 9. 2 ff.; cf. 8. 17). In a
word, she wishes to embody herself, to become flesh in the moral
and religious life of men.

The exact degree of individuality ascribed to Wisdom in the
eighth chapter of the Proverbs is a matter of dispute among
commentators. The most generally accepted idea is that the
passages point to a poetical personification of the qualities of
God.[1] On the other hand, Kautzsch thinks that Wisdom in this
chapter has passed beyond mere poetical personification and
possesses a real personal existence apart from God.[2] The mediat-
ing position of Toy seems to be the most reasonable. After

---

[1] Cf., e.g., Gregg, *The Wisdom of Solomon*, p. xxxii.
[2] *H.D.B.*, v, 729.

pointing out the influence which this chapter has had upon Christian writers, he says: "It seems obvious that it gives a personification, intended to affirm the wisdom manifest in the creation of the world—an approach (under Greek influence) to hypostasis, but not more than an approach".[1]

In the Books of the Apocrypha further developments along the same lines may be traced. Wisdom is with God from eternity, the partner of his throne and knowing all his thoughts (Ecclus. 1. 1; Wisd. Sol. 8. 3 f.; 9. 4, 9). She is an emanation from God's glory (Wisd. Sol. 7. 25, ἀπόρροια, ἀτμίς), the brightness of his everlasting light (Wisd. Sol. 7. 26, ἀπαύγασμα φωτὸς ἀιδίου), the mirror of his power and goodness (Wisd. Sol. 7. 26, εἴσοπτρον, εἰκών). She is one and yet can do everything; she remains within herself, and yet makes all things new (Wisd. Sol. 7. 26). She is of resplendent purity (Wisd. Sol. 6. 13), and has a spirit that is reasonable, holy, only begotten . . . beneficent, absolute and independent, almighty and all-observant (Wisd. Sol. 7. 22 ff., νοερόν, ἅγιον, μονογενές, λεπτόν, πολυμερές, ὀξύ). She is more in motion than any motion (Wisd. Sol. 7. 23). She was created before all things (Ecclus. 1. 4, 7 ff.; 24. 14), and boasts herself in the presence of God before his powers (Ecclus. 24. 1 ff.). She is everywhere (Ecclus. 24. 4-9). She is the principle of creation, especially of man's creation, for she has a spirit of love to men (Ecclus. 24. 10 ff.; 42. 21; Wisd. Sol. 7. 21; 9. 2; cf. 1. 6). She is the artificer of the universe, poured out by God on all his works (Ecclus. 1. 2; Wisd. Sol. 7. 21). She is the principle of redemption. She invites the righteous to heavenly possessions (Ecclus. 4. 12; 6. 24 ff.; 15. 2 ff.; 24. 7 ff., 18-22), makes those who love her sons of God (Ecclus. 4. 11), searches out those who deserve her (Wisd. Sol. 1. 4, 6; 6. 16), descends into the souls of God's servants, and makes them God's friends and prophets (Wisd. Sol. 7. 27; 8. 1 ff., 21; 11). She is the principle of divine revelation that seeks rest in and takes up her abode with men, and especially with the holy people (Ecclus. 24. 7 ff.; Wisd. Sol. 10. 1 ff.; 11). It is especially important to notice those places where she appears in connexion with the "Word of God" (Ecclus. 1.

[1] *Proverbs*, p. 181.

5; 24. 3 f.; Wisd. Sol. 16. 12, 26; 18. 15; cf. 6. 12; 7. 22 f.; 9. 1 ff.), which is clearly the most active form of revelation. In Enoch also there are found allusions to these thoughts in connexion with the Messiah, in whom dwells the Spirit of wisdom (Enoch 42. 1 f.; 49. 3).

In view of this development of the idea of Wisdom it is not surprising that Dr. Rendel Harris should argue that the Prologue is based upon a previous existing hymn in praise of Wisdom, which eventually leads back to Proverbs 8. He has pointed out the many similarities in the language and theology between the Wisdom literature and the Prologue. He has found a parallel from the Wisdom Books for almost every phrase of the Prologue.[1] He reinforces his argument by evidence which shows that it was a characteristic of early Church writers to call Jesus the Wisdom of God.

It is reasonable, therefore, to suppose that John has taken a hymn in praise of Wisdom and applied it to Jesus. The chief difficulty of accepting this view is that the Prologue does not begin with the words Ἐν ἀρχῇ ἦν ἡ Σοφία. But, as Dr. Harris says, there is nothing very much involved in replacing a feminine expression by a masculine one in Greek. Philo occasionally identifies the Logos with Wisdom (*Leg. Alleg.* 1. 19; 2. 21; *Quis rer. div. haer.* 41). But he also prefers the term Logos because the masculine qualities were more appropriate to the nature and function of the Logos (*De profugis* 9). And clearly the masculine term was more suitable when applied to Jesus. Whether John adapted an actual Wisdom-hymn to his own purposes or not we do not know, but the theology of the Wisdom Books must have prepared the way for the Christian conception of the Logos and the fuller revelation of the New Testament.

vii. *The Torah*

There is another possible source of influence which must be considered. If Christians saw in Jesus the Wisdom of God, the Jews had already identified Wisdom with the Torah. In Ecclesiasticus we read: "Without deceit shall the law be

---

[1] *The Origin of the Prologue to St. John's Gospel*, p. 43.

fulfilled, and Wisdom is perfect in a mouth that is faithful"
(34. 8); "He that keepeth the law controlleth his natural
tendency, and the fear of the Lord is the consummation of
Wisdom" (21. 11); "All Wisdom is the fear of the Lord, and all
Wisdom is the fulfilling of the Law" (19. 20). The Torah was
more than a code of commandments. It was, in the words of
C. G. Montefiore, "the middle term between Israel and God",[1]
and therefore fulfilled the same purpose as Philo's Logos and the
Old Testament "Word of the Lord". The things which the
Rabbis said about the Torah were surprisingly like the things said
about the Logos (Wisdom) in the Prologue. I set them out in
parallel columns [2]:

THE LOGOS	THE TORAH
In the beginning.	Seven things were created before the world was created; namely, the Torah. . . .
The Logos was with God.	The Torah lay on God's bosom, while God sat on the throne of glory.
All things were made through him.	Through the firstborn God created the heaven and the earth, and the firstborn is none other than the Torah.
In him was life.	The words of the Torah are life for the world.
And the life was the light of men.	For the world is set in darkness and they that dwell therein are without light, for thy Torah is burnt, therefore no man knoweth the things that are done by thee.
Full of truth.	Truth, by this the Torah is meant.

It would appear that John was aware of this identification
of the Torah with Wisdom, and, if he was moulding his Prologue

[1] Peake's *Commentary*, p. 620.
[2] See Howard, *Christianity according to St. John*, pp. 50 f.

on a previous existing hymn in praise of Wisdom, he makes it quite clear that the Logos is superior to the Torah: "For the Torah was given by Moses; grace and truth came by Jesus Christ".

We find, therefore, in Jewish literature, "the Word", "Wisdom," and the "Torah," all fulfilling to some extent the purpose which Christ came to fulfil. Wisdom, in particular, assumed a semi-personal independence. Such was the way John's first problem was met in Hebrew thought. The development of these conceptions also provided a scheme of thought into which the personal Logos of Christianity might be fitted without suggesting too great a break with Jewish monotheism. At certain points the Johannine conception of the Logos coincided with both Hebrew and Hellenistic ideas, but in the historic Jesus John found the completion and fulfilment of the gropings towards the truth on the part of both these groups of people. All that the Jews had believed about God as proceeding forth by his Word and Wisdom to create and govern nature, and to reveal himself to men by his prophets, belongs to Jesus and is consummated in him. All that the Greeks had imagined of a divine activity in the world, all their speculations about a divine mediator between the immutable and timeless God and the created world, find in Jesus their justification, their fulfilment, and their correction.

All these different currents of thought may, therefore, have had some influence upon John when he identified Jesus with the Logos. But the primary factor in arriving at this conclusion was Jesus himself. "The Evangelist stands under the creative power of the words of Jesus, words that, so far from being haphazard and disjointed, proceed from one source. The Fourth Evangelist does not personify the Word of God. The Word had created him, not he the Word; and the Word of God had confronted the apostles in the person of Jesus, the Son of God." [1]

viii. *The Johannine Conception of the Word*

We are now in a position to consider John's own distinctive contribution to religious thought in his conception of the Logos.

[1] Hoskyns, *The Fourth Gospel*, p. 163.

In this chapter we shall limit the discussion to the relation of the Logos with God: in another chapter we shall consider the relation of the Logos with men. We shall begin by studying the first three verses of the first Epistle: "That which was from the beginning, that which we have heard, that which we have seen with our eyes, that which we beheld, and our hands handled, concerning the Word of life (and the life was manifested, and we have seen, and bear witness, and declare unto you the life, the eternal life, which was with the Father, and was manifested unto us); that which we have seen and heard declare we unto you also, that ye also may have fellowship with us; yea, and our fellowship is with the Father, and with his Son Jesus Christ".

It is uncertain whether the "Word of life" in this passage is used in the same personal sense which it has in the Prologue, or merely in the sense of life-giving revelation which Christ brought. Westcott,[1] Brooke,[2] and Moffatt[3] interpret ὁ λόγος τῆς ζωῆς, "the revelation of life". Prof. Dodd regards the "Word of life" as a definition of the whole Gospel.[4] Bernard,[5] Hoskyns,[6] and Robert Law[7] take the Logos as in the Prologue of the Gospel. The difference of opinion shows how readily this expression might rise from the designation of Christ's saving revelation to the name for the Revealer Himself. According to the New Testament, the "word of the Lord", the "word of God", or simply the "word", denotes the powerful life-giving revelation of the Gospel (Heb. 4. 12); it is not applied to the Old Testament as a whole, but only to such sayings as contain a prophecy of the Gospel, or are actually the expression of God's own words to the prophets. With John, especially, all the words of Christ are a powerful revelation; all Christ's sayings are thought of as a unit (1 John 2. 7); it is the truth, and as such sanctifies (17. 17); its reception delivers from death (8. 51) and from judgement (12. 47); the words (ῥήματα) of Christ are spirit and life (6. 63). We may also compare 5. 24, 38; 8. 31, 37, 43, 55; 10. 34; 14. 22; 15. 3; 17. 6, 14, 21-22. In all

[1] *The Epistles of St. John*, p. 6.
[2] *The Johannine Epistles* (I.C.C.), p. 5.
[3] *I.L.N.T.*, p. 591.
[4] *The Johannine Epistles*, p. 5.
[5] *St. John* (I.C.C.), p. lx.
[6] *New Commentary*, iii, p. 660.
[7] *The Tests of Life*, pp. 44 and 370.

these passages the "word" expresses the real, essential mind of Jesus. Those who have this have eternal life. Men do not understand the "speech" of Jesus because they are not in accord with his mind. The "word" reveals the mind of Jesus.

When we notice how closely "the Word of life" in 1 John seems to be related to this usage we can realize how natural it was for John to use the name Word both in a personal sense and as the revelation of life. Nevertheless the expression in 1 John means something much more than the revelation of life. If that were all it meant we should be unable to explain the extraordinary grammatical construction, and in particular the change from the relative construction to the prepositional phrase "concerning the Word of life". The verb of the whole sentence is "we declare" ($\dot{a}\pi a\gamma\gamma\acute{\epsilon}\lambda\lambda o\mu\epsilon\nu$), and if it had been simply a question of the message he had heard from Jesus, John must inevitably have construed it as the direct object of the verb, as in verse 5. Furthermore, the content of this clause is defined by the relative clauses which precede it, "that which was from the beginning, which we have heard, seen, handled, etc.". He cannot mean by these clauses the Son of God himself, or why should he express himself so strangely in the neuter? Moreover, in this case we should have in 1 John 1. 1 something presented as the object of his declaration which would be different from what is named in verse 2. The content, therefore, of the first verse must be substantially the same as that eternal life mentioned in the second verse. In the second verse eternal life is declared to have been with the Father and to have been manifested to us. But John is here thinking, in abstract terms, of that life which constituted the eternal nature of the Son of God. He then goes on to say that this eternal life has been manifested in the historic Person of Jesus.

The Son of God was the subject of the saving message of the Gospel precisely in so far as in him was, and was manifested, that eternal life which being manifested became light (1. 4). It seems that John is grappling with the second problem which was set out above, and it is this essential nature of the Son of God which he would represent as the content of his declaration. In order to embrace this in one word, he breaks the relative construction with the clause "concerning the Word of life". There the Word himself was not the subject of the declaration but that which had been manifested as his essential nature. The essential nature of the Son is marked not only by the fact that he has eternal life in himself, but that he is able to impart it to men. Hence, in the relative clause the fact of his existence in the beginning is associated with the historical manifestation; and the life is spoken of as that "which was with the Father and was manifested unto us". The conclusion seems to be that in the first verse of the Epistle the term Word, though it is strictly the personal title of Jesus, designates him not so much according to his personality as according to his essential nature, in virtue of which he is one with the Father (πρὸς τὸν πατέρα).

In the Prologue we find the term Word employed in the same way. In both cases the Word is an expression of an essential characteristic of God. In the second verse of the Epistle it is the life that is πρὸς τὸν πατέρα; in the Prologue it is the Word that is πρὸς τὸν θεόν. Many attempts have been made to translate the phrase πρὸς τὸν θεόν. Bernard thinks that we cannot better "the Word was with God". Westcott paraphrases it as: "The personal being of the Word was realized in active intercourse with and in perfect communion with God". Abbott urges that the phrase carries with it the sense of "looking towards God". Lock says that it implies one who has the values of God himself. The phrase is so difficult that Dr. Rendel Harris would reject it altogether and substitute for it the easier preposition παρά.[1] According to all these commentators, the general sense is that of union with God conveying also the impression of a distinction within the Godhead.

Dr. F. C. Burkitt, however, interprets the phrase in such a way as to obliterate the idea of distinction.[2] He paraphrases the verse as follows: "In the beginning was the Word and the

---

[1] *The Origin of the Prologue to St. John's Gospel*, p. 5. Dr. Burney points out that if the Greek text represents a translation from the Aramaic, πρός and παρά may both be used to represent the Aramaic *lᵉwāth*. Schlatter agrees that John has the Hebrew phrase in mind (*Der Evangelist Johannes*, p. 2).

[2] *Church and Gnosis*, pp. 94 ff.

Word was addressed to God and the Word was divine". Thus "the Evangelist introduces us to no new theology, but the familiar, though lofty, conception of Genesis, namely, that of the One only God producing the creation by consulting himself, yet bringing forth into visible form nothing without announcing his formulated intention". In this way the unity of the Hebrew conception of God was safeguarded, and this was John's problem. But if the suggestion of distinction is at this point obliterated by this particular interpretation, it rises later when (in Dr. Burkitt's translation) John goes on to say: "I mean to say the Word itself became human and we saw him". Thus both in the Epistle and in the Prologue the Word is so identified with God that there can be no suggestion of a δεύτερος θεός. John has succeeded in describing the relation of Jesus to God in a way which maintains the monotheistic belief of the Hebrews.

The next verse in the Prologue indicates that, however close was the relationship of the Word with God in the eternal sphere, he possessed an independent activity in the world of space and time: "All things were made through him, and apart from him nothing was made; what was made in him was life".[1] Furthermore, "the life was the light of men". This is in harmony with the second verse of the Epistle: "In him was life". The Prologue affirms that the Word is also the medium of revelation. This will be discussed more fully under a later topic. We now notice that the same thought is continued down to verse 14: "The light shineth in the darkness; and the darkness apprehended it not" (1. 5).[2] The true light is the light that lightens every man.[3] He was in the world and the world was made through him, and the world knew him not. He came unto his own and his own received

---

[1] Nearly all the Fathers before the end of the fourth century agree on this reading It is to be preferred on the grounds of grammar, and the rhythmical balance of the sentence. The words " what was made in him was life " are paraphrased by Bacon as " through him the creation was infused with life " (*The Gospel of the Hellenists*, p. 243).

[2] W. L. Knox interprets καταλαμβάνειν as understanding God : " the darkness had never succeeded in understanding the light " (*Some Hell. Elements in Prim. Christianity*, p. 55).

[3] Schlatter points out in *Der Evangelist Johannes* that " every man coming into the world " is a Rabbinic circumlocution for " all men ", p. 15.

him not (1. 9-11). It is here affirmed that in accordance with the universal relation which the Logos has to the world as creator, he is also universally the mediator of revelation. The continued action of the light upon the world provided men with the opportunity of knowing the truth at all times. The Jewish people are called "his own" on the ground of his special revelation to them through the Old Testament prophets; but all who accept the revelation which he personally brings become truly the children of God (1. 12). The Evangelist then goes on to affirm that all the scattered and broken gleams that had been shed on nature, history, and conscience have been focused in the glory of the only begotten Son of God, the Word made flesh. The exact meaning of ἐγένετο is difficult to determine. Dr. Bernard says: "to explain the exact significance of ἐγένετο in this sentence is beyond the power of any interpreter".[1] But it is at least clear that in the light of the Evangelist's whole teaching it cannot be held to mean that by becoming man the Logos ceased to be divine. "The Logos became a real man, and that without ceasing to be himself."[2] Before bringing the Prologue to an end, John repeats what he has already indicated in verse 1: Jesus Christ is in the bosom of the Father. The Greek εἰς τὸν κόλπον suggests movement in the eternal relationship of the divine persons. The current of the Son's life is set towards the Father.[3] The words may refer to the present exaltation of Jesus, but, as Dr. Stevens argues, the purpose of the verse is to "show how the Son is fitted to reveal God to mankind, and it is his essential and eternal relation with the Father that would constitute the ground of that fitness".[4] The whole pagan world was tantalized with stories

[1] St. John, p. 20. According to Dr. Jannaris in Zeitschrift für die neutestamentliche Wissenschaft, ii, p. 13, this sentence means that the empowering Word of God became flesh by lodging in our bodies, i.e. in our hearts; cf. John 15. 4; 1 John 1. 10.

[2] Macgregor, The Gospel of John, p. 16; cf. Schlatter, Der Evangelist Johannes, p. 22: "By using ἐγένετο any schism between the Divine Word and the living man Jesus as flesh is avoided. The fact that in Jesus the unity of the Divine Word with the human life was complete and ever effective gives to the Divine Sonship of Jesus wholeness".

[3] Though the force of εἰς is emphasized here, there is usually no distinction between εἰς and ἐν in Hellenistic Greek; see T.W.z.N.T., ii, p. 431, article by Oepke on "εἰς".

[4] Johannine Theology, p. 90.

of the appearances of the gods to men,[1] and it is to Greek and Jew alike that John makes his claim that Jesus is the final interpreter of the Father. Jesus, in the mind of John, was the final and complete revelation of God. In Christ alone do we find the true *exegesis* of God.[2]

The above exposition has shown how appropriate the choice of the term Logos was to express (*a*) the oneness of nature with God; (*b*) the participation of the Logos in the creation of the world; and (*c*) Jesus as the Logos, the medium of revelation. The Word which was in the beginning with God, and which for the Hebrew expressed the activity of God in creation and the work of the prophets, and for the Greek supplied the intermediary between God and creation, has been shown to be at one with God himself and is now brought into relation with the historic Jesus in the affirmation, ὁ λόγος σὰρξ ἐγένετο.

With this statement we pass from the contemplation of the Logos with God to the Logos in relation to the world. But before considering this we must first discuss John's conception of the world into which Jesus came.

[1] See pp. 129 ff.
[2] Cf. the function of the Holy Spirit as guide in 16. 13. ἐξηγεῖσθαι was the technical word used by the Jewish Rabbis for the interpretation of the Scriptures. See Schlatter, *Der Evangelist Johannes*, p. 36 ; cf. Büchsel, *T.W.z.N.T.*, ii, p. 910.

5

THE WORLD LYING IN DARKNESS

i. *The World in Johannine Literature*

John conceives very vividly the contrast between the divine nature and the created world. As God is light, and in the light, so is the world characterized as darkness. But, though the contrast is strongly marked, it has no point of contact with metaphysical dualism. Indeed, Irenaeus says that the main purpose of the Gospel was to refute such Gnostic teaching: "In the course of preaching this faith, John the disciple of the Lord, desirous by preaching of the Gospel to remove the error which Cerinthus had been sowing among men; and long before him those who are called Nicolaitans, who are an offshoot of the knowledge (*gnosis*) falsely so-called; to confound them and persuade men that there is but one God, who made all things by his word, and not, as they affirm, that the Creator is one person, the Father of the Lord another, and that there is a difference of persons between the Son of the Creator and the Christ of the higher Æons, who doth remain impassible, descending on Jesus, the Son of the Creator, and glided back again to his own pleroma; and that the Beginning is the Only Begotten and that the created system to which we belong was not made by the First Deity, but by some power brought very far down below it and cut off from communion in the things which are beyond sight and name. All such things, I say, the Lord's disciple desiring to cut off, and to establish in the Church the rule of truth, namely, that there is one God Almighty, who by his word hath made all things visible and invisible; indicating also that by the Word whereby God wrought creation, in the same also he provided salvation for the men who are part of creation; thus did he begin in that instruction which the Gospel contains" (here follows John 1. 1-5). In the next section he quotes verses 10,

11, and 14 against Marcion and Valentinus and other Gnostics who held that the world was made by angels or demi-gods.[1] Irenaeus emphasizes the full significance of the phrase "all things" in verse 3 when he says: "Now from 'all things' there is no subtraction made; but the Father made all things by him, whether things visible or invisible, sensible or intelligible, temporal (on account of a certain character they possess) or eternal; not by angels or any powers separated from his *sententia* . . . but making all things by his Word and Spirit" (1. xxii. 1).[2]

We have seen that John needed no intermediary to bridge the gulf between the invisible God and the sensible world. The Word which became flesh was God. The reason for this is that human nature itself as it is physically constituted is not evil. God, through the Logos, created the world, and there is nothing which is excepted from the relationship between the created world and the Creator. There is, therefore, no radical opposition between the world as such and God; and even the world of human existence which has fallen into rebellion against him is the object of his love and saving effort.

The world in the Johannine writings means that system which answers to the circumstances of man's present life. The phrase τὰ ἐν τῷ κόσμῳ shows that ὁ κόσμος carries with it a wider significance than humanity fallen from God. But generally speaking it is limited to men and society as organized apart from God. "It is the whole system considered in itself apart from its Maker, though in many cases the context shows that its meaning is narrowed down to humanity." [3]

This conception of the world as fallen away from God involves the writer in a strong religious dualism. The Gospel is, according to Dr. E. F. Scott, "pervaded from end to end by one grand antinomy".[4] At first sight the world appears as something wholly evil. Without Christ it is darkness and not light (1. 9; 8. 12). It has refused to know the Word, its creator (1. 10). Its

[1] *Adv. Haer.*, 3. xi, Oxford Trans., pp. 229 ff.

[2] Cf. Sanders, *The Fourth Gospel in the Early Church*, pp. 72 ff.

[3] Brooke, *The Johannine Epistles* (I.C.C.), p. 47 ; see also Westcott, *St. John*, pp. 31 ff. ; Strachan, *The Fourth Gospel*, p. 100 ; and Sasse, *T.W.z.N.T.*, iii, p. 894.

[4] *The Fourth Gospel*, p. 12.

ruler is the Devil, and it appears to tolerate his rule with equanimity, so that both together are destined to suffer the same fate (12. 31; 16. 11; 1 John 5. 19). Everything that is in the world, being lust of the flesh and lust of the eyes, is of the world and not of God (1 John 2. 16). The world has given birth to false prophets; they speak of the world and the world heareth them (1 John 4. 3-5). Christ cannot or will not pray for it (17. 9); and its hatred is focused on him (7. 7; 15. 18), and his disciples (15. 18; 17. 14; 1 John 3. 13). Though Christians are bidden to love one another, they are commanded not to love the world: "If any man love the world, the love of the Father is not in him" (1 John 2. 15). The business of the Christian appears to be not to save the world, but to overcome the world (1 John 5. 4, 5).

Over against these passages there are others which speak of the world as the object of God's peculiar favour and love. Though the Christian, as we have just seen, is not to love the world, we are told that God so loved it that he gave his only begotten Son, that the world should be saved through him (3. 16, 17; 1. 29; 12. 47; 1 John 2. 2). The life of the world is God's special interest; to give life to the world is the purpose of the Son's coming. And the Samaritans confess that in Jesus they find one who is "indeed the Saviour of the world" (4. 42).

It is to be noticed that in the Gospel the love of God for the world is grounded in the love which he had for the Son. The disciples must abide in the Son's love, as he abides in the love of the Father. In the Epistle, on the other hand, we find a slight change in emphasis. In 1 John 4. 9-11 the stress is laid on the love of God for the world. But the close connexion of this passage with John 3. 16 implies that no fundamental difference of view is to be found between the two conceptions.

Attempts have been made to resolve the difference between these two attitudes to the world. Bauer, for example, commenting on 3. 16, says that John is not here expressing his own mind; that is to be found in 1 John 4. 9, where it is said that God sent his Son into the world that we (not the world) might live through

him.[1] Bauer would also take away the force of the phrase
"Saviour of the world" by saying that it is just a hackneyed title
taken over from the Graeco-Roman emperor-worship of the cults
of the heathen gods.[2] On the other hand, A. D. Nock comes to
the conclusion that "the application of *Soter* to Jesus is not in
origin connected with non-Jewish religious use of the word".[3]
Odeberg quotes extensively from current Jewish and Hellenistic
literature to show that in contemporary belief there was a similar
dualistic attitude towards the world. And he says that "it is
evident that John is merely adopting the language of the times in
his use of the word κόσμος. Hence there is in the Johannine
use of the word no indication of the meeting of two incompatible
lines of thought as peculiar to John. He simply adopts, and
finds appropriate, the duplicity in the current use of the word".[4]
As these opposite interpretations of God's attitude towards the
universe are found in John's most fundamental conceptions they
must be allowed their full weight. The dualism is, however, an
ethical dualism, and is neither absolute nor final. The opposition
is already abolished in the sphere of spiritual reality to which the
faithful spirit rises when it freely turns away from the darkness to
the true life and light.

Dr. W. R. Inge, commenting upon this characteristic of
John's religious thought, says: "The intense ethical dualism
of the Fourth Gospel is another perplexing phenomenon to those
who look for philosophical consistency in a religious treatise. . . .
Although the Logos is the immanent cause of all life, so that
'without him nothing whatever came into being', the 'darkness'
in which the light shines is no absence of colour, but a positive
malignant thing, a rival kingdom which has its own subjects and
its own sphere". "The sources of this ethical dualism may be
found partly in the spiritual struggles of an intensely devout

---

[1] *Das Johannes Evangelium*, p. 54.

[2] Op. cit., p. 71.

[3] In *Essays on the Trinity and the Incarnation* (ed. Rawlinson), pp. 87-94 ; cf. Knox,
Some Hell. Elements in Prim. Christianity, pp. 37-42. It is significant that Schlatter does
not quote an exact parallel from Rabbinic literature for the phrase " the Saviour of
the world " when commenting on 4. 42 (*Der Evangelist Johannes*, pp. 134 f.).

[4] *The Fourth Gospel* etc., p. 129.

nature, but to a greater extent probably, in the furious antagonism of Judaism to nascent Christianity." [1]

But his experiences being what they were led John to see in this contrast between light and darkness, between God and the world, a matter of prime importance. Both heaven and earth are represented in Genesis 1. 1 as equally the creation of God; and John no doubt comprises both in the third verse of the Prologue. He does not, however, think of them so much as constituting one universe, but rather as exhibiting the moral contrast that has come about within God's creation. He thinks of the world as an object requiring salvation out of the evil and darkness into which it has fallen. Darkness, as an ethical condition, could not have been the original and necessary character of the world; it came about as an historical development and in no other way than that represented in the Book of Genesis, namely, through sin. But however it came about, darkness is the character of the world as Jesus finds it. It is into a realm of spiritual darkness and death that he comes to bring light and life. John conceives this darkness after the analogy of the chaos which preceded the material creation: it is the object of God's saving work, the matter of a new creation.

ii. *Parallel with Genesis*

As this parallel with Genesis furnishes luminous points of suggestion for the construction of Johannine thought, we shall examine its features in some detail.[2]

The first hint of this relation of thought is, of course, the very first phrase of the Gospel, "In the beginning". But even the style is modelled on that of Genesis. Dr. E. A. Abbott, explaining the use of the Hebraic narrative καί, remarks: "In the opening of the Gospel John follows the style of the opening of Genesis, not in affectation, but with a symbolism natural to him, sympathetically describing what was 'in the beginning' of Spiritual

---

[1] *D.C.G.*, i, p. 889 ; cf. Howard, *Christianity according to St. John*, p. 85.

[2] See Burney, *The Aramaic Origin of the Fourth Gospel*, pp. 43 ff ; Burkitt, *Church and Gnosis*, pp. 94 ff. C. H. Dodd draws an interesting parallel between Genesis and the cosmogony of the *Poimandres* in *The Bible and the Greeks*, pp. 99 ff. Even if the Hebrew of Gen. 1. 1-3 be translated strictly according to the syntax the parallel is not materially affected ; see Skinner, *Genesis* (I.C.C.), p. 13.

H

Being, as Genesis describes what was in the beginning of material creation. But after the resurrection, when the Apostles are receiving their morning meal before going forth to convert the whole world, Greeks as well as Jews, 'all things become new', and the old-world Hebraic style is thrown aside".[1] The relation to the Prologue is, however, not primarily one of grammar or of vocabulary. Nor does he merely reproduce the Hebrew account of creation in a Christian setting. He is rather using the Old Testament account of the creation of the physical world as the basis for his parallel account of the spiritual re-creation of man.

Different meanings have been given to the words "In the beginning". According to Westcott, John lifts our thoughts beyond the beginning of time and dwells on that which "was" before time began its course.[2] With this Bernard agrees: "Before anything is said about creation, he proclaims that the Logos was in being originally".[3] Hoskyns, on the other hand, identifies it with the moment of creation: the Word of God was not first made audible when Jesus spoke and acted. The Word made known then is the Word audible in the whole creation: "In the beginning was the Word".[4] If, however, in the Prologue we have a *parallel* with Genesis, the phrase must in the first instance denote not the same, but a different time. It refers rather to the beginning of the New Creation, the New Dispensation, which came into being with the coming of Jesus in the flesh. Hoskyns points out the close association of "beginning" with the Gospel dispensation in both Mark and Luke. St. Mark's Gospel opens with "The beginning of the Gospel", and in St. Luke we have "those who from the beginning were eyewitnesses and ministers of the word".[5] The word is often used in this sense in the Johannine writings—John 16. 4; 1 John 2. 7, 24; 2 John 5, 6.

The several ideas which are common to the first chapter of Genesis and to the Prologue are: The creative voice—the Word; light and darkness, and the various manifestations of life. "The Spirit of God" in Genesis 1. 5 may be another point

---

[1] *Johannine Grammar*, pp. 135, 136.
[2] *St. John*, p. 2.
[3] Ibid., p. 1.
[4] *The Fourth Gospel*, pp. 135, 136.
[5] Ibid., p. 166.

of contact with the Gospel re-creation; and it is at least not improbable that Christ's act of breathing out the Holy Spirit upon his disciples (20. 22) was associated in John's mind with God breathing into man the breath of life as recounted in Genesis 2. 7. "Jesus as the Logos is the instrument of a new spiritual creation, the Church, of which the assembled disciples are the nucleus." [1] We may account it likely that John's idea of eternal life was associated with "The Tree of Life"; and it is possible that his close association of knowledge and life has some connexion with the two trees in the Garden of Eden.

These common ideas in the two accounts are worked out as follows: In Genesis we are directed to God as the Creator of the heavens and the earth. Before us lies a material chaos enveloped in darkness; into which presently, at the utterance of the creative Word, the light shines which later appears in concrete manifestation as "lights". The creation proceeds by the instrumentality of the Word to effect a still further division, of the waters from the waters, and of the waters from the land. The first part of creation is thus effected by means of simple mechanical separation; further development is wrought by the introduction of the various stages of life—from the green herb to the beast wherein is a living soul. Man is not only the climax of this order of living souls; but he is constituted a different kind by the breath of God. This supreme and unique product of creation proceeds, according to the divine command, to multiply and fill the earth.

The world for John, as we have seen, is considered to be for the most part simply the dwelling-place of mankind, the sphere of human souls. This psychical sphere has been thrown by sin into a state of spiritual chaos; it is under the power of darkness and of the Evil One; and hence it is the object of Salvation, which John thinks of as a New Creation. Accordingly, quite parallel with Genesis, his description takes for its beginning the commencement of the New Creation. As in Genesis, the Only

---

[1] Strachan, *The Fourth Gospel*, p. 329. Bauer, when commenting on John 20. 22 in *Das Johannes Evangelium*, points out that the idea of new birth is contained in the use of the word ἐμφυσάω in the early baptismal rites.

God is represented as consulting himself.[1] In Genesis "the earth was without form and void, and darkness was upon the face of the deep",[2] so in the Gospel there lies before us a spiritual chaos which is enveloped in spiritual darkness. As in Genesis the first moment of creation is the creative Word, "Let there be light", so in the Prologue the Word is the personal creator, and he also was light—a spiritual light, the light of men. By him a separation is effected between the different elements of the world, and order is brought out of chaos. But not only was he light; "in him was life". He brings eternal life to men, and this is thought of not as mere prolongation of physical existence, but as an entirely new and superadded gift, which has its beginning in the new birth. This new birth ("not of blood, nor of the will of the flesh, nor of the will of man, but of God" [3]) is parallel to this first divine gift of psychical life in Genesis 2. 7. This life consists in the knowledge of and fellowship with God [4]; it is truly possessed from the moment of new birth, and there is a development of it corresponding to the growth in knowledge. The detailed process of physical life recorded in Genesis has its counterpart in the development of this spiritual life described in the Gospel. Furthermore, the separate moments of creation in both accounts are blended in the continuous operation of the Personal Word. These thoughts, set out briefly in the Prologue, are expanded and developed in the rest of the Gospel so that it may well be called the second book of Genesis. The exposition which follows will have this fact constantly in mind, and, first, we must consider in greater detail what constitutes the darkness in the Johannine scheme of re-creation.

iii. *The Darkness*

Important as this antithesis between God and the world,

[1] πρὸς τὸν θεόν; see Burkitt, *Church and Gnosis*, pp. 94 ff.

[2] It should be noticed, however, that the Hebrew *tohū wābohū* suggests indiscriminate monotony rather than confusion; barrenness rather than beauty.

[3] The variant ὃς ἐγεννήθη in the Latin versions may be due to a desire to "eliminate the Gnostic suggestion of the text" (Knox, *Some Hell. Elements in Prim. Christianity*, p. 57).

[4] See pp. 195 ff. ; cf. Charles, *Eschatology* etc., p. 369 : " eternal life consists in a growing personal knowledge of God and of his Son ".

between light and darkness, certainly was in the mind of John, the absoluteness of the antithesis must not blind us to the presence of light in the world even before Jesus came. Although the "darkness apprehended not the light" (1. 5) "and his own received him not" (1. 11), there were nevertheless those who did receive him (1. 12), and, before they became his, they belonged to the Father (17. 6). There were in fact already at his coming two classes of men: those who hate the light because they do evil, and those who come to the light because they do the truth (3. 20, 21). John also recognizes that the world had in the Jewish Scriptures a revelation from God,[1] and in the Jewish nation a chosen people who have a special knowledge of God.

The ninth verse of the Prologue means that the Logos is the medium of God's universal revelation of himself to the world. "From the first he was (so to speak) on his way to the world, advancing towards the Incarnation by preparatory revelations. He came in type and prophecy and judgement." [2] Hence "Isaiah saw his glory, and he spake of him" (12. 41); Moses wrote of him (5. 46) and also the prophets.[3] The divine mission of John the Baptist (1. 6) is specially emphasized in the Fourth Gospel; though not the light (1. 8), he nevertheless was himself "the lamp which burneth and shineth" (5. 35). John's interpretation of the counsel of Caiaphas (11. 51 ff.) shows very strikingly his conception of prophecy as the official distinction of the Jewish nation even in the moment when they were con-summating the disruption of the covenant relation. The gift of prophecy in primitive days belonged traditionally to the priest-hood, and that the prophet should be unconscious of his prophecy is an idea found in Rabbinic writings. For example, in the Midrash known as *Mekhilta* the commentator says on Exodus

[1] For the use of the Old Testament in the Fourth Gospel see Bernard, *St. John*, pp. cxlvii ff., and Westcott, *St. John*, pp. vi ff. and lxvi ff.; for the use of the Old Testament generally by Jesus see B. H. Branscombe, *Jesus and the Law of Moses*.

[2] Westcott, *St. John*, p. 7.

[3] Cf. Phythian-Adams, *The Church Quarterly Review*, Oct.-Dec. 1944, pp. 12 ff., where he points out that it was an ancient belief of the Church that it was the Logos who called Abraham out of Ur, who revealed himself to Moses in the Bush, who delivered Israel out of Egypt.

15. 17: "Our fathers prophesied and knew not what they prophesied; only Moses and Isaiah knew".[1] This incident and its interpretation suggest a much deeper view of Old Testament prophecy on the part of John than was conceived by the other writers of the New Testament. It is difficult to understand Dr. Scott's conclusion that "his allusions to it [the Old Testament] are comparatively few and of a somewhat perfunctory and superficial nature".[2] For if we find in the Fourth Gospel fewer references to the Old Testament than in, say, Matthew, "we must also observe", as Dr. Rendel Harris points out, "that when they do occur they betray acquaintance quite clearly with the method and the contents of the primitive *Testimony Book*"[3] which contained the so-called Messianic proof texts from the Old Testament.

iv. *The Revelation of the Old Testament*

The Old Testament is frequently quoted to establish a fact, or to clinch an argument, or to illustrate something that has been said. In particular, John reveals his knowledge that the Jews believed that the Old Testament Scriptures pointed forward to the Messiah. He represents the people as expecting that the Messiah would come one day, because the prophets had so predicted, and they expected him to be born in Bethlehem (7. 42 ; cf. Mic. 5. 2); that he would vindicate himself by wonderful works (6. 14, 30)[4]; and that he would abide for ever (12. 34 ; cf. Ps. 110. 4; Is. 9. 6; 1 Enoch 41. 1). The disciples are represented as applying Messianic Scriptures to Jesus both before (2. 17) and after his resurrection (2. 22; 12. 16). There can be no doubt that John sees in Jesus the fulfilment of the Old Testament Scriptures which prophesy the coming of the Messiah. "Moses wrote of me" and the Scriptures "bear witness of me" (5. 39, 46; cf. Acts 3. 22; 7. 37).

[1] See Strachan, *The Fourth Gospel*, pp. 174 ff., 244, and 245.

[2] *The Fourth Gospel*, p. 197.

[3] *Testimonies*, ii, p. 71 ; cf. Dr. Torrey's remarks on p. 16 above and Schlatter, *Der Evangelist Johannes*, p. viii.

[4] The provision of Manna was especially associated with the Messianic age; see Schlatter, op. cit., pp. 172, 173, for examples.

The Scriptures of the Old Testament possess a value as a revelation of truth quite apart from any particular words spoken by the prophets. The various writings are thought of as a unit, as the Scripture, ἡ γραφή,[1] a term which is used to denote the Old Testament as a whole (7. 38) and its individual utterances (19. 37), and this Scripture cannot be broken (10. 35). The Scriptures as a whole testify of Christ (5. 39); and this witness is found not only in those passages which are expressly prophetic, but in the Psalms (19. 24, 28-37). So complete was the witness to Jesus that, had the disciples really known the Scriptures, they would have known what must happen to him (20. 9). We may agree with Westcott that without accepting the Old Testament basis for the Fourth Gospel it remains an insoluble riddle.[2] That the Scriptures were fulfilled in Jesus is a fundamental conception of the Fourth Gospel.

The term Law, or Teaching, is used to describe the Scriptures when they have a special reference to the Jewish nation or beliefs.[3] Christ in addressing the Jews speaks of "your law" (8. 17; 10. 35), and of "Moses' law" (7. 23), whereas in his use of the word Scripture there is no such narrowing of meaning. Dr. Odeberg offers the following explanation of the term "your law"[4]: "Jesus declares himself expressly in both contexts (5. 30-47 and 8. 14) to be a celestial being, the Son of his Father. God never says 'our law', but either 'my law' or 'your law'. Jesus stands in the same relation to the Torah as his Father. The Torah is secondary to Jesus, and this was especially the case with the Torah as manifested in writing and tradition to the Jews. Jesus' position in regard to the Torah is similar to his position in regard to Abraham or Moses. He certainly does not reject Abraham or Moses . . . but: 'before Abraham was, I am'." Nevertheless this distinction between the Scriptures and the Law does not mean that Jesus repudiated the obligation of the Law for himself or for his disciples; for when he says, "which of you convicteth me

---

[1] See Schrenk, *T.W.z.N.T.*, i, pp. 750 ff.

[2] *St. John*, p. lxix.

[3] In Rabbinic literature the Law embraced the whole of the Old Testament Scriptures ; see Hoskyns, *The Fourth Gospel*, pp. 454, 455.

[4] *The Fourth Gospel* etc., p. 292.

of sin?" (8. 46), he must be understood as challenging comparison between his conduct and the Law, which was the presumed basis for the accusation. In the alleged cases of Sabbath-breaking he justifies his actions by a right interpretation of the Law (7. 22). Nor is it to be supposed that John sharply distinguished the two principal divisions of the Scripture, the Law and the Prophets; for in Philip's call to Nathanael (1. 45) the two are intimately combined: "of whom Moses in the Law and the Prophets did write". John did not, like St. Paul, think of the Law as being in fundamental conflict with the Gospel (Rom. 4. 16; 6. 14, 15; Gal. 5. 4). The contrast expressed in 1. 17 is Pauline in form only: "For the law was given by Moses; grace and truth came by Jesus Christ". Here the Law is supposed to be a good thing in itself, or else the particular excellence of the gift of Christ would not be made to be better by comparison. The point of comparison is suggested by the preceding verse, "of his fulness we have all received, and grace for grace". It is as the inexhaustible gift of God that the Gospel is contrasted with the Law, which in the opinion of the Jews was static and complete. In the Rabbinical schools it was "an uncontested axiom that every syllable of the Scripture had the verity and authority of God. . . . The notion of progressive revelation was impossible; the revelation to Moses was complete and final".[1] In Rabbinic literature the Law was regarded as the source of salvation and life. "This is the book of the commandments of God and the law that endureth for ever. All they that hold it fast are appointed to life, but such as leave it shall die" (1 Bar. 4. 1, 2); "If food which is your life but for an hour requires a blessing before and after it be eaten, how much does the Torah, in which lies the world that is to be, require a blessing" (Rabbi Ishmael, c. 135); "He who has gained for himself the words of the Law has gained for himself the life in the world to come" (Aboth, 2. 7). These quotations show that for the Jew the Law was the predominant note of religion; the essence of religion was to be found in the Law. But John shows that nearly everything which was ascribed to the Torah has now been

[1] G. F. Moore, *Judaism* etc., i, p. 239.

transferred to Christ; that the Scriptures find their fulfilment in him.[1]

v. *The Jews in the Fourth Gospel*

The Jews had, therefore, in the Scriptures a light shining in the darkness, a veritable witness to Jesus. Because of them the Jews could be presumed to have some knowledge of God even before Christ came. And in the Fourth Gospel such knowledge is allowed. Christ affirms that salvation is of the Jews and that they possessed a belief in God which was distinguished from other contemporary religions in that it demanded a worship which combined in a unique way both religion and morality (4. 22).[2] He asserts that, if they were truly Abraham's children, they would do the works of Abraham (8. 39).[3] If they had believed on Moses they would have believed on him (5. 46). There is frequent reference to belief among the Jews extending even to the highest circles (12. 42). The resurrection of Lazarus leads many Jews to faith in Jesus (11. 45). Even the covert faith of Nicodemus and of Joseph of Arimathaea comes finally to public expression (3. 2; 19. 38, 39). John recognizes that it is primarily in "this fold" that Jesus finds his sheep (10. 16).

But side by side with these individual expressions of faith in Christ the Jews are regarded in the Fourth Gospel as the representatives of the darkness of this world. There are about twenty-five instances in which the term is used in this hostile sense. From beginning to end John's representation moves along the line of opposition between Christ and the Jews. So prominent is this that one Jewish writer has called it "the Gospel of Christian love and Jew hatred".[4] It should be noticed, however, that there is nothing in the Fourth Gospel to match the "woes" recorded by the Synoptists. The Synoptists make it

---

[1] Cf. Hoskyns, *The Fourth Gospel*, p. 305, and also pp. 100 f. above.

[2] Cf. Temple, *Readings in the Fourth Gospel*, p. 64 ; according to Schlatter, the worship of the Samaritans was based upon the " custom and tradition of the fathers, not a movement of the will, based upon genuine apprehension " as was the case with the Jews (*Der Evangelist Johannes*, p. 125).

[3] " It was the distinction of Abraham to have received the emissaries of God with faith and obedience ", Hoskyns, op. cit., p. 392.

[4] *Jewish Ency.*, ix, p. 251.

clear that the Jews were less ready to believe than the Galileans, who were not so directly under the influence of the scribes and priests who gave the dominant tone to Judaism. Jewish opposition naturally comes in for more extended notice in the Fourth Gospel, as the author dwells particularly upon the episodes of Jesus' ministry in Judaea.

Nevertheless the tone of the controversial passages in the Fourth Gospel suggests that John saw in the attitude of the Jews the epitome of the opposition of the world to Christ. And it was probably a subordinate aim to bring out the opposition as clearly as possible. But it must not be supposed that the attitude of the Jews in Jesus' day was alone responsible for this emphasis upon their unbelief.[1] It was probably provoked by the great body of organized opposition in the Hellenic Judaism of the Dispersion. "His anger is the inverted patriotism of the prophet rebuking his people."[2] *The Martyrdom of Polycarp* reveals the intense hatred of the Jews towards the Christians in Asia Minor. From A.D. 50-150 the real battleground of Christianity was in Asia Minor, and, among all the inimical forces, Judaism was the chief instigator of the persecution of the Church. The dialogues and discourses in the Fourth Gospel reflect a situation which the earliest Christian preachers would meet when brought into contact with the Jews of Ephesus and elsewhere. The writings of Justin Martyr indicate what were the subjects of controversy between the Jews and the Christians. His *Dialogue with Trypho the Jew* deals with such subjects as: the obscure birth of Jesus (8; cf. John 7. 27); his birthplace (108; cf. John 7. 41 ff.); Sabbath observance (22, 26 f.; cf. John 9. 14 f.; 7. 19); the coming of Elijah (49 f.; cf. John 1. 21); Jews and Samaritans (78; cf. John 4. 1 f.; 7. 48).[3] If the above references are compared they will show that the same subjects were debated in both works.

Yet it was of the Jews of his own time that Jesus affirmed,

[1] Cf. Burkitt : " It is quite impossible that the historical Jesus of the Synoptic Gospels could have argued and quibbled with opponents as he is represented to have done in the Fourth Gospel ", *The Gospel History and its Transmission*, pp. 227 ff.

[2] Lord Charnwood, *According to St. John*, p. 52.

[3] See Strachan, *The Fourth Gospel*, pp. 50 f.

"Ye have neither heard his voice at any time, nor seen his face" (5. 37). There is no reference here to the *Bath Qōl*, which in Jewish theology represented the Voice of God. The meaning is that the Jews have not heard the voice of God nor seen his form, because they do not recognize that Jesus reveals the Father to them. They do not even understand the Scriptures which they have inherited and which they study (5. 39, 40),[1] and hence they do not receive the witness which the Father bears to the Son (5. 37), because God's words find no abiding place in them (5. 38). As they are unable to perceive God's witness, so they cannot understand Christ's speech, because they cannot hear his word (8. 43). The Jews are therefore characterized as darkness, not because the light has not shone upon them but because they have not apprehended the light (1. 5).

vi. *The Nature of Sin*

Christ's coming into the world was itself a judgement, and the decision which men make for or against him lays bare the inmost disposition of the heart. In the opinion of Dr. E. F. Scott, "sin" in the Fourth Gospel "is conceived not as a positive principle, but as a privation, a limitation. . . . To the mind of John, sin in itself involves no moral culpability. . . . Sin in itself is a mere privation, and only assumes the darker character when the freedom offered through Christ is refused".[2] It is true that unbelief is not a category that includes all sins; but it is the test which cuts deepest, and which most conclusively manifests the bent of the heart. "The virtuous man fulfils the law of his own being"[3]; so do men's reactions to Jesus reveal their moral state. Hence the incapacity of the Jews to know Jesus reveals the essential evil in their nature (3. 20, 21). On two occasions John traces this unbelief to pride. Men do not care for the honour that comes from God, but rather seek their own glory (δόξα, 5. 44;

---

[1] Cf. *J. T. Berekhoth*, 4 *d* : " Thou knowest how to read, but not how to search ", quoted by Schlatter, *Der Evangelist Johannes*, p. 158. Hence Jesus says, " *Search* the scriptures " (imp.) ; see Field's *Notes on the Translation of the New Testament*, pp. 88 ff.

[2] *The Fourth Gospel*, pp. 219-221.

[3] Marcus Aurelius, *Meditations*, 9. 42.

12. 43).[1] So prominent is this idea of sin as unbelief that Jesus says: "If I had not come and spoken unto them, they had not had sin: but now they have no excuse for their sin. He that hateth me hateth my Father also. If I had not done among them the works none other did, they had not had sin: but now have they both seen and hated both me and my Father" (15. 22-24). And when at the last he promises that "the Paraclete will convict the world in respect of sin" he defines sin in the clause "of sin because they believe not on me" (16. 8, 9). The sin of Antichrist is variously stated as the denial "that Jesus Christ is come in the flesh" (1 John 4. 2), "that Jesus is the Christ" (1 John 2. 22), or as the denial "of the Father and the Son". In the same way we must understand the "sin unto death" (1 John 5. 16, 17). We cannot understand it as anything other than a deliberate apostasy from Christ which involves a definite crisis of the soul.[2] It is the sin not of the outsider, but of the "brother" who has seen Christ and hated him. "In the author's view any sin which involves a deliberate rejection of the claims of the Christ may be described as 'unto death'."[3]

John does not, however, confine himself to the consideration of the sin of unbelief. In the last passage quoted above he contrasts sin unto death with sin in general: "All unrighteousness is sin; and there is a sin not unto death". The expression "sin is lawlessness", which we find in 1 John 3. 4, shows his fundamental adherence to the Old Testament conception of sin. In the Old Testament deliberate transgression was opposed to sins committed unwittingly (Num. 15. 30), and the former was punished by the sinner being cut off "from among his people". And according to John, sin is not limited to those who are guilty of deliberate and wilful rejection of Christ (15. 22); even those to whom the manifestation of Christ's light has not come are in a state of sin; for it is into a world already sinful that Christ comes "to take away the sin of the world" (1. 29; 1 John 3. 5).

---

[1] Cf. Kittel in *T.W.z.N.T.*, ii, p. 251, article "δόξα".
[2] Cf. Dodd, *The Johannine Epistles*, p. 136.
[3] Brooke, *The Johannine Epistles*, p. 146.

It is a world completely sinful; for sin is co-extensive with darkness, and it is expressly stated of the world, after the Christian
community has been separated from it, that it lieth all of it in
the Evil One (1 John 5. 19). The condition of sin is compared to
bondage (8. 34). Sin is in a negative sense the absence of life,
and it is only by faith that we pass out "of death into life"
(5. 24; 1 John 3. 14). It is out of a perishing condition that
Christ saves us (3. 16). In a certain sense it is natural for men to
sin; for in a way quite familiar to the Old Testament the pleasures
of the world are regarded as enticements away from God, "For
all that is in the world, the lust of the flesh, the lust of the eyes,
and the vainglory of life, is not of the Father, but of the world"
(1 John 2. 16). Flesh, however, is not thought of as an evil
principle, any more than is the eye. Christ's sentence in 3. 6,
"that which is born of the flesh is flesh", is not to be taken to
mean the essential sinfulness of mankind. It means that the
earthborn is unable to transcend the earthly sphere without a
begetting from above.[1] Flesh is contrasted with spirit in
6. 63, where the property of "quickening" is ascribed to spirit,
while flesh has no such quality where eternal life is concerned.
Σάρξ in the New Testament means more than material flesh. It
means that part of human nature which belongs to the world. It
is an essential constituent of man, and as such a part of Christ's
nature (1 Pet. 3. 18). While not being evil in itself, if the flesh
is made supreme and sufficient it is almost certain to become the
occasion of sin. "Ye must be born anew" (3. 7).

John uses the phrase ἁμαρτίαν ἔχειν and the verb ἁμαρτάνειν in
two senses: to denote the power or principle of sin, and to denote
concrete acts of sin.[2] The latter sense he generally expresses by
the plural, sins; but it is not always possible to distinguish which
idea is uppermost in his mind. This distinction helps in part to
explain how in the Epistle he can denounce the claim to sin-
lessness (1 John 1. 8), and yet assert that "he that sinneth hath

---

[1] Cf. Hoskyns, *The Fourth Gospel*, p. 231 : "Flesh is flesh, and spirit is spirit ; and
what is and has been begotten or born of each remains and must remain within the
capacity of that which has begotten it or given it birth ".

[2] See Brooke, *The Johannine Epistles*, p. 17 ; cf. Westcott, *The Epistles of St. John*,
pp. 37 ff., and Dodd, *The Johannine Epistles*, pp. 78 ff.

not seen him, hath not known him" (1 John 3. 6). Even the
Christian is often guilty of particular sins for which confession
and forgiveness are required; but he has been freed from the
bondage of sin (8. 36), and is no longer under its slavish control;
he cannot habitually practise it, nor abide in it, still less can he
be guilty of sin in its superlative form—the denial of Christ. The
same distinction is found in 13. 10. The suggestion is that he
that has been bathed by the water of Baptism, λελουμένος λουτρῷ
παλιγγενεσίας (Tit. 3. 5; Eph. 5. 26; Heb. 10. 22), is wholly
washed. His affections are, however, sullied by contact with the
world; he must therefore constantly wash his feet by repentance.[1]
Bauer sees in the incident a reference to both Baptism and Holy
Communion. "The deeper meaning of this episode", he says,
"concerns the two Christian mysteries, Baptism, which effects
a general cleansing of the unbeliever, and the Lord's Supper,
which repeatedly cleanses the Christian, whose feet are ever
soiled by contact with this finite world." [2] Strachan, however,
rejects any reference to the Sacraments in this passage. He
interprets the washing of Peter's feet as showing that, although
Peter has yielded himself in spirit to Christ, i.e. he is bathed in
love, he must further yield himself in action and allow life's travel
stains to be washed away.[3] But in view of the distinction we have
already seen to be characteristic of John, the former interpretation seems to fit more easily into the Johannine system of thought.

We have already seen that sin, according to John, is lawlessness (1 John 3. 4), and in this expression there is to be found a
deeper conception than at first appears. The Law, for John, is
no longer contained in a number of precepts, but is summed up
in Christ's example of love (13. 14). As sin against God is
thought of chiefly as rejection of his light, so sin against man is
included in the idea of hate, the transgression of the law of love.
This sin is traced back to Cain, "who was of the Evil One, and
slew his brother" (1 John 3. 12). It is not likely that John
thought so much of the unity of the sinful race as derived from

---

[1] Cf. Hoskyns, *The Fourth Gospel*, pp. 510 ff.
[2] *Das Johannes Evangelium*, p. 167.
[3] *The Fourth Gospel*, p. 267.

Adam in the Pauline sense, but rather of the moral contrast within the race, between the children of God and the children of the Devil; of this contrast Cain was the representative, and his sin was for John the antitypal sin.

But even Cain's sin is traced to the fact that he was of the Evil One, who himself "was a murderer from the beginning" (8. 44).[1] "He that doeth sin is from the devil; for the devil sinneth from the beginning" (1 John 3. 8). "Ye are of your father the devil, and the lusts of your father it is your will to do" (8. 44). As to the origin of the Devil himself, John shows no sign that he ever speculated about it. But we may assume that he did not intend to represent the Devil as in any sense co-ordinate with God, as the eternal principle of evil. There is no sign of metaphysical dualism in his writings. And although John dwells upon the contrast within the human race between the children of God and the children of the Devil, and often represents this difference as something which antedated their conscious choice of Jesus (10. 3, 5, 16), we must not read into this a fatalism which predetermines their relation to Christ. For, though this difference is traced to God's choice and they were his before they were Christ's (17. 6), yet their own choice remains one of perfect freedom. It is because men love darkness rather than light that they reject Christ and are therefore justly judged (3. 19). "Nowhere in the Johannine writings does the problem of the relation between the will of God and human freedom appear above the horizon, and it is therefore important for their interpretation to avoid the temptation of reading them in the light of later controversies." [2]

---

[1] For the meaning of ἀπ' ἀρχῆς see Stevens, *The Theology of the New Testament*, p. 195; Brooke, *The Johannine Epistles*, p. 88; Delling, *T.W.z.N.T.*, i, pp. 479 f.

[2] Hoskyns, *The Fourth Gospel*, p. 502; cf. Bernard on John 9. 3 : "The doctrine of predestination is apparent at every point in the Fourth Gospel, every incident being viewed *sub specie aeternitatis* as predestined in the mind of God"; cf. pp. cliii. ff.

6

THE LIGHT IN THE DARKNESS

i. *Introduction*

We have now before us the two great generic ideas of darkness and light, which represent the contrast between the human and the divine, between the world and God. We have been able with reasonable certitude to deduce, even from John's indirect utterances, his view of the nature and disposition of God, and of the condition of the world. But, fundamental as these topics are, they are only the introduction to the themes with which John most expressly and predominantly deals. Light and darkness, as we have come to understand them, are in a sense the postulates of John's theology; they are the colours with which his picture is painted. The contrast involved in these two facts represents also the problem which John's doctrine solves. The all-absorbing fact to John is not that the world lieth in darkness, nor even that God is light; but that the divine light has actually come into the darkness. He sees the world perishing in darkness and death; he sees God as One who is light and in whom is no darkness at all: but he does not speculate upon these facts, he does not strive to delineate them; he is content to name them in two words. What he does minutely describe is the process by which the light overcomes the darkness and saves the world. And the first step in this process is the manifestation of the light in the world. It is upon the fact of the Word made flesh that eternal life, the new birth, the conditions and fruits of divine sonship, depend. It is with these themes that John is constantly occupied; and upon them that the majority of his utterances in the Gospel and Epistles directly bear. This is the point round which all other themes circle. This is the region of Johannine thought with which we have yet to deal; and here it is that we find the most obvious, as well as the most interesting, of the Johannine peculiarities. But before we proceed to study more closely these things it will help us to appreciate the distinctive teaching of John if we examine the contemporary desire to see God, its content and the means by which men sought to satisfy it.

ii. The Vision of God in Pagan Literature

(a) The *Metamorphoses* of Apuleius has already been referred to in connexion with rebirth,[1] and this is also our chief authority for the experiences which were encouraged by the Mystery Religions. In the eleventh book of the *Metamorphoses* Lucius sees the goddess in no less than three different ways: sometimes in contemplation of her sacred statue; sometimes in dreams at night; and at the culminating point of his initiation in the mystic ritual of the shrine (*Met.* 11. 18, 19, 20, 24; 19, 26, 29, 30).

He describes his vision of the goddess as follows [2]: "When I had ended this oration, discovering my plaints to the goddess, I fortuned to fall again asleep upon that same bed; and by and by (for mine eyes were but newly closed) appeared to me from the midst of the sea a divine and venerable face, worshipped even of the gods themselves. Then, by little and little, I seemed to see the whole figure of her body, bright and mounting out of the sea and standing before me; wherefore I purpose to describe her divine semblance, if the poverty of my human speech will suffer me, or her divine power give me a power of eloquence rich enough to express it" (*Met.* 11. 3). Then follows a long and detailed description, based no doubt upon the conventional features and ornaments of the statue he had come to love so well.

In the last chapter of the book (*Met.* 11. 31) the Great Osiris appears to him "which is the more powerful god of the great gods, the highest of the greater, the greatest of the highest, and the ruler of the greatest". The revelation given, however, is

---

[1] Pp. 46. For this section I am much indebted to K. E. Kirk, *The Vision of God*, pp. 30 ff.

[2] *The Golden Ass* (*Metamorphoses*), in Loeb Classical Library, trans. by W. Adlington, revised by S. Gaselee (1919).

I

singularly inept and shows how difficult it must have been to keep upon the highest planes of religious exaltation for long.

A further illustration may be found in the Mithras Liturgy.[1] This is a magic papyrus of the beginning of the fourth century but contains earlier material. It professes to give an account of the appearance of the great god Helios Mithras and the stages which lead up to the final vision. The final stage is described as follows:

"When these have set themselves hither and thither in order, look up into the air, and thou shalt see lightnings flashing down, and the gleams of lights and the earth quaking, and a great god coming down, with a shining countenance, young and golden headed, in tunic white and golden crown and buskins, with golden shoulder-blade of an ox in his right hand. . . . Then shalt thou see lightnings glance from his eyes and stars from his body. . . . Then gaze upon the god and bellow long, and greet him thus: 'Hail, Lord, Master of the Water; hail, founder of the earth; hail, ruler of the Spirit. Lord, born again am I, and so in my exaltation depart; and being exalted die. Born in life-giving birth and dissolved in death, I go my way as thou hast ordained, as thou hast commanded and hast made mystery'."

(b) What the mysteries did for the eye, the Hermetic Sects professed to do for the ear. By word of mouth, by exhortation, by instruction, rather than by religious ecstasy, they proposed to bring men to the vision of God. Mr. W. Scott says: "If one were to try to sum up the Hermetic teaching in one sentence, I can think of none that would serve the purpose better than the sentence, 'Blessed are the pure in heart, for they shall see God'".[2]

The agent by whom the knowledge of God was conveyed to the people was in Greek Hermes, and in Egyptian Thoth, the messenger of the gods. The message derived from him was passed on to disciples by the anonymous writers of the Hermetic tracts.

It is not difficult, one writer says, "to contemplate God in thought, or even to see him. Look at the arrangement of

---

[1] The relevant portion is printed in *The Vision of God*, by Kirk, pp. 473 ff.
[2] *Hermetica*, i, p. 14.

the universe and its orderliness. Look at the necessity which governs all that is presented in our sight, and the providence shown in what has been and what came to be. Look at the material world filled to the brim with life, and see this great God in movement in all things" (*Corp. Herm.* 12. 21, 22; Scott, *Hermetica*, i, p. 236).

From the beginning to the end of the *Corpus Hermeticum* purity of heart and moral rectitude are represented as the essential conditions of seeing God. "There is but one way to worship God, my son, and it is to be devoid of evil . . . you must cleanse yourself of irrational torments of matter . . . ignorance, incontinent desires, injustice, covetousness, deceitfulness, envy, fraud, rashness, vice" (*Corp. Herm.* 13. 7 ff.; Scott, i, p. 238). "To be righteous is to see God" (*Corp. Herm.* 9. 4 *a*; Scott, i, p. 180).[1]

There are some passages which suggest that the vision of God must be deferred until the soul has entered the eighth and highest sphere of heaven; it is then that the soul "sings together with those who dwell there, hymning the Father . . . and with them in turn mounts up to the Father, giving itself up to the powers and itself becoming a power, and so enters into God" (*Corp. Herm.* 1. 26; Scott, i, p. 128). Other passages are more optimistic: "Man is more immortal than aught else that lives, for he can receive God and hold intercourse with God" (*Corp. Herm.* 12. 18; Scott, i, p. 234).

The vision itself is accompanied by ecstatic experiences. "Father God has given me a new being, and I perceive now not with bodily eyesight but by the working of the mind. I am in heaven and in earth, in water and in the air; I am in beasts and in plants. . . . I am present everywhere. Father, I see the whole, and myself in the mind" (*Corp. Herm.* 10. 6; Scott, i, p. 190). In one tractate, however, ecstasy is not considered as the test of the vision. "The vision of God is not a thing of fire, as are the sun's rays. It does not blaze down upon us, and force us to close our eyes. It shines forth much or little according as he who gazes

---

[1] Cf. *The Bible and the Greeks*, pp. 173 ff., where Prof. Dodd discusses the ethical vocabulary of the *Poimandres*.

on it is able to receive the inflow. . . . It cannot harm us, it is full of all immortal life" (*Corp. Herm.* 10. 4 *b*, 5; Scott, i, pp. 188, 190).

iii. *The Vision of God in Philo*

(*c*) This desire to see God in pagan circles is more than equalled in the writings of Philo. To see God was his aim, and he thought of this vision as a "vision of peace"; for "God alone is perfect peace" (*De Somn.* 2. 38). No physical eye can see God; that can be achieved only through the eye of the soul (*De Conf. Ling.* 20). The name Israel meant for him "seeing God" (*De Mut. Nom.* 12). The title "sons of Israel" means "hearers of him who saw" (*De Conf. Ling.* 28). Philo writes to encourage the people of Israel to "aim at the vision of him who is, to go beyond the visible sun, and never leave the road that leads to perfect happiness" (*De Vit. Cont.* 2).

In one of Philo's finest passages he expresses the doubt whether men will ever see God: "Whether by seeking thou shalt find God is uncertain, for to many he has not made himself known and their labour seems without reward. Yet the bare search avails to the attainment of God; high aspirations, even though they fail, bring joy to those who pursue them" (*Leg. Alleg.* 3. 15). Yet generally he is more optimistic: "When God perceived how fruitful it would be to the creature to know its creator (for this is the sublimity of all joy and blessedness) he breathed into it some spark of his divinity from above, which working invisibly, sealed with its impress the soul invisible . . . so that it no longer received mortal but immortal thought . . . and now it comprehends the very bounds of earth and sea, of air and heaven. . . . The universe itself is too narrow for its soaring ambitions. Further, it penetrates in its striving, to grasp the incomprehensible nature of God, if it can" (*De Pot. Ins.* 24).

The nature of this vision is ecstatic: "A Bacchic frenzy has filled me with ecstasy; I knew no more the place where I sat, my company, myself—nay even what I said or wrote. A flow of exposition comes upon me at such seasons, a delectable light, the vision of the keenest. . . . Then is revealed to me that

which is most worthy to be seen and contemplated and loved—
the perfect good, which changes the soul's bitterness to honey"
(*De Migr. Abr.* 7).

It will be clear from the foregoing that John was writing in a
world which desired passionately to see God. It was encouraged
in this by the belief that some men had attained the vision and
had found therein the sum of human happiness. This stimulated
the hope that the same vision might be attained by all who sought
it. It is against this background that we can understand the
significance of John's declaration that "the Word was made
flesh". The Gospel is, in the words of Loisy, "a perpetual
theophany".[1]

It is true that John reminds us that "no man hath seen God
at any time" (1. 18; 6. 46; 1 John 4. 12) and he looks forward
to a day in which we shall see him as he is (1 John 3. 12). But
what is implied here is a difference of degree and not of kind.
"In so far as the age to come has already dawned upon the world
in the coming of Christ, the Fourth Gospel finds a place for the
vision of God, not in the sense of mystical rapture, but in the
sense that in the incarnate Christ one beheld the glory of the
Lord".[2] Already it is the case that "he that hath seen me hath
seen the Father" (14. 7, 9). "One who is God, only begotten,
which is in the bosom of the Father, he hath declared him"
(1. 18).[3] By using the word ἐξηγεῖσθαι (*pe'resh*) John retains
the essentially Hebraic conception that God is heard by the ear
rather than "seen" (θεωρία) by religious experience. God is
"declared" by the incarnate Word of God. The pagan mysteries
claimed that God could be known through ecstasy and contemplation. In the Fourth Gospel God was revealed through
the words and deeds of Jesus upon the plane of history.[4]

The characteristic word in the Fourth Gospel to indicate
this revelation of God in and through the incarnate Word is

---

[1] *Le Quatrième Évangile*, p. 104.

[2] Dodd, *The Johannine Epistles*, p. 113.

[3] For the translation see p. 76. "Verse 18 was added to make it clear that
Christianity has not abandoned the claim of Judaism to have the true revelation of
the 'invisible God'," Knox, *Some Hell. Elements in Prim. Christianity*, p. 58 n.

[4] Cf. Bultmann, *T.W.z.N.T.*, i, pp. 690 ff.

"glory". This is a word which has a very long history.[1] In its Hebrew form it suggests weight and was used to denote authority and majesty. All that transcended the ordinary conditions of humanity was supposed to throw out a kind of radiance. God was pre-eminently the King of Glory. Glory was not just one of his attributes—it was common to all. His power, his mercy, his wisdom, all reflect the glory of his nature. For those who had eyes to see, this glory irradiated all his works. The glory which belonged to his essential being streamed out from him and was made manifest in nature, in history, and in the activities of chosen men. God was regarded as dwelling in light in an almost physical sense. When Moses communed with him on Sinai a mysterious light overspread the mountain. This belief that light possessed some kind of "body" was held by the Jewish contemporaries of John. We have already drawn attention to the fact that light indicates not only the essence of God but also the *sphere* of goodness, the *element* in which God lives. When therefore Jesus claimed to be the Light of the World, he meant that in his Person the divine world had broken through into the realm of darkness. And all who are born again and united with Jesus by faith pass into that realm of light. The purpose of the Gospel is to show that the glory of God was revealed in the Person and Work of Jesus. When the Word was made flesh we beheld his glory, that is God's manifest presence, "the glory as of the only begotten from the Father, full of grace and truth" (1. 14).

We may agree, therefore, with the conclusion of Heitmüller: "The Gospel is to show by what means Christians saw the Divine majesty of the Logos—by his miracle-working power, his supernatural knowledge, his physical inviolability, the spiritual efficacy of his preaching, and, not least of all, by his voluntary suffering and death, and his resurrection".[2] The manifestation of God in Christ is thus contrasted with the earlier and contemporary manifestations, and shown to be different, not only in degree but in kind. Every other manifestation has now been superseded in the great Christian declaration that the "only be-

[1] See Kittel, *T.W.z.N.T.*, ii, pp. 251 ff., article "δόξα," and Strachan, *The Fourth Gospel*, pp. 103 ff.

[2] *Die Schriften des Neuen Testaments*, iv, pp. 45, 46.

gotten Son who is in the bosom of the Father", that is admitted to God's inmost counsels and participating in his very nature, "he hath declared him".[1] It is with this fact in mind that we proceed to examine in more detail what is involved in the statement that "the Word was made flesh".

iv. *The Word was made Flesh*

This is the corner-stone upon which the whole structure of Johannine thought depends. The visible historical Jesus is the place in history where the glory of God was manifested. John was faced with the dangers of a false spirituality. Some of his contemporaries were convinced that any materialistic notions in religion would clog the movement of the spirit. John succeeds in a remarkable way in holding the tension between a false spirituality and a gross materialism. He does not say that the spirit is reduced to the level of the flesh and therefore become profitless; nor does he say that the spirit has become something that is visible to the naked eye. But he does mean men to understand that it is in the man Jesus that the spirit is encountered, and through belief in the historic Jesus that eternal life is received.[2]

Polycarp, quoted by Irenaeus, tells us that the chief exponent of this false spirituality was Cerinthus. He informs us that Cerinthus separated Christ, the divine aeon, from Jesus, the good but mortal and finite man. The two, he said, met at the waters of Jordan, upon the day of Baptism, when Christ united himself to Jesus for a few years, after which he left him for ever. Before the passion the divine ideal Christ withdrew; the man Jesus suffered, while the impassible, immortal Christ was far away in heaven (*Adv. Haer.* 1. 26). In the quaint words of Jerome: "While the Apostles yet remained upon the earth, while the blood of Jesus was almost smoking upon the soil of Judaea, some asserted that the body of the Lord was a phantom" (*Adv. Lucif.* 23).

Further encouragement for this depreciation of the flesh of Jesus would no doubt be given by certain aspects of pagan

---

[1] Cf. E. F. Scott, *The Fourth Gospel*, p. 211.
[2] Cf. Hoskyns, *The Fourth Gospel*, pp. 56 ff.

thought. The Mystery Religions and the Hermetic Sects believed in a world of visions, ecstasies, secret revelations, and deification. Communion with God was only possible by way of the temporary annihilation of sense perception and worldly experience. The body is the prison-house of the soul. The aspirant must purge himself of the "irrational torments of matter". No aspect of terrestial existence had any good in it (see especially *Corp. Herm.* 7). Even Philo lent himself to this kind of thought. The body to him was a "foul dungeon", a "prison cell", "a cage", "a burden", "a fetter", "a coffin". It was to oppose this conception of a purely spiritual religion that John was moved to place so much emphasis upon the flesh of Jesus.

In the sixth chapter, for instance, the Jews are confronted in the crudest possible manner with the flesh of Jesus. To them this seemed blasphemy, but so important was the point that Jesus faced the disciples with the same test and the Apostles alone remained. In the Epistle John condemns "spirits, false prophets, antichrists" (1 John 4. 1-3). Christians must learn to distinguish between true spirits and false spirituality. "Beloved, believe not every spirit, but test the spirits" (1 John 4. 1). No spirit that refuses to confess Jesus in the flesh can be of God (1 John 4. 3). To deny the incarnate Son of God is to deny the Father also and to usher in the last hour (1 John 2. 22, 23).

"The Fourth Evangelist saw clearly that, unless historical reality was to be surrendered to religious speculation, the perplexities apparent in the minds of his hearers must be met as to the relationship between the historic Jesus and the risen Christ. Disastrous compromise with the thought of the time must not take place. The only hope for the Christian faith was to restore it to the assurance of the abiding significance of the earthly life of Jesus." [1]

That this was no passing danger to the Church is made evident by the same emphasis which we find in the Epistles of Ignatius. He writes to the Trallians of the Christ who "was

---

[1] E. F. Scott, *The Fourth Gospel*, p. 372 ; cf. Inge in *D.C.G.*, p. 886 : " The author of this Gospel interposed his powerful influence to save Christianity from being swamped in a mythology or sublimated into a theosophy ".

truly born, ate and drank; truly suffered; truly was crucified and
died; truly rose"; then, playing upon the name Docetists, he
says: "λέγουσιν τὸ δοκεῖν πεπονθέναι αὐτόν, ὄντες αὐτοὶ τὸ δοκεῖν"
(*Ad Trall.* 10).   In the Epistle to the Church of Smyrna we find
this form of error stigmatized as not confessing that "Jesus bore
real human flesh" (μὴ ὁμολογῶν αὐτὸν σαρκοφόρον, *Ad Smyrn.* 5. 2).
This heresy about the reality of the flesh of Jesus was logically
bound to involve anti-sacramental views, and docetic Christians
eventually ceased to observe the Eucharist.   Herein lies the
significance of John's declaration that Jesus came by water and
blood, "not by water only, but by water and blood".   The water
centres in the Baptism (3. 5), and the blood is symbolized,
exhibited, and applied in the Holy Communion (6); and the
Spirit, by his divine power, perpetually makes them effective.
The water and the blood warn the Church not to spiritualize
the material.   The Spirit saves the Church from materializing
the spiritual.[1]

John was aware that the flesh of Jesus in itself "profiteth
nothing".   The Jesus of history could not exhaust the Christian
message.   Historical knowledge by itself was "from below", and
could be appreciated as such by both Jews and Christians
(3. 1-15).   This had been the drawback of the portrait of
Christ drawn by the Synoptic Gospels.   True, these earlier
narratives revealed that their authors saw something more than
history in the ministry of Jesus.   The voice from heaven at the
Baptism, the narrative of the Transfiguration, the appearance of
the angels, reveal that they were trying to convey spiritual or
absolute truth through the medium of an historical life.   But the
narratives as a whole fix the attention upon the historical and
earthly side of Jesus' life.   The Synoptic Gospels are filled with
homely details—Jesus mixing with publicans and sinners and
blessing little children.   He is represented pre-eminently as one
who "went about doing good".   And John was aware that if the
minds of men were limited to this conception of an historical,
earthly Christ, they would never perceive the full significance

---

[1] See additional note in *Speaker's Commentary* on 1 John 5. 6, p. 348, and cf. what
was said on pp. 7 and 29 f.

of the Incarnation. They would never rise to the belief in Jesus as the "Saviour of the world". He therefore proclaimed that "it is the spirit that quickeneth; the flesh profiteth nothing". Only in relation to the Spirit are the words of Jesus significant (6. 63). His actual words require for their understanding the interpretation that the Spirit of Truth alone can provide (14. 16). His words, his actions are, as merely historical episodes, trivial and meaningless (7. 16-18). For the same reason important events are omitted from the Fourth Gospel—the Baptism and Transfiguration, the Temptation of Jesus and his Agony in the Garden, the narrative of the Institution of the Last Supper. Not that they are unimportant, but because they are so important, so pregnant with meaning, that no historical event can contain their full significance. "The Fourth Gospel is less an apostolic witness to history than an apostolic witness to that which is beyond history, but which is, nevertheless, the meaning of the Jesus of history, and therefore the meaning of all History." [1] It is in this sense that we must understand the words of Clement of Alexandria as quoted by Eusebius: "John, last of all, perceiving that what had reference to the body in the Gospel of our Saviour was sufficiently detailed; and being encouraged by his familiar friends and urged by the Spirit, he wrote a spiritual Gospel" (*Hist. Eccles.* 6. 14).

v. *The Son of Man*

In spite of the fact that John in the Prologue lets us into the secret of Jesus' divine nature, and that he composes his Gospel with the distinct purpose of establishing belief in him as the Son of God, he nevertheless dramatizes him before us as a man. It is not altogether true to say with Dr. Scott that the humanity of Jesus is different in essence from that of the men around him.[2] He is nearer the mark when he says: "Behind all his speculative thinking there is the remembrance of the actual life which had arrested him as it had done the first disciples, and been to him the true revelation of God. His worship is directed in the last

---

[1] Hoskyns, *The Fourth Gospel*, p. 66.
[2] *The Fourth Gospel*, p. 163.

resort not to the Logos, whom he discovers in Jesus, but to Jesus himself ".[1] As we have seen, it is impossible to separate the historical and spiritual aspects in the Fourth Gospel, or the divine and human natures of Christ.[2] The two sides of John's witness must be given their full weight without suggesting that one or the other predominates. If we approach this problem from the spiritual side we are led inevitably to the material; if we approach it from the material and historical side we are led just as inevitably to the spiritual. We propose to follow the latter course and we shall see how the Incarnation implies and involves the manifestation of the glory of the Logos.

As a man, Jesus appears in the family relations of family life: with his mother and his brethren he attends a wedding, and evidently within the circle of his friends or relatives (2. 12); he abides for a time in the family circle at Capernaum (2. 12); his brethren even undertake to lecture him about his conduct (7. 3-8); and from the cross he displays his care for his mother (19. 25, 26). As a man Jesus wept at the grave of Lazarus (11. 35); he was troubled in soul at the thought of death (12. 27); and shows even a momentary hesitation whether he shall not pray to be delivered from this hour. In 8. 40 he actually calls himself a man. But his truly human consciousness is nowhere so clearly expressed as in his relation to God. Notwithstanding the exalted character of his self-witness, in his human existence he bears even to the Father the relation of a man to God (20. 17); he prays to his Father (12. 27; 17); he thanks him for his gifts (6. 11); and also for hearing his petitions (11. 41).[3] Though John thinks of the Logos as the creator of all things, he represents the miracles of Jesus, not as proceeding from his own power, but as given him by the Father, in answer to his prayer, and for a special occasion (11. 22, 41; 5. 36; 14. 10). When Jesus says

---

[1] *The Fourth Gospel*, p. 174.

[2] See above, pp. 27 ff., 107 f.

[3] Loisy denies that the prayers of Jesus in the Fourth Gospel are natural and spontaneous : " The Johannine Christ could not pray as the Synoptic Christ could. Since his divine will was that of the Father, he could no more submit to the agony of Gethsemane than to the temptations by the Devil in the desert. He was above human conditions " (*Le Quatrième Évangile*, p. 689).

he seeks not his own will, but the will of him that sent him (6. 37; 5. 30), he postulates the double possibility of following his own will, or the will of God. When he says that he seeks not his own honour, but that of his Father (8. 49, 50), he implies that the mastering of self-will and self-gratification was for him, as for other men, a moral task. The Father's will is expressed for him, as it is for other men, as an external will, as a commandment (12. 49, 50); and his life, therefore, like that of other men, lies under the stress of obligation; he includes himself with the disciples under the ethical "ought": "We must work the works of him that sent me" (9. 4). This, however, is no irksome duty, for the fulfilment of the Father's will is his greatest joy (4. 34).

To express the fact of Christ's truly human condition, John, like the Synoptists, uses Jesus' self-chosen name "Son of Man". "The expression understood in the natural sense of the word denotes one who, though a man, holds nevertheless a unique position among men. . . . The title . . . designates Jesus as the man in whom human nature was more fully and deeply realized and who was the most complete exponent of its capacities, warm and broad in his sympathies, ready to minister and suffer for others, sharing to the full the needs and deprivations which are the common lot of humanity, but conscious at the same time of the dignity and greatness of human nature, and destined ultimately to exalt it to unexpected majesty and glory." [1]

Though this may be the natural sense of the words, the title in a technical sense is a great deal more significant; it is indeed one of the most difficult and complex problems of the New Testament, and the amount of agreement in regard to its meaning is very slight as compared with the amount of research which has been made on the subject. No attempt, therefore, can be made to discuss fully the many questions involved. To do so would be to throw the rest of the book out of proportion and exaggerate the importance of the title in the scheme of John.

It is clear that John understood the title in the same way as the Synoptists; we must turn, therefore, to the Synoptic Gospels

[1] Driver, *H.D.B.*, iv, pp. 579 ff.

and examine them in order to understand the meaning of the term. In the first three Gospels the passages which contain the words fall into three classes: in one group the title is used with reference to Jesus' earthly life; in the second group it is associated with the sufferings of Christ; and in the third group it is used in connexion with the *Parousia*. Not all of the instances, however, where the words occur, are used in any special sense. After an exhaustive examination of the instances where the title occurs before the confession of Peter both Dr. Gould and Dr. T. W. Manson [1] agree that "in the instances in which our Lord's designation appears in the Synoptic Gospels prior to their recital of Peter's confession at Caesarea Philippi there is not one which can on examination be held to afford proof that this Messianic title was used by him to be the Messiah or to invalidate the assumption that the use of the title by our Lord began at the time of that declaration, not earlier". [2] We are therefore limited to the following passages in our discussion of the meaning of the technical term: Sayings referring to the Passion—Mark 8. 31; 9. 9; 9. 12; 9. 31; 10. 33; 10. 45; 14. 31; 14. 41; Luke 22. 69; 24. 7; Sayings referring to the *Parousia*—Mark 8. 38; 13. 26; 14. 62; Matt. 24. 30; 25. 31; 19. 28; Luke 12. 8; 12. 40; 17. 24; 17. 26; 17. 30; 21. 36; 22. 69.

When these passages are examined and we ask for a definition which will embrace them all, a great variety of answers are given by scholars. Meyer [3] thinks that it means simply the Messiah and that it was derived directly from Daniel 7. 13. But Jesus never openly called himself the Messiah, whereas he did openly call himself the Son of Man. It would seem, therefore, that Jesus did not identify the title with the Messiah. Neander [4] takes it to mean the ideal representative man. This conception seems somewhat remote from the Jewish habit of thought. Wendt [5] regards it as being primarily connected with the Old Testament

[1] Gould, *D.C.G.*, ii, p. 659; T. W. Manson, *The Teaching of Jesus*, pp. 211 ff.; cf. Cadoux, *The Historic Mission of Jesus*, pp. 94 ff.

[2] Gould, op. cit., p. 663.

[3] *Commentary on Matthew*, 8. 20.

[4] *Life of Christ*, p. 99.

[5] *The Teaching of Jesus*, ii, p. 139.

representations which emphasize lowliness and weakness. But this hardly does justice to the special use which Jesus made of the term. Charles [1] combines the Old Testament conception of the Servant of Jahweh and the notion of majesty found in Daniel. "These two conceptions," he says, "though outwardly antithetic, are, through the transformation of the former, reconciled and fulfilled in a deeper unity in the New Testament Son of Man." [2] Dr. Rudolph Otto prefers to think that the Similitudes of Enoch rather than the Book of Daniel influenced the teaching of Jesus.[3] There is, however, no other evidence that Jesus had ever read the Book of Enoch. And it does not appear to have been known in the circle in which he lived.[4] Dr. T. W. Manson, basing his exegesis on Daniel, finds in the Son of Man not a personal title but a designation of the Remnant. The Son of Man is "an ideal figure and stands for the manifestation of the Kingdom of God on earth in a people wholly devoted to their heavenly king". The mission of Jesus is to "create the Son of Man", that is, the Kingdom of the Saints of the Most High.[5] And it must be agreed that such a representation of a whole group by a single individual was not unknown among the ancient Hebrews. "When Israel was a child, then I loved him, and called my son out of Egypt" (Hos. 11. 1). The identification between our Lord and Israel is unmistakable in his whole Messianic work. Our Lord is not only the Messiah; he is also Israel, the people of God.[6]

These references reveal the very great difference of opinion among Biblical theologians on this matter. And none of the theories put forward appear to explain adequately the use of the title in all the passages under review. No doubt each definition contains an element of truth, in particular the theory of Dr. Manson, but none of them seem to be comprehensive enough. A simple and apparently adequate definition is that Jesus used

---

[1] *The Book of Enoch*, Appendix B.

[2] Ibid., p. 315.

[3] *The Kingdom of God and the Son of Man*, pp. 201 ff., 382 ff.

[4] Moore, *Judaism*, i, pp. 131, 186.

[5] *The Teaching of Jesus*, p. 227.

[6] See H. Wheeler Robinson's article "The Hebrew Conception of Corporate Personality" in *Beihefte zur Z.A.W.*, lxvi, pp. 49 ff.

the title in those circumstances when he conceived himself as the Head and Founder of the Kingdom of God. The sources which may have influenced Jesus accord with this definition. In Daniel it is the theocratic king who is likened to a Son of Man. In Enoch the Son of Man appears as the glorious Founder and Head of God's Kingdom. The extreme novelty in Jesus' conception of the title is his association of the Messianic dignity with the Suffering Servant of Jahweh in Deutero-Isaiah. But there is nothing inconsistent in the combination of the two ideas. "Suffering and death for the actual possessor of the Messianic dignity are in fact unimaginable according to the testimony of the prophets. . . . But the 'One like unto the Son of Man' of Daniel 7. 13 has still to receive the sovereignty. It was possible that he should also be one who had undergone suffering and death." [1]

There are, therefore, these two broad conceptions, one derived from Daniel or Enoch (or both), which depicts the Kingdom of the Saints of which the Son of Man is the glorified head. This idea of glory and exaltation is repeated in those passages which refer to the *Parousia* in the Gospels, e.g. "And then shall they see the Son of Man coming in clouds with great power and glory" (Mark 13. 26). The other conception is derived from the Suffering Servant of Jahweh as presented in Deutero-Isaiah, and is reflected in such passages as "The Son of Man must suffer many things, and be rejected by the elders, and chief priests, and the scribes, and be killed, and after three days rise again" (Mark 8. 31). These two conceptions are united in the Person of Jesus as the Head and Founder of the New Israel. We may also add that in the isolation of Calvary, Jesus alone was Israel, the Son, the Servant.

It has been argued by some scholars that Christ's claim to be the Son of Man carries with it the idea of pre-existence. For example, Dr. Rashdall, quoting Weiss, says: "Wrede and Brüchner have conclusively shown that Paul before his conversion held the belief, as a Pharisee, that the Messiah existed from all eternity with God in Heaven".[2] Similarly, Dr. Stanton

---

[1] Dalman, *The Words of Jesus*, p. 265.
[2] *The Idea of Atonement*, pp. 127-129.

says "that the pre-existence of Jesus was inevitably suggested by the identification of Jesus with the heavenly Son of Man".[1] On the other hand, we must reckon with the verdict of Dalman, who says: "Judaism has never known anything of a pre-existence peculiar to the Messiah, antecedent to his birth as a human being". He denies that Judaism knew anything of a pre-existent ideal man.[2]

The only pre-Christian ground for such an idea appears to be the Similitudes of Enoch. And in relying upon this document much care is required, for our existing version is greatly interpolated.[3] All that can be safely assumed is that the pre-Christian author of the Similitudes borrowed from Daniel the idea of a celestial figure "like unto a Son of Man". This celestial being was conceived as pre-existing, and the idea would have been known to the people who were familiar with the Similitudes. This circle does not appear to have been a large one. The conception of a pre-existing man does not appear in the New Testament. We cannot claim, therefore, with any certitude that John intended his readers to include the idea of pre-existence in his ascription to Jesus of the title Son of Man.

Dr. C. J. Wright denies that the title has any technical or theological associations in the Fourth Gospel.[4] It is used by John, he says, "to express the real, though exceptional humanity of Jesus". Sonship means "partaking of the nature of", and the Evangelist would have us understand by this title that the Eternal Word has spoken in one who was truly man; and not, as the Docetists were beginning to say, in one whose humanity was but an illusory garment. No doubt the title is intended to convey the real humanity of Jesus as set forth in the Synoptic Gospels, and we have already seen that John emphasizes to the full the human characteristics of Jesus. But it would be to

---

[1] *The Gospels as Historical Documents*, iii, p. 171 ; cf. Bousset, *Kyrios Christos*, pp. 140 ff. and 203 f.

[2] *The Words of Jesus*, pp. 128-132, 248 and 252 ; see also discussion by J. M. Creed in *J.T.S.*, Jan. 1925, entitled "The Heavenly Man", and W. Manson, *Jesus the Messiah*, pp. 8-11, 174 ff.

[3] See Charles, *The Book of Enoch*, pp. 64, 65.

[4] *The Message and Mission of Jesus*, pp. 683 ff.

over-simplify a most pregnant term to limit it to this one meaning. An examination of the use of the term in the Fourth Gospel shows that the references fall into the same categories as in the Synoptic Gospels. Those which refer to the passion are as follows: 3. 14; 8. 28; 12. 23, 34; 13. 31. And the following have reference to eschatological ideas: 1. 51; 3. 13; 5. 27; 6. 62. It is as One who is Founder of the Kingdom of Heaven on earth that Jesus brings eternal life to men and provides them with spiritual food (6. 27, 53). We may reasonably claim, therefore, that the testimony of Jesus concerning himself which stands connected with the title Son of Man is in substance the same in both forms of our Gospel tradition. It is hardly likely that John would have simplified the meaning to this extent without some good reason.

vi. *The Glory of the Logos*

There is, however, one important difference which reveals an essential characteristic of the Fourth Gospel. In the Synoptic Gospels Jesus is represented as saying that after his death he would be exalted to the throne of power and glory whence he would come to judge the world (Matt. 24. 31; 25. 31).[1] In the Fourth Gospel the sufferings and death of Christ are the glorification and not merely preliminary to it.

The revelation of the glory of the Logos through humiliation is suggested when Jesus speaks of the lifting up of the Son of Man (3. 14; 8. 28; 12. 32). It raises the mind at once to the cross and the Heavenly throne.[2]

In the first reference (3. 14) the immediate context deals with the New Birth. Hence the primary meaning is no doubt connected with a spiritual experience such as being lifted up in the thoughts and hearts of men. But John himself goes further and associates the lifting up with the cross. In 12. 32 Christ says, "And I, if I be lifted up from the earth, will draw all men unto

---

[1] Although the Synoptic Gospels represent the powers of the kingdom as being revealed during our Lord's earthly activities, and supremely as the result of his death and resurrection, it should be noted that Matthew and Mark never use the word δόξα of the earthly Jesus, and that Luke speaks only twice of the divine glory (2. 9 ; 9. 31 f.).

[2] Cf. Bauer, *Das Johannes Evangelium*, p. 53, and Loisy, *Le Quatrième Évangile*, p. 166.

K

myself", and John adds the comment, "But this he spake, signifying by what manner of death he would die". There is here an unmistakable allusion to the crucifixion. The other reference (8. 28), "When ye shall have lifted up the Son of Man, then shall ye know that I am", refers clearly to the Jews as the agent by which the Son of Man shall be "lifted up".

The great difficulty in regard to 3. 14 is the reference to the serpent. From the Jewish point of view the serpent could not possibly be connected with the idea of salvation. Schlatter quotes the following passage from *Mekhilta* on Exodus 17. 11 showing how the Jews interpreted the incident connected with the serpent [1]: "It was not assuredly the uplifted hands of Moses that invigorated Israel and laid Amalek low. So long as he lifted up his hands, Israel looked at him and believed on him who had given Moses the command to act thus. God it was who did the signs and wonders on their behalf. Nor was it the serpent that killed and gave life. Israel looked on, and so long as Moses lifted up the serpent, they believed on him who had commanded Moses to act thus". In Rabbinic literature generally the serpent is regarded as the symbol of envy (*T.B. Sanh.* 29 *a*); he introduced evil seed into mankind (*T.B. 'Ab. Zar.* 22 *b*); he is the symbol of evil inclinations (*Tanh. B.* 7).

There were, however, interpretations current which regarded the serpent as the symbol of a saviour. For example, the symbolic use of the serpent of Moses for the Logos is found in the allegorical interpretation of Numbers 21. 7-9 in Philo's *Leg. Alleg.* 2. 20, 79. Here the serpent of Eve is contrasted with the serpent of Moses, the ἡδονή with the σωφροσύνη, the σῶμα with the νοῦς. Dr. Odeberg, after quoting a long passage from Hippolytus (*Refut.* 5. 16) about the speculations of the Ophitic sect, called Peratae, says: "It must be concluded that probably there existed a Gnostic interpretation—of pre-Johannine origin—of Num. 21. 8-9 reading in that passage a reference to the 'true and perfect serpent who was also the Mediator, the Son, the λόγος'." [2] But the difficulty in regard to the serpent in the Fourth Gospel is not so

---

[1] *Der Evangelist Johannes*, pp. 95, 96.
[2] See Odeberg, *The Fourth Gospel* etc., pp. 105 f.

great as might be imagined. The emphasis in John 3. 14 is actually upon the elevation, and not on the serpent, which takes secondary place. The elevation of the serpent is paralleled with the elevation of the Son of Man; the serpent itself is not paralleled with the Son of Man. It would appear also that this elevation referred to the elevation upon the cross.

Such was also the general interpretation given by the Fathers of the early Church. For example, in the *Epistle of Barnabas* the reference to Moses and the serpent in John 3. 14 is clearly understood to refer to the cross. Barnabas says (12) that Moses made a brazen serpent the τύπος of Jesus, and set it up conspicuously (τίθησιν ἐνδόξως), and bade any man that had been bitten to "come to the serpent which is placed on the tree (ἐπὶ τοῦ ξύλου ἐπικείμενον) and let him hope in faith that the serpent being himself dead can yet make him alive (αὐτὸς ὢν νεκρὸς δύναται ζωοποιῆσαι) and straightway he shall be saved". Origen (*Exhort. ad Martyr.*, 50) argues that death by martyrdom may be called ὕψωσις. Cyprian also applies John 3. 14 to the crucifixion of Jesus. Westcott gives other examples from the Fathers which interpret the lifting up of the Son of Man as referring to the cross.[1]

Other associations of the verb ὑψοῦν suggest the idea of exaltation. The verb may have been taken from Isaiah 52. 13 where the Servant of the Lord is said to be exalted and glorified (ὑψωθήσεται καὶ δοξασθήσεται σφόδρα). This is followed almost immediately by predictions of suffering and contempt and death, which are to be crowned with triumph and division of "the spoils". The same word is used by St. Peter in his sermon on the day of Pentecost when he said that Jesus had been exalted to the right hand of God (τῇ δεξιᾷ οὖν τοῦ θεοῦ ὑψωθείς). Elsewhere he says that "the God of our fathers raised up Jesus . . . him did God exalt (ὕψωσε) with his right hand to be a Prince and a Saviour" (Acts 5. 30, 31).

Bernard, however, denies that ὑψοῦν is used in the Fourth Gospel in the sense of exaltation as at the time of the ascension.[2] And Burkitt argues that the Aramaic word meaning "to exalt"

[1] *St. John*, pp. 63 ff.   [2] *St. John*, p. 13.

('*ᵃrim*) cannot also mean "to crucify" and that the Aramaic word meaning "to crucify" (*zᵉqoph*) cannot also mean "to exalt".[1] This is the weakness of Abbott's argument when he says that the word rendered by ὑψοῦν may actually have the double meaning "to exalt" and "to crucify".[2] Schlatter argues that the positive meaning of the word in 3. 14 is that of glorification revealed in Jesus. He says that although ὑψωθῆναι, from 'ezdᵉqeph="to be raised on high", was a customary term for crucifixion in Northern Syria, it remains uncertain whether that is the meaning here, for it is not established that this form of speech was customary in Jerusalem also.[3]

But whatever may be the result of the linguistic argument, we cannot confine the thought of John to such narrow dimensions. Every great and original thinker uses current modes of speech, but it would be a profound mistake to imagine that the use of current modes of speech also indicates the acceptance of current modes of thought. John constantly struggles with the language of his day to express ideas which transcend the ideas of his contemporaries. In the mind of John the exaltation of Jesus does not take place at the ascension, but in the death on the cross. This is such a novel idea that no verbal arguments should be used to tie down his thought to a literal and prosaic interpretation. Certain it is that John elsewhere combines the two ideas of exaltation and crucifixion, of glory and humiliation. In close connexion with the passion he represents Jesus as saying "The hour is come, that the Son of Man should be glorified" (12. 23); "Now is the Son of Man glorified, and God is glorified in him" (13. 31). Furthermore, the Judgement which in the Synoptic Gospels is associated with the *Parousia* and is deferred until the coming of the Son of Man is in the Fourth Gospel exercised here and now by the attitude of men to Christ. In 5. 27 Jesus says that the Father gave the Son authority to execute judgement "because he is the Son of man". The judgement which is here spoken of consists in this, that some hear, while others do not hear,

---

[1] *J.T.S.*, July 1919, p. 337.
[2] *The Son of Man*, par. 3402, and *Johannine Grammar*, par. 2211 *c*, 2642 *b*.
[3] *Der Evangelist Johannes*, p. 96.

Christ's word (6. 25). This characteristic thought of John will be discussed more fully later, but it illustrates the idea that the conception of glory and majesty and judgement which are derived from the Jewish Apocalyptic writings are in the Fourth Gospel considered as something present and not future. This was, in fact, John's answer to those who still expected the Lord to appear on the clouds of heaven at the end of the world. The glory of Jesus is not revealed in lightnings and thunderings, but in service, humiliation, and death.

To these references we may add 3. 13. Dr. W. Lock says that the words "who is in heaven" may be understood in two ways: (a) as our Lord's own words, "who while on earth still has heart and home in heaven", or (b) by the Evangelist, "who (while I write) has returned to heaven and is there".[1] In our opinion (a) is to be preferred as being in complete harmony with the Johannine conception of the eternal and spiritual world. "The spiritual world is not to be thought of as something beyond space and time; it must be admitted that the spiritual world, according to John, is manifested in some kind of space, allowing the application to it of spiritual terms in a literal sense." [2] The Son of Man descends from the spiritual world and lives in the spiritual world and carries about with him the glory of heaven because the spiritual world and the plane of history are embraced in one complete unity.[3] It is this which enables us to see in the historical person of Jesus the supramundane glory of God.

Prof. Manson thinks that this bringing into the present what in the Synoptic Gospels was deferred to the future was brought about by the obvious fact that Jesus did not return in glory and power to judge the nations within the lifetime

---

[1] *New Commentary*, iii, p. 251.

[2] Odeberg, *The Fourth Gospel* etc., p. 114; cf. Hoskyns, *The Fourth Gospel*, p. 235: " If these words belonged to the original text of verse 13 they cannot have referred to the time after the Ascension, since the Evangelist is not accustomed to forget the historical context of the narrative altogether. They must, therefore, be understood to belong to the range of thought in which heaven means that invisible existence in or with God (1. 1, cf. 17. 21-23), and which makes possible the assertion that those who believed possess eternal life here and now ".

[3] This also explains the apparently contradictory statements of 14. 10 and 14. 12. The journey to the Father is intended to be taken realistically, yet it is implied that there is no separation between the Father and the Son.

of the first generation of Christians.[1] There is no doubt that the failure of our Lord to return in the apocalyptic manner depicted in some passages in the Synoptic Gospels led both St. Paul and John to reconsider our Lord's teaching on the subject. And it is our opinion that John more accurately represents the actual teaching of Christ in regard to the ideas associated with the current apocalyptic imagery; that, in the words of Wendt, we have here "an interpretation and explanation of the inner meaning which these ideas had for the consciousness of Jesus himself".[2]

This is the general outlook of the Fourth Gospel. The Incarnation is not only a manifestation of life, it is also the manifestation of the glory of God. In the Word incarnate "we beheld his glory, glory as of the only begotten from the Father" (1. 14). In the historical person of Jesus we see the spiritual glory of God. It was in the man Jesus that John learned to know what God was like, and his earthly manifestation was not regarded as the obscuration of divinity, but as the only means whereby the divine character could be adequately manifested to men.

In this connexion the phrase ἐσκήνωσεν ἐν ἡμῖν (1. 14) is of particular interest, for it suggests the *Shekinah*, the glory with which God himself appeared among his people in the tent in the wilderness.[3] In contemporary Judaism the Word was used in the Targums to denote the invisible presence of God, and "the glory" for the visible presence of God. But *Shekinah* stood for both the visible and the invisible presence. In the words of Dr. I. Abrahams it "applied to both as a continuous religious experience . . . to local and universal, to earthly and heavenly, to visible and invisible, manifestation of the Holy Spirit".[4] In the Fourth Gospel the invisible *Shekinah* is regarded as dwelling in the tabernacle of the flesh of Jesus, for "we have seen his glory", which is the manifestation of the *Shekinah* among men. Hence

---

[1] *The Teaching of Jesus*, p. 278.

[2] *The Teaching of Jesus*, ii, p. 307 ; see further pp. 204 ff.

[3] See Burney, *The Aramaic Origin of the Fourth Gospel*, pp. 35 ff., and Schlatter, *Der Evangelist Johannes*, pp. 23, 24.

[4] *The Glory of God*, pp. 51 ff.

"glory in this Gospel is God in action through Jesus Christ, bringing the whole 'weight' of riches of the love of the Father to bear on the world of men".[1] Though the Temple may have been destroyed the presence of God has not been withdrawn, for Jesus has taken the place of the Temple; in him the glory of God shone.[2]

The very fact that Jesus revealed God in his own Person not so much in terms of might as of love is proof that this is the most exalted attribute of God, his peculiar glory, and the very character of his nature as light (1 John 1. 5). Because, therefore, the love of Christ was shown supremely in just those moments which from another point of view might be regarded as the very depths of his humiliation—his menial service (13. 3-17), his betrayal and death—John regards them as the highest expression of his glorification among men, which was at the same time the glorification of the Father (13. 31).

We see then the close connexion between sacrifice and glory in the "lifting up" of the Son of Man. And in the Fourth Gospel the Son of Man is lifted up whenever he performs what men of the world would call an act of condescension, and most of all when he performs the special act of "lifting up" implied in the offering of himself upon the cross. In the Synoptic Gospels the disciples are called the light of the world in so far as they manifest their good works to the world. They are bidden to let their light shine before men (Matt. 5. 14). Similarly Christ as light of the world (8. 12) reveals his glory in acts of condescension, and supremely when he is raised upon the cross. Then it is that light shines from the cross; the glory of God is revealed to all the world. If it is the case that the Book of Revelation was written by a disciple of John, and there appears to have been some kind of contact between the two men,[3] then it is no coincidence that we read of the New Jerusalem that "the city hath no need of the sun, neither of the moon, to shine upon it: for the glory of God did lighten it, and the lamp thereof is

---

[1] Strachan, *The Fourth Gospel*, p. 106.
[2] Cf. Schlatter, *Der Evangelist Johannes*, p. 24.
[3] See Charles, *The Revelation* (I.C.C.), p. xxxiii.

the Lamb" (Rev. 21. 23). And the Lamb is the Lamb that hath been slain in virtue of which he is worthy of glory (Rev. 5. 12; cf. John 1. 36).

vii. *The Messiah*

We have seen how John represents Jesus as having fulfilled the yearnings of contemporary pagans to see God. The vision of God which they sought to attain in philosophy and the ecstatic rites associated with the Mystery Religions is given once and for all in the manifestation of Jesus in the flesh. "He that hath seen me hath seen the Father" (14. 9). We have also seen in our discussion on the Logos that John wished to prove to his contemporaries who had remained in the liberal and philosophical Judaism of the Diaspora that, in Jesus Christ, the revelation of the Logos, admitted by them in the Old Testament, has its full and definite fulfilment.[1] It now remains for us to consider whether John regards Jesus as having likewise fulfilled the Messianic hopes of the Jewish people.

It has already been pointed out in the discussion on the Johannine use of the Old Testament that John finds in Jesus the fulfilment of the Old Testament prophecies of the Messiah. "Moses wrote of me", and the Scriptures "bear witness of me". Yet it has been charged that John suffered the idea of the Messiah, and its corollary the Kingdom of God, to fall into the background; and has superseded it with the higher conceptions involved in the terms Logos and Son. Dr. E. F. Scott, for instance, asserts that "in the Fourth Gospel the Messianic idea is replaced by that of the Logos", and that "throughout the Gospel the Messianic title denotes nothing more definite than the higher nature and dignity of Jesus as the Son of God".[2] On the other hand, Archbishop Bernard claims that the idea of Jesus as Messiah is fundamental to the thought of John. "This thesis is continually present, while we might antecedently have expected that it would be kept in the background by one who had reached a more profound doctrine of Jesus as the Logos of God. Yet that Jesus is

---

[1] Cf. Réville, quoted by W. R. Inge, *D.C.G.*, i, p. 886.
[2] *The Fourth Gospel*, pp. 6 and 183.

the Christ, was for John, as it was for Paul, the essential germ of a fuller belief that he was the Saviour of the world." [1]   And this seems to reveal a deeper insight into the complex nature of the Fourth Gospel.   The way in which ideas are generally developed and enriched as the Gospel proceeds has already been observed. There is a further illustration of this in the gradual unfolding of the Messianic idea in conflict with popular expectations.

There is a division of opinion among scholars as to whether the title Son of Man was a current title for the Messiah.   Dr. S. R. Driver in an article in the *Dictionary of the Bible* [2] gives a long list of the opinions of scholars for and against its being a Messianic title.   Dr. Driver himself decides against the supposition that it was a popular description of the Messiah.[3]   On the other hand, Dr. Gould says emphatically that "the multitudes are familiar with the title Son of Man; to them it is a designation of the Messiah; their difficulty is to reconcile Messiahship with exaltation through death".[4]   On the whole it seems that it cannot be called a popular designation, and if the title was traditional it awaited final interpretation.   We shall not, therefore, employ this as evidence that Jesus claimed to be the Messiah in the Fourth Gospel.

After the Prologue the Gospel opens with the testimony of John the Baptist in consequence of which some of the disciples of John followed Jesus.   At this period there are several confessions of belief in the Messiahship of Jesus.   Andrew tells his brother Simon, "We have found the Messiah" (1. 41).   Philip again says to his friend Nathanael, "We have found him of whom Moses in the law and the prophets did write"; and Nathanael acknowledges him as the Son of God, the King of Israel, and Jesus accepts the homage (1. 45-51).   The Fourth Gospel at the very outset places into clearest relief the consciousness of Messianic vocation possessed by Jesus; this is emphasized by the three declarations by John the Baptist that he is not the Messiah.   In the Synoptic Gospels the Messiahship is not confessed until the crisis at Caesarea Philippi (Mark 8. 29; Matt. 16. 16).   But when

---

[1] *St. John*, p. lxxxi.
[2] Vol. iv, pp. 586 ff.
[3] Op. cit., p. 586.
[4] *D.C.G.*, ii, p. 659.

John wrote it was an "open secret", and he would have his readers know that Jesus was aware that he was the anointed of the Lord from the beginning. He wishes us to understand that the whole life of Jesus was controlled by this sense of divine vocation. That which the disciples came only slowly to realize was known to Jesus from the earliest days of his ministry. This shows how fundamental the Messianic idea was to the author of the Fourth Gospel. It is that which dominates the whole ministry.

Next we find Jesus making himself known directly as the Messiah to the woman of Samaria (4. 26). That Jesus should reveal himself in this manner so early in his ministry is probably to be explained, as already suggested, by John's reading the end into the beginning. But in this case there are certain local circumstances which make it possible that Jesus did actually proclaim his Messiahship to these people. The Samaritans were cut off from the general life of the Jewish people, and there would not be any reason to fear that dangerous consequences would follow from proclaiming that he was the Messiah. There is reason to believe that the Samaritans regarded the Messiah as fulfilling a prophetic role rather than being of a kingly character.[1] Their Messianic hopes would not therefore be such as to encourage a revolt against the civil power [2] or an attempt to force Jesus to adopt a policy alien to his own conception of Messiahship (cf. 6. 15).

We again find Jesus using language which can hardly fail to have been understood to involve a claim to be the Messiah at Jerusalem at the time of the Jewish feast to which chapter 5 relates. His words appear to have been addressed to his opponents, and they may have been heard by them and his disciples only. In chapter 6 there is narrated the crisis which involved the disciples in a decisive act of faith in Jesus as "the Holy One of God" (6. 69; cf. Mark 8. 27 f.; Matt. 16. 31 f.; Luke 9. 18 f.). This confession is of the highest importance for the understanding of John's mind. "Words

[1] See Stanton, *The Jewish and the Christian Messiah*, pp. 127 ff. The Samaritans rested their expectations of the advent of the Messiah upon Deut. 18. 15-18 ; he would therefore be above all things a teacher of righteousness ; cf. John 4. 25.

[2] Cf. Westcott, *St. John*, pp. lxix f.

which had been spoken before (chap. 1) have now a wholly different meaning. To believe in Christ now was to accept with utter faith the necessity of complete self-surrender to him who had finally rejected the homage of force." [1] John here penetrates below the external office of Messiah to the essential nature of Jesus. Jesus is the Messiah not because he is a wonder-worker (cf. 6. 30), but because he is holy. Holiness is the true sign that Jesus is the Lord's anointed.[2] In contrast, Judas desires to find not holiness, but power in the Messiah; not the light of truth that is self-luminous, but the thunderbolt of authority which compels men to acquiesce.

The importance which the Messianic hope had for John is shown generally in the conflicts between Jesus and the Jews which he reports. When Jesus appeared in Jerusalem he created a division among the people (7. 30 ff., 43). Some thought that he was the Christ because of his works (7. 3), others because of his teaching (7. 26, 37 ff., 46). But he did not satisfy their popular expectations of the Messiah (7. 27, 42, 52). In the end they asked him : "If thou art the Christ, tell us plainly" (10. 24). And Jesus' reply is, "I told you, and ye believe not" (10. 24, 25), implying that this had been all along the substance of his claim. In the same manner he acknowledges Pilate's question, "Art thou a king then?" (18. 37).

The reason why Jesus' familiar word "the Kingdom of God" only occurs in two passages in the Fourth Gospel (3. 3, 5; 18. 36) may have been the fear of rousing the ready suspicion of the Roman Empire against the Church as a political faction (cf. 19. 12). There may also have been a deeper reason in harmony with what we have already seen to be the character of this Gospel. A king requires the service, if not of slaves, at least of servants. This was not the kind of service which Jesus desired (15. 15).[3]

When John speaks of "Jesus Christ" it is always with the

---

[1] Westcott, *St. John*, p. lxx.

[2] Cf. Hoskyns, *The Fourth Gospel*, p. 342 : " In the Fourth Gospel it [the title, Holy One of God] expresses the consecration of the Son to be Saviour of the World ".

[3] Ibid., p. 228.

signification of Jesus the Messiah: Christ never becomes for him a mere personal name, the adjunct of the name Jesus. Although it is true that the confession which is made in the Epistle is a test of orthodoxy, that Jesus is the Christ come in the flesh, and is directed especially against the gnostic denial that the heavenly aeon Christ was identical with the man Jesus, yet it at least includes the assertion of his real Messianic character. Jesus does not expressly say to the world, "I am the Christ"; but neither does he do so in the Synoptic accounts.

We may reasonably claim, therefore, that John fulfils his purpose in writing the Gospel, "that ye may believe that Jesus is the Christ, the Son of God" (20. 31). John shows how Christ satisfied the hopes and aspirations of the people of Israel, though they were both fatally at variance with the current and dominant Judaism. Especially in one respect does John emphasize the difference between the Jewish and Christian conceptions of the Messiah. John never refers to Jesus as "the Son of David". The national aspect implied by such a title was too narrow a conception for the Christ who, in the mind of John, was "the Saviour of the World".

7

SALVATION

i. *The Saviour of the World*

One cannot fail to be struck with the universal reference which John's language attributes to Christ's saving work in the world. Not only is he in the world as Saviour; but he is sent as "Saviour of the World" (4. 42; 1 John 4. 14). Loisy says that this formula belongs neither to the Jewish nor to the Evangelic tradition; rather its style and mysticism show that it is pagan in origin.[1] We have already pointed out that such a theory is not necessary and that there is evidence that the title was not unknown in Jewish circles.[2] In the words of Hoskyns: "The theory that the Fourth Evangelist has simply borrowed a phrase from Philo or transferred to Jesus a current Hellenistic title underestimates his capacity for crystallizing the meaning of Christian tradition into a short and pregnant phrase".[3] This universalism is a characteristic of the Fourth Gospel. Schlatter points out that the phrase in the Prologue, "every man coming into the world", is a Rabbinic circumlocution for "all men".[4] The verse would then be translated, "there was the true light that lightens all men". This would be in accord with the universalism of the Fourth Gospel: see e.g. 10. 16; 12. 32; 17. 2. The fourth chapter is probably the most universal chapter in the whole of the New Testament. Dr. Knox suggests that the infrequency of the title "Saviour of the World" in the earlier books of the New Testament is probably due to the fact that, if Christ had been preached as such, he would have been in danger of being

---

[1] *Le Quatrième Évangile*, p. 191 ; cf. Bauer, *Das Johannes Evangelium*, p. 71.

[2] See p. 112. In Philo, *Quod deus sit immut.* 156, God is referred to as " the Saviour of the Universe ". There may even be a conscious reference to Joseph's new name (Gen. 41. 45), Zaphenath-Paneah, the Vulgate translation of which is *Salvator Mundi*.

[3] *The Fourth Gospel*, p. 272. Dr. Knox thinks that the Evangelist has taken a title with pagan associations and put it into the mouth of the half-heathen Samaritan woman (*Some Hell. Elements in Prim. Christianity*, p. 42 n.).

[4] *Der Evangelist Johannes*, p. 15.

reckoned as only one of the many saviours recognized in the Hellenistic world.[1] The language of John is remarkable in one respect. There is no saying in the Synoptic Gospels which asserts with the same directness the universal effect of the work of Jesus. There are utterances in the Synoptic Gospels which, if pressed, might involve such universalism. But it was the Fourth Evangelist who gave clear expression to the belief. This was no doubt due to the pressure of the Hellenistic environment.

There is evidence from contemporary Rabbinical literature of such a saving attitude towards the whole world. For example, the Palestinian R. Hanina bar Hama, commenting on Genesis I. 31, pictures God's concern for the world as follows: "It may be likened unto a king who built a palace; he looked at it and it pleased him; he said: Palace! Palace! O that you might always obtain favour before me as you obtain favour before me at this hour; so the Holy One, blessed be he, said to his world: O my world! my world, would that thou mayest always obtain favour before me as thou obtainest favour before me in this hour". Dr. Odeberg, commenting on this passage, says: "The underlying idea is that the Holy One loves his newly created world, and wishes that it would remain in such a state that it would always find favour in his sight. The implication is that with man's sin the whole world is defiled. Yet it always remains his world, the object of his pleasure".[2] It is therefore not surprising that John should claim similar universality for the saving work of Christ, and make explicit what was implicit in the Synoptic tradition.

But the language is also remarkable, because according to John's predominant use of the word "world" in both Gospel and Epistle it denotes not the totality of human existence, but the evil remnant which is left after the Christian community has been gathered out. It is the evil world power, in contrast to the Church; it is not merely an unbelieving world, but a persecuting world (17. 14; 1 John 3. 13), which openly and

[1] *Some Hell. Elements in Prim. Christianity*, p. 41.

[2] *The Fourth Gospel* etc., p. 115. Schlatter draws attention to the common Jewish belief that " what God does in Israel is done for all mankind " (*Der Evangelist Johannes*, p. 50).

violently displayed its antagonism to Christ and to all who are his. John beholds the whole world lying in the Evil One (1 John 5. 19). This indicates more than that subjection to darkness and sin which characterized the world at the coming of Christ. The world had already seen and rejected Christ; it is therefore ripe for judgement (12. 31), for the reproof of its sin of unbelief (16. 8, 9); and Christ's attitude towards it is only that of conqueror (16. 33). In the last hour Christ even forbears to pray for it (17. 9), although he still looks forward to an ultimate turning of the world to belief through the ministry of his disciples (17. 20, 21).

It is, of course, not in this exclusive sense, denoting particularly the evil residue, that John uses the word when he speaks of the Logos coming into the world, and of Christ as Saviour of the world: but it is in a sense which includes this evil element also; for it is the whole world. This universal reference is put beyond doubt when he says: "He is the propitiation for our sins; and not for ours only, but also for the whole world" (1 John 2. 2). It is not as though he were Saviour of both the good and the bad; for the whole world was in darkness and sin, and the discrimination of the two classes was subsequent to his manifestation, and a result of it, though not the purpose of it. Although Christ's manifestation in the world is actually a judgement, and although what he actually accomplishes is in 9. 39 represented as the purpose of his coming, there is really nothing in John's representation to contradict the solemn assertion: "God sent not his Son into the world to condemn the world; but that the world should be saved through him" (3. 17; 12. 47). For Christ's judgement of the world consists simply in this, that God's loving gift of light to the world has as its inevitable consequence the revealing of the darkness, or rather, it presents the test which reveals the fundamental bent of the heart. "And this is the judgement, that the light is come into the world, and men loved the darkness rather than the light" (3. 19). It is this figure of the light which makes John's meaning clear and consistent. Jesus proclaims himself the light of the world (8. 12; 12. 46), and in 9. 5 he says that, being in the world, he must be its light. It is this perfectly objective mode of thought which explains John's meaning. Just as the light shines in the world, and shines none the less because the darkness does not apprehend it, so, in the simplicity and directness of his thought, he beholds Jesus lying objectively before the world as the sacrifice and "propitiation" [1] for its sin; and none the less for all—intended for all, available for all—that some do not accept the gift he offers. As the Baptist in the early days pointed to Jesus as "the lamb of God, which taketh away the sin of the world", so finally John sees him hang on the cross, "lifted up" before the eyes of the world, "as Moses lifted up the serpent in the wilderness", "that every one that believeth on him may have eternal life" (3. 14, 15).

ii. *The Division Among Men*

The Fourth Gospel records no more striking saying of Jesus, considering the circumstance of its utterance, than that before Pilate and the rulers of the Jewish nation: "to this end have I been born, and to this end am I come into the world, that I should bear witness unto the truth. Every one that is of the truth heareth my voice" (18. 37). At this word, the apparent relationship in that Hall of Judgement is dissolved, inverted, and Jesus appears as Judge for the condemnation of his judge and of his accusers, who thereby proved that they were not of the truth, because they heard not his voice.

It is characteristic of John that he represents the apostasy of the nation as culminating in the official act of its chiefs in delivering Jesus up to the Roman power. He does not record the extenuating words from the cross, "they know not what they do" (Luke 23. 34), nor in any way admit that the rulers and people were acting in ignorance (cf. Acts 3. 17): it was the clear rejection on the part of the nation and its rulers of the Messianic King. It is rather Pilate whose conduct is pityingly extenuated on the ground that he exercised his power only subordinately (19. 11), and under the dread of offending his master (19. 12); whereas it is Jesus' own nation and the chief priests who have delivered him unto him who have the "greater sin" (18. 35;

[1] For a discussion on the meaning of " propitiation " see pp. 179 f. below.

19. 11). This, as we have seen, is in accordance with John's constant representation, that the very manifestation of the Truth (which is the Light) is in itself the judgement of the world.[1] In 8. 43 Jesus says: "Why do ye not understand my speech? Even because ye cannot hear my word". This, however, is not a pre-determined deafness, although it is traced back to the fact that the devil is their father; for it is expressly said: "The lusts of your father it is your *will* to do" (8. 44). Consistently with this claim that he is not in the world as judge (although a judgement is accomplished by his presence), he says: "If any man hear my sayings, and keep them not, I judge him not: for I came not to judge the world, but to save the world. He that rejecteth me, and receiveth not my sayings, hath one that judgeth him: the word that I spake, the same shall judge him in the last day" (12. 47, 48). The judgement ascribed to Jesus' word, his truth, and his light, is in the above instances represented as a judgement of condemnation, for John uses the word judgement almost always with this implication. As Loisy remarks, in the term judgement there is always present the threefold meaning of discrimination, verdict, and condemnation.[2] In the third chapter, for example, where Jesus speaks of the judgement accomplished through the light, although the word is used simply in the sense of condemnation (3. 18; cf. 3. 9), he nevertheless notices the double effect of the light: upon them who come to it, as well as upon them who hate it (3. 20, 21). The judgement which Christ is actually accomplishing in the world is one which includes blessing as well as ban: "that they which see not may see; and they which see may become blind" (9. 39). This is parallel to the saying recorded in Luke: "not to give peace but division" (12. 51 ff.). This also reminds us that, according to the Synoptic tradition, Jesus' earthly manifestation in some sense forestalls the final judgement. But it is a

[1] Dr. Odeberg suggests that the Hebrew conception of *dīn*, judgement, may have been in the mind of John as he thought of men's attitude towards the light. The Jews thought of judgement as consisting of two divine relations to man : (i) That of *dīn* or *mĭshpāt*, judgement or justice, and (ii) *hĕsĕd* or *răhamīm*, love or mercy. He who by his correct attitude towards God has put himself under the attribute *hĕsĕd* is not judged. See *The Fourth Gospel* etc., p. 147.

[2] *Le Quatrième Évangile*, p. 168.

L

characteristic of the Fourth Gospel that the blessings of the Gospel (salvation and eternal life) are regarded as substantially present here and now, and therefore that the judgement must also be realized in the present. This does not merely mean that the final judgement has only to pronounce upon works already done on earth. The division itself, the segregation of good and evil (cf. Matt. 25. 32), is in some sort accomplished by Christ's manifestation on earth.

This idea of division accomplished by Jesus amongst the men who heard his words is one which to a very marked degree determines the plan of the Fourth Gospel. Not only is it apparent in the passages upon which we have commented, but we see that the whole Gospel is arranged with a view to demonstrating the diverse effects which the word of Jesus had upon his hearers, and to displaying the division which from the beginning of his ministry it began to accomplish amongst men. For this reason it is expressly mentioned, after many of his notable sayings or works, that "there arose a division among the multitudes concerning him" (7. 43; 9. 16; 10. 19; cf. 7. 12). This division proceeded even to the sifting of his own followers (6. 66); Judas finally "went out" and left Jesus at the last hour alone with his friends (13. 3). This sifting continued in the Apostolic Church; and the apostasy of its members was regarded as a sign that they never really belonged to the community: "They went out from us, but they were not of us; for if they had been of us, they would have continued with us: but they went out that they might be made manifest how that they all are not of us" (1 John 2. 19).

The division thus accomplished in the world is not a mere incident in Christ's manifestation; as regards the children of God it is an essential step in the work of salvation. It has already been suggested that we may perhaps find a parallel here to the Genesis account of the creation, according to which the mechanical division of the elements of the world preceded the production of life.[1] In the Fourth Gospel it is considered a matter of real importance that the children of God should be

---

[1] See pp. 113 ff. above.

separated from the evil elements in the world. It is especially
in Jesus' final discourse with his true friends, and in his prayer
for them, that the contrast between the disciples and the world
is expressed. Just as surely as they are "in the world" (13. 1;
17. 11), just so surely are they "not of the world" (15. 19).
"They are not of the world, even as I am not of the world" (17. 16).
And this is explained by the fact that he has chosen them (or that
God has given them to him, 17. 15) "out of the world" (15. 19).

At the end of his Epistle John expresses the vivid consciousness
which the Christian community had of its separateness from the
world: "We know that we are of God, and the whole world
lieth in the Evil One" (5. 19). There is more than a negative
advantage in this separation of the children from the world; or,
rather, this very act includes the formation of a Christian community, which can oppose itself as a unit to the world; while
the world is for its part conceived as a unity represented in the
person of the prince of this world, and constituting a power that
not only tempts but persecutes the Church. The formation of a
community out of the darkness scattered abroad in the world is
expressed in the saying, "that he might also gather together
into one the children of God who are scattered abroad" (11. 52).
This is expressed also in the tenth chapter in Christ's allegory
of the Shepherd. There, too, it is the voice of Christ which
collects the flock (10. 5), and there are other sheep besides those
of the Jewish fold which he must bring, and they shall become
one flock and one shepherd (10. 16).

This idea of unity is profoundly emphasized in Jesus' prayer
in which, looking into the future and beyond the circle of his
present disciples, he entreats "for them also who believe on me
through their word; that they may all be one; even as thou,
Father, art in me, and I in thee, that they also may be in us: that
the world may believe that thou didst send me" (17. 20, 21). We
see from this quotation, and in general by a reference to the whole
prayer, that this unity of the disciples is of the highest importance
in manifold directions. In the first place, it is a positive good
in itself, and is the condition of fellowship with one another,
and with God in Christ. It is further of importance not only

for protection against the world, and as a means of overcoming it, but as a means of gaining disciples out of the world and even of winning the world itself to faith. In this is seen the reason why, though Christ leaves the world, the disciples must remain in it; why they must be in it, though not of it; for Christ has sent them into the world, even as the Father sent him into the world (17. 18; cf. 1 John 4. 17).

We see, therefore, that this division which is brought about by the shining of the light of truth in the world, thereby gathering together into one the scattered children of God, as against the collective might of darkness, is the first and fundamental effect of Christ's work of salvation, in regard both to the individual and to the community. Notwithstanding the mystical element in John's thought, and his vivid sense of personal communion with Christ and God, salvation is not to be thought of apart from the community, which is the expression of separation out of the world and of adherence to Christ.

iii. *The Last Day*

We have seen how slight a stress John lays upon the developments of the future and that he does not dwell upon the conceptions of now and then, but of here and there, above and below, heaven and earth. There would appear to be in the expression "this world" (ὁ κόσμος οὗτος) the implication of another and future world. But John is probably distinguishing between the world of Domitian with its impermanence and the real life of the Kingdom which is possible here and now. In John the contrast between present and future worlds (αἰῶνες) seems to be wholly merged in the contrast between this evil world (κόσμος) which passes away and the eternal truth of God which has been revealed in the darkness.

There are, however, expressions which appear to suggest that Christ will come again at the last day. Are we to understand by these expressions that a great cosmic event will herald the last day? It is generally considered that John wishes his readers to understand that he has arrived at a more profound interpretation of our Lord's references to his "coming again".

For instance, Dr. C. J. Wright says: "The Evangelist is using the language of time to convey that which is not of time". "What he means when he speaks of the 'last day' is the quality of finality. The life which belongs to the spiritually regenerate man has in it the quality of eternity; and that quality will be completely sifted from every trace of evil in a consummation which indwells the thought and purpose of God." [1] "Jesus did not mean what we mean by 'coming' and 'going'. What he says is that the divine Spirit which constitutes his own essential life will be their guide and their stay." [2]   Other scholars regard all references to the "last day" as interpolations into the text. Wendt adopts this view and is followed by Dr. Charles, who believes, for instance, that 5. 27, 29 is at variance with its context and in fundamental conflict with the general tendency of the Gospel.[3]

An examination of the references to the "last day" in the Gospel confirms the view that John has arrived at a more spiritual interpretation of the final judgement. It is to be noticed that his references to the "last day" are always balanced by words which make it clear that he is not thinking of the future but of the present. When Martha says of Lazarus, "I know that he shall rise again in the resurrection at the last day", Jesus at once replies, "I am the resurrection and the life: he that believeth on me, though he die, yet shall he live: and whosoever liveth and believeth on me shall never die. Believest thou this?" (11. 24, 25). Our Lord's words to the Jews in chapter 5 (verses 25-29) need not refer to an historical event that was still in the future when he spoke. The "coming forth out of the tombs" cannot be anything else than a graphic description of the awakening of souls to accept or reject the light. It is only on this interpretation that we can understand the words, "the hour cometh and now is" (verse 25). Those who hear the voice of Jesus stand even now within the final order of God. Similarly in the sixth chapter, when our Lord says, "I will raise him up at the last day", these words are qualified by what follows: "Verily, verily, I say unto you, he that believeth hath eternal life" (verses 40, 44, 47). The terms of primitive

---

[1] *The Message and Mission of Jesus*, pp. 696 f.
[2] Ibid., p. 880.
[3] Wendt, *The Teaching of Jesus*, i, pp. 249 ff. ; Charles, *Eschatology*, p. 429.

eschatology are put on the lips of our Lord, but these are reinterpreted in such a way that the "last day" is no longer an apocalyptic event of some future date, but a fact realized by the present attitude of men to Christ. The "last day" of which Jesus spoke is, according to the Evangelist, that moment when men accept or reject the light that is already shining in the world. As Sir Edwyn Hoskyns says: "In Jesus the world is confronted by the End. This does not mean that the eschatology of the earlier tradition has been transmuted into an inner, present, spiritual mysticism: it means that the Evangelist judges the heart of Christian eschatology to lie less in the expectations of a second coming on the clouds of heaven than in the historical fact of Jesus; there the final decision is made".[1] The eschatology of Jesus in the Fourth Gospel thus expresses the absoluteness and vital urgency of God's demand on us through Jesus Christ.[2] This sense of urgency and crisis when confronted by Jesus also finds expression in the Epistle where the author speaks of a "sin unto death" (1 John 5. 16-17). The denial of Christ, manifested in the flesh, is, in the mind of John, so deadly a sin that it places a man beyond the pale, and may well represent for him the "last day". The same conception is found in the Epistle to the Hebrews where it is said that those who deny their Christian faith are beyond the power of the Church's forgiveness (Heb. 6. 4-6; 12. 16-17; cf. Mark 3. 24-29; Matt. 12. 31-32; Luke 12. 10).

When Jesus asserts that he has come not to judge but to save the world, he is expressly contradicting the Jewish expectation that the Messiah would come in power and glory to judge the world; in particular, to right the wrongs of his people, and execute judgement upon their enemies. Jesus repudiates this interpretation of his mission, but he by no means denies the necessity of a definite judgement of mankind. The decisive sundering of the wicked from the righteous is essential to the idea of completed salvation. Jesus, therefore, claims that "the Father hath committed all judgement unto the Son" (5. 22); and again, "he gave him authority to execute judgement,

---

[1] *The Fourth Gospel*, p. 298.
[2] Cf. Cadoux, *The Historic Mission of Jesus*, p. 349.

because he is the Son of Man" (5. 27). This judgement is accomplished by men's attitude to Christ. Though Jesus was not sent to judge the world, this was in fact the result of his coming: "He that believeth on him is not judged: he that believeth not hath been judged already, because he hath not believed on the name of the only begotten Son of God. And this is the judgement, that the light is come into the world, and men loved the darkness rather than the light; for their works were evil" (3. 17-20). This is quite different from the Synoptic conception of the coming of the Son of Man on the clouds of heaven (cf. Matt. 25. 31-46). In the Fourth Gospel "the place of life and of judgement, the place where the final eschatological decision is made, is no transcendental, mystical, supernatural activity of the Son or Word of God. The place of decision is the flesh of Jesus, his audible words and visible death (12. 31-33, 19. 30), in fact, the historical event of his mission".[1]

In the Synoptic Gospels there are to be found traces of a similar conception of judgement pronounced by men's attitude to Christ here and now. In both Q and Mark it is he who acknowledges Jesus that will be acknowledged by the Son of Man; he who denies Jesus will be denied by the Son of Man. Furthermore, each generation in the past will be judged by its response to the degree of revelation open to it at the time. In the days of the Queen of Sheba it was the wisdom with which Solomon was endowed that was the criterion of judgement. To the generation of Ninevites to whom Jonah preached, the principle of judgement was the response made to the call to repentance and amendment of life. But a greater than Jonah is here. To the generation that saw the ministry of Jesus, his words and works and all that Jesus was in himself were the principles of judgement.[2]

This conception is very similar to that found in the Fourth Gospel. But the idea was in the early days of the Church overshadowed by the Jewish apocalyptic conceptions incorporated in the Synoptic Gospels. In the Fourth Gospel the crude apocalyptic ideas are completely done away. The belief in a final judgement has

---

[1] Hoskyns, *The Fourth Gospel*, p. 300.
[2] See T. W. Manson, *The Teaching of Jesus*, pp. 270 ff.

been subjected to a profound reinterpretation in the mind of John, and in accordance with elements found in the Synoptic Gospels.

It is in harmony with the general tenor of John's mind that he does not dwell with predilection upon the nature of the punishment meted out to the unbelieving world. It is in general sufficient to know that the world is judged: this judgement is, however, further expressed by the fact that "the prince of this world shall be cast out" (12. 31; cf. 16. 11). Christ has "overcome the world" (16. 33), and John, as he writes his Epistle, sees the world as a power which is indeed still able to persecute and tempt the Church, but which the Church can overcome by the superior might of Christ (4. 4), and which is already passing away with its lusts (2. 17). In his allegory of the vine Jesus says, "If a man abide not in me, he is cast forth as a branch, and is withered; and they gather them, and cast them into the fire, and they are burned" (15. 6). The very phraseology of this verse recalls the saying, likewise parabolic, of Matthew 13. 40, according to which the gathering and burning of the tares occurs "in the consummation of the age". Both Jewish and Christian theology represented the "last judgement" as a partition of life and death, and the "resurrection of judgement" which John contrasts with the "resurrection of life" (5. 29) would seem to indicate the same conception. As eternal life is the specific gift which Christ brings into the world, we can hardly conceive that the punishment of the wicked could consist in anything but the deprivation of this gift, namely in abandonment to death. This would seem to accord peculiarly well with the characteristics of Johannine thought. The "sin unto death" of which John speaks in his Epistle (5. 16) refers primarily to the Jewish discrimination between those sins for which the legal penalty was death, and those that admitted of ritual atonement: but John doubtless thought of eternal death, which is God's final punishment for sin. As the immunity of believers from judgement is founded upon the fact that they have already "passed out of death unto life", so the doom of him that loveth not is simply expressed as an abiding in death (1 John 3. 14). The condemnation of the world, so far as it concerns the positive completion of salvation, is satisfied in this, that every evil thing opposed to God is abolished.

iv. *The Election of the Children of God*

We have seen that the division which is brought about by Christ's appearance among men results, on the one hand, in the dissolution of the previous relation of the Jews by their own rejection of the Messiah; and, on the other hand, in the establishment of a new family of God's children upon the ground of their believing reception of him. The company which is thus drawn together, separated from the world, and drawn to God, by their loving reception of the light, is nothing less than a new covenant congregation which steps into the place vacated by the old. They also are Jesus' own (cf. 1. 12 with 13. 1); and, being his, they are the Father's possession and the people of God (10. 14, 26, 29; 17. 10). But no people can by its own choice become God's possession: it is only by God's free grace that men are called into his fellowship. It was a maxim of Israel that God had not chosen the nation on account of its excellence or its might, but because he loved his people. In the Old Testament it is always looked upon as an act of condescension and love of God for Israel that he rescued them from bondage and purified them from sin (Deut. 7. 8; 10. 15; Is. 44. 21, 22). It was not otherwise in the new covenant relation: it was Jesus' choice, and not their own, which constituted the disciples his possession (15. 16, 19); and in the last resort it was God himself who separated them from the world and brought them to Jesus (17. 6); they were his because they were the Father's and were given to him (6. 37, 39; 10. 29; 17. 2). This time, however, God's election was not a national one but an individual one. His choice was indifferent to the question of race (1. 13); the Jews themselves were accorded no privilege above other peoples, but as many of them as were truly Christ's flock were "put forth" (10. 4; cf. 9. 34), in order that they, as well as the children of God who were scattered throughout the world, might be gathered together as one flock under one shepherd (10. 16; 11. 52; cf. Ezek. 34. 20-24; 37. 21-24).

John's use of the word "flock" emphasizes the unity of God's people. They were even more thoroughly sundered from the world, more radically contrasted with the world, than were the covenant race of old. Because they are not of the world, God's people must expect the world's hatred (15. 20); while they are in the world they must endure persecution, but they may nevertheless be of good cheer, for Jesus has "overcome the world" (16. 33); or, as John says in his Epistle, "greater is he that is in you than he that is in the world" (1 John 4. 4).

This separation of the people of God from the world is not a nominal, but a real one: they are not only called the children of God, but such they are (1 John 3. 1). They are "in truth" what the people of the Old Covenant were in a figure. The Christian is God's child because he is actually begotten of God. This relation manifests itself in ethical likeness to God (1 John 2. 29; 3. 9; 4. 7), which in heaven will be perfected (1 John 3. 2), and which on earth constitutes a family in which brotherly love is perfectly spontaneous and natural (1 John 5. 1, 2). Israel was called God's vine (Ps. 80; Jer. 2. 21; Hos. 10. 1), but Christ is the "true vine" and his disciples are the branches (15. 1 ff.).[1] In contrast to the Jews—whose worship is nevertheless an intelligent one—the Christians are the true worshippers and "worship the Father in spirit and in truth" (4. 23). Instead of the figurative temple, Jesus' body is the true temple (2. 21) because it more really represents God's presence among men. The essential importance of the temple is that it represents God's presence among men. As Schlatter says, "it was a sign and guarantee of the presence of God in their midst".[2] But in the Christian community, as in the heavenly Jerusalem, there is no temple needed, "for God Himself and the Lamb are the temple thereof". Even when Jesus has ascended to heaven, it is still true that God is in the midst of his people (1 John 4. 4);

---

[1] Behm, in *T.W.z.N.T.*, i, p. 346, gives many examples from Mandaean and pagan literature of the symbolic use of the vine. But the imagery is almost certainly taken from the Old Testament. For examples from Jewish literature see Schlatter, *Der Evangelist Johannes*, pp. 304, 305. Jesus is denying the claim of the Jews to be the vine of God.

[2] *Der Evangelist Johannes*, pp. 79 ff.

and the idea of the temple is completed, fulfilled, in the mystical union of the believer with God, in his taking up his abode in each disciple (14. 23), of which we are assured "by the Spirit which he gave us" (1 John 3. 24; 4. 13).

The people of God, who in reality do not belong to the world, are sent into the world, even as Christ was sent into the world (17. 18); and for the purpose of this mission they must be sanctified "in truth", as Christ sanctified himself (17. 19). They are to be a holy people, as Israel was of old, set apart and consecrated to God. This sanctification is wrought by God (17. 17) and by Christ (17. 19); but it also demands from the believer continuous ethical effort to preserve himself from all the contamination of the world (1 John 3. 3; cf. 15. 2). Christians are engaged in an ethical struggle with the world. They must keep themselves pure, not only from idolatry, but from every such relation with the world and the things that are in the world as would prove essential relation with it. They may not love the world, nor the pleasures which it affords, "for all that is in the world, the lust of the flesh, the lust of the eyes, and the vainglory of life, is not of the Father, but is of the world. And the world passeth away, and the lust thereof" (1 John 2. 16, 17). The result of this struggle is not doubtful, for in the last resort it is God's might and not man's which gains the victory. Christ has overcome the world, and his victory is the ground of the disciples' confidence (16. 33). The victory of the children of God over the world is grounded in the fact that "greater is he that is in you than he that is in the world" (1 John 4. 4). "We know that whosoever is begotten of God sinneth not; but he that was begotten of God [Jesus] keepeth him, and the Evil One toucheth him not" (1 John 5. 18). It is clear from this last verse that John cannot think of the possibility of a true member of the family of God falling into apostasy. The more decidedly man's relation is traced back to God's own choice and work, so much the more difficult is it to think of the continuance of this relationship as dependent upon human fickleness. However, the very fact of the extension of the Christian community in the world brings with it the possibility that heterogeneous elements may mix with it. Deceivers (1 John 2. 4), and deceived (1 John 1. 8), Christians only in tongue (1 John 3. 18), false teachers and lying prophets, even children of the devil (1 John 3. 10), can for a time appear as members of the community, although they are of the world, and finally return to the world where they belong and where they find a hearing (1 John 4. 5). The community, like the individual, must continually purify itself from the contamination of the world; and John sees in the severing of these false members from the Church the proof "that they all are not of us" (1 John 2. 19).

Not only is the final victory assured for the children of God; they are altogether kept from sin. Upon this point John's statements are clear and emphatic, but they seem to be involved in a radical contradiction. On the one hand he says: "Whosoever is begotten of God doeth no sin, because his seed abideth in him: and he cannot sin, because he is begotten of God" (1 John 3. 9). It is only in appearance that this contradicts 1 John 1. 7-10, for this is in a sense the continuation of the Baptist's preaching of repentance, and may perhaps be specially referred to sins committed before the cleansing of the blood of Jesus,[1] which is received upon entrance into the Christian community, and he goes on to warn those who have become Christians against sin. This requires him, however, either to leave quite hopeless the brother who does nevertheless commit sin; and with his absolute, "he that sinneth hath not seen him, neither knoweth him", to cut him off from communion with God; or to point out to him some still further possibility of forgiveness. This latter he does by pointing to Jesus and his priestly intercession with God (1 John 2. 1): Jesus' sacrifice was made once and for all (1 John 2. 2), and his priesthood is perpetual and eternal.[2] The contradiction which is here involved in John's expression is only partly resolved

---

[1] This limitation of πάσης ἁμαρτίας to pre-Christian sins is denied by Brooke (*The Johannine Epistles*, p. 16). Westcott understands the singular to signify the spring or the principle of sin in contrast to separate manifestations (*The Epistles of St. John*, p. 22). Dodd says: "The Evangelist thinks of *sin* as a principle or quality of life, expressing itself variously in thought, word, and deed; the author of the Epistle thinks of *sins*, the multiform outward expression of the sinful principle" (*The Johannine Epistles*, p. 73).

[2] The present of the verb "to be" is used in John to signify not an isolated fact, but an abiding and present reality, e.g. 1 John 3. 3, 5, 7; cf. Westcott, op. cit., p. 44.

by distinguishing between sin as a habit and particular acts of sin,[1] for John's language does not consistently observe this discrimination. For John, as for the Jews, sin is transgression of the Law (ἀνομία, 1 John 3. 4). The old covenant discriminated between sins of ignorance, for which pardon might be had through ritual atonement (Num. 15. 27), and sins done "with a high hand", for which there was no forgiveness (Num. 15. 30, 31). So John also distinguished between the wilful breach of God's covenant, which irretrievably forfeits that eternal life which is to be had only within the Christian community, and sins for which a brother's intercession may still avail to obtain restoration to the communion in the brotherhood, and to participation in life (1 John 5. 16).

The distinction is not quite the same, however, in the two cases. The Christian law is no longer expressed in external ordinances which a man transgresses in ignorance. It is contained in the principle of likeness to God, of love. As love is so inward an affair it is at bottom impossible to conceive of any transgression of it which is not a presumptuous breach of the covenant. To deny the law of love would be a manifestation of radical subjection to the darkness and the dominion of the devil, to whom all hatred is traced.

But sin means more than this—"all unrighteousness is sin" (1 John 5. 17); every instance of yielding to the temptations of the world, of straying away from absolute rectitude, although it does not involve a radical deflexion of the heart from God, is sin—"and there is a sin not unto death". This, as we have already pointed out, is explained symbolically in the Gospel when Jesus washed the disciples' feet: "He that is bathed needeth not save to wash his feet, but is clean every whit" (13. 10). The Baptism of the New Covenant cleanses perfectly and for ever; there is needed no second radical cleansing, but only a washing of the feet from such contamination as is inevitable to all who walk in the world.[2]

[1] Cf. 1 John 3. 9 with 1 John 2. 1. The aorist is used of isolated actions, but the present infinitive is generally employed to express an action frequently repeated : see Westcott, op. cit., p. 42 ; Dodd, *The Johannine Epistles*, p. 78.

[2] See pp. 125 f. above.

There is, however, one instance in which even the necessity of confession and forgiveness for the Christian is quite left out of account. In 1 John 3. 18-20 it is said, "Children, let us not love in word, neither with the tongue; but in deed and truth. Hereby shall we know that we are of the truth, and shall assure our hearts before him, whereinsoever our heart condemn us; because God is greater than our heart, and knoweth all things". In the consciousness of fulfilling God's commandment by a genuine love of the brethren, the Christian need not be for ever perturbed by his own conscience convicting him of particular delinquencies, for God who knoweth all judgeth according to the inward disposition of the heart. It was in this thought that Peter found relief, when after his fall Jesus examines him: "Lovest thou me?"—his own heart testified against him, accusing him of denial, but in the assurance of true love he appeals to the superior knowledge of him who knows all: "Lord, thou knowest all things; thou knowest that I love thee" (21. 15-17).[1]

The foregoing discussion will have shown how readily John

---

[1] This may be called the "soothing" interpretation. It is an antidote to what moral theologians call a scrupulous conscience. It is adopted by Brooke, *The Johannine Epistles*, p. 98, and Westcott, *The Epistles of St. John*, p. 118. A different interpretation sees in the passage an appeal to awaken the conscience. If we cannot in God's sight "persuade" our conscience, how can it be supposed that we can succeed in persuading God who is greater than conscience itself? Therefore we ought to examine our conscience thoroughly so that the verdict of conscience and God coincide. But, as Dodd says, "it does not seem to be the intention of the passage as a whole to awaken a sense of sin which would amount almost to despair". See the whole discussion in *The Johannine Epistles*, pp. 88-92.

The critical questions involved in this passage are five in number : (i) Whether καὶ ἔμπροσθεν αὐτοῦ begins a new and independent clause, so that the future πείσομεν is so co-ordinated with the future γνωσόμεθα, or whether πείσομεν, like ἐσμέν, still depends on ὅτι ; and, in the former case, whether ἐν τούτῳ is to be referred to γνωσόμεθα, or also to πείσομεν. (ii) Whether πείθειν means to convince, or has an object following ; or whether it means to persuade and stands absolutely. (iii) Whether ὅτι is generally a particle, and then also ἐάν a conditional particle, the second ὅτι being a resumptive of the first ; or whether ἐάν stands for ἄν and ὅ, τι must be read. (iv) Whether God is called μείζων because he is more merciful than our heart, or because he is more rigorous in judgement upon us. (v) Whether in verse 21, by means of the words ἐὰν ἡ καρδία κτλ., a second proposition is introduced in opposition to that contained in verse 20 ; or whether, rather, this ἐάν stands in the sense of "if then now", and introduces a deduction from what is said in verse 20.

These problems are fully discussed in *Commentary on St. John's Epistles*, by J. H. A. Ebrahard, pp. 258 ff.

applies to the Christian community the ideas of covenant relationship which were familiar to the Jews. It is therefore surprising that John does not use the word "covenant", nor does he expressly contrast the Jewish community with the Christian. This seems to indicate that, although he felt for himself a personal necessity of constructing his theology in terms of Hebrew thought, he did not find in the idea of the covenant the highest expression of salvation brought by Christ; and that in this instance, as in so many others, he avoided the use of words and ideas that were alien to his Hellenistic environment.

How unserviceable the word was for the expression of the idea of salvation to the Gentiles we can see from the devices by which St. Paul (Gal. 3. 15) and the author of Hebrews (9. 16 ff.) sought to adapt it to their modes of thought.

It is also a ground for some surprise that he omits the name which designates Christ's people, in their organized unity, the people of God. The word ἐκκλησία occurs only in the Third Epistle, and then only in relation to the individual congregation (3 John 6, 9, 10). There was, of course, no reason for its use in the Gospel, and the omission in the Epistle may have been accidental. At any rate, no one could lay more emphasis than does John upon the conceptions which were most fundamental to the Christian idea of the Church; in particular upon the unity of the whole brotherhood, the very idea which the name church in its universal reference was meant to express. The pre-eminence of the Apostles is also clearly recognized (13. 20; 15. 16; 17. 18; 20. 21; 1 John 1. 3; 4. 6; 2 John 10; 3 John 9 ff.). It is recorded in 20. 23 how Christ bestowed upon the Apostles plenipotentiary authority; though their unique function in the Church is more commonly referred to the fact that they are true witnesses to the historical manifestation of Jesus, having been with him from the beginning (15. 27; 19. 35; 1 John 1. 5). As, however, it is God's power which protects the disciples from evil, and as direct fellowship with him is the highest Christian ideal, so too it is the distinction of the people of the New Covenant, as the prophet foretold (Jer. 31. 34), that "they shall all be taught of God" (6. 45). It is no longer necessary for every man to teach his brother, for the Holy Spirit directly teaches them all things (14. 26). In the same way it is said in the Epistle: "Ye have an anointing from the Holy One, and ye know all things" (1 John 2. 20).[1] This sentence means that Christians have a chrism from Christ, no doubt bestowed at Baptism, because the Holy Spirit proceeds from the Holy One. This first baptismal anointing is maintained by a continued anointing through their union with Christ which renders the children of God independent of the Apostolic teaching: "And as for you, the anointing which ye received of him abideth in you, and ye need not that any one should teach you; but as his anointing teacheth you concerning all things, and it is true, and is no lie, and even as it is taught you, ye abide in him" (1 John 2. 27).

v. *The Death of Christ*

We have studied a number of traits in Johannine thought which mark the Christian community as God's covenant people; but we have still to discuss the most important element in the covenant. If a company of sinful men gathered out of the world was to be brought into real communion with God, it could be accomplished, according to the ideas of the Old Testament, only by doing away with that which on the part of men constituted an absolute impediment to such communion. This condition determined the conception of the foundation of the Old Covenant: it also determines the ideas associated with the foundation of the New Covenant; hence the presence of the ideas of purification and expiation in the Johannine writings. It is the more necessary to emphasize this point because it is sometimes asserted that the idea of atonement has absolutely no place in these writings, and that Christ's death has importance only as a manifestation of his love.

As an example of this way of thinking we may quote Dr. E. F.

---

[1] But the older and better texts have : " You all possess knowledge ". Prof. Dodd does not think that the reference here is to the Holy Spirit. He argues that it means the Word of God, or the revelation of God in Christ, confessed at Baptism. So long as the Word remains in the Christian and continues to be a living power in him, he really needs no teaching from anyone (*The Johannine Epistles*, pp. 58 ff.).

Scott: "He accepts the fundamental idea of a redeeming sacrifice, with the difference that he connects it with the incarnation instead of with the death". "His appearances in the flesh constituted his sacrifice. The death at the close could not add to it anything that was essential." "In the true Johannine doctrine there is no logical place for the view of the death of Christ as an atonement." [1] (NO)

It is readily admitted that the idea of the atonement does not, as with St. Paul and the writer of the Epistle to the Hebrews, occupy the foremost place in John's representation; that indeed it recedes before the dominant representation of the moral efficacy of Christ's revelation.[2] Nevertheless there are to be found in the Gospel and the Epistle distinctive expressions of the objective significance of Christ's death, and evidence that it is an organic part of the work of Christ.

In the first place we notice that John perceives a rational necessity in the death of Christ. The Son of Man must ($\delta\epsilon\hat{\iota}$) be lifted up if he is to save those that believe (3. 14). The corn of wheat must ($\delta\epsilon\hat{\iota}$) fall to the ground and die if it is not to abide alone (12. 24). Oneness of purpose with the divine will is indicated when Jesus says: "Therefore doth the Father love me, because I lay down my life, that I may take it again" (10. 17). This is in harmony with those references to the "hour" of Jesus in which he indicates an unfolding of the divine purpose (12. 23; 17. 1).

The death of Christ is also an essential element in the defeat of Satan. It is in regard to death and its consequences that Jesus says: "Now is the judgement of the world: now shall the prince of this world be cast out. And I, if I be lifted up from the earth, will draw all men unto myself" (12. 31 f.). As his hour draws near he says: "I will no more speak much with you, for the prince of the world cometh, and he hath nothing in me" (14. 30). In the description of the work and power of the Holy Spirit the same conception occurs: "He when he is come will convict

[1] *The Fourth Gospel*, pp. 208, 225.

[2] For a discussion of the limitations of the Johannine conception of the atonement as compared with the rest of the New Testament see Vincent Taylor, *The Atonement in New Testament Teaching*, pp. 226 ff.

M

the world . . . of judgement, because the prince of this world is judged" (16. 11). The idea contained in these passages is that Jesus demonstrates by his death that the prince of this world has no right in it at all; he has nothing in Christ, he is judged, he is cast out. Through the death of Christ the Kingdom of this world is taken from him. The same conception appears in the Epistle. The world "lieth in the Evil One" (1 John 5. 19), but the Son of God was manifested that he might destroy the works of the devil (1 John 3. 8). Powerful though the prince of this world may be, "greater is he that is in you than he that is in the world" (1 John 4. 4). Such a faith in the victory of Christ over the world leads to the thought that God's children will share that victory. "For whatsoever is begotten of God overcometh the world: and this is the victory that hath overcome the world, even our faith. And who is he that overcometh the world, but he that believeth that Jesus is the Son of God?" (1 John 5. 4-5). It is the chief point in Aulen's book *Christus Victor* that the idea of the conquest of Satan by the death of Christ is rooted in the Gospel tradition, and the above passages show that it is a prominent idea in the Johannine writings.

The death is regarded as the means by which Christ enters into his glory. This has already been discussed in an earlier chapter,[1] but the relevant passages may be recalled here. "The Spirit was not yet" because "Jesus was not yet glorified" (7. 39). The disciples remembered what was written of him (12. 16) when Jesus was glorified. When the Greeks came to Jesus he says: "The hour is come, that the Son of Man should be glorified" (12. 23). When Judas went out into the night to betray Jesus, our Lord rejoiced because "now is the Son of Man glorified, and God is glorified in him" (13. 31). In the High Priestly prayer he says: "Father, glorify the Son, that the Son may glorify thee" (17. 1). To the same order of thought belong those passages which speak of the exaltation of the Son in death (3. 14; 8. 28; 12. 32). The death of Christ is, therefore, an integral part in the process by which Christ is liberated from the self-imposed conditions of this world: it is the exaltation.

[1] Pp. 145 ff.

That the death of Christ is regarded by John as vicarious is seen by the frequency with which he uses the technical sacrificial word ὑπέρ.[1] "The good shepherd layeth down his life for (ὑπέρ) the sheep" (10. 11; cf. 15).[2] "It is expedient for you that one man should die for (ὑπέρ) the people" (11. 50; cf. 18. 14). "Hereby know we love, because he laid down his life for (ὑπέρ) us" (1 John 3. 16).

One of the most disputed points in the interpretation of Johannine thought is to be found in the verse where Jesus is represented as the "propitiation for our sins" (1 John 2. 2). In 1 John 4. 10 this is said to be the purpose of God sending the Son into the world.

In the New Testament "propitiation" is only used in this Epistle, in the form ἱλασμός, and once in the Epistle to the Romans, in the form ἱλαστήριον (Rom. 3. 25). Dr. Driver discusses the meaning of *kipper*, which in the LXX is translated ἱλάσκεσθαι, from the Old Testament point of view in Hastings' *Dictionary of the Bible*.[3] There he points out that the ritual term *kipper* is usually rendered "covering". God graciously "covers" over the sins of men. But God himself is not said to be propitiated. Sacrifice does not render God propitious in the sense of transforming him into a merciful God, as if he had not been so before. Many complex meanings are, however, associated with the word *kipper*, and it is difficult to arrive at a single comprehensive meaning of the word. Dr. Driver regards the actual word as colourless in meaning, and while admitting that "propitiation" accentuates too much one particular side of what is involved, he considers that this is on the whole the best rendering.

Prof. C. H. Dodd approaches the question from the point of view of Hellenistic Judaism. And after an exhaustive examina-

---

[1] It should be noticed, however, that in Hellenistic Greek even the original meaning of ὑπέρ as "in the interest of" is sometimes greatly weakened. Cf., for instance, ὑπέρ ὧν ἠβουλόμεθα meaning "as regards those things we wished", in *Selections from the Greek Papyri* by Milligan, p. 24.

[2] Hoskyns points out that the Rabbinic parallels cited by Strack-Billerbeck suggest that the two verbs *lay down* and *give* may reproduce the two Hebrew words *masar* and *nathan* which were used to express surrender of life for the sanctification of the divine name (*The Fourth Gospel*, p. 436).

[3] Vol. iii, pp. 128-132.

tion of the general use of the word ἱλάσκεσθαι and its derivatives in the LXX, he says that "Hellenistic Judaism as represented in the LXX does not regard the cultus as a means of pacifying the displeasure of the Deity, but as a means of delivering man from sin, and it looks in the last resort to God himself to perform that deliverance". He says that ἱλασμός should be interpreted in the same sense as καθαρίζειν, and regards the Johannine use of the term as falling into line with this usage.[1] A similar view is taken by Dr. Moffatt.[2] This interpretation, which appears to be generally accepted by modern scholars, serves to show that the barrier against reconciliation is on man's side, not on God's.

Nevertheless we must beware of seeking to interpret Biblical language in the terms of modern thought, and it would seem that the meaning of the word is not exhausted by a purely subjective interpretation. Although John speaks in 1 John 1. 7 of the cleansing power of the blood of Jesus, there is no indication in 1 John 2. 1 f. that he is primarily thinking of the moral effects which are wrought by Christ in the consciousness of sinners. John does not say that Christ provides a means of expiation, but that he himself is the expiation. This is a usage which is not found elsewhere in the New Testament, and warns us that lexical research regarding the use of a word cannot finally settle a theological problem. To say that Christ is the expiation is thoroughly in accord with the method of John as a whole. Jesus is represented to us as the Word of God, the Way, the Truth, the Life, the Door, Spiritual Food and Drink. The meaning of ἱλασμός would appear to be, therefore, that in Christ (not merely in the consciousness of sinners) sins are cancelled so that they no longer stand between God and ourselves.[3]

In the Gospel the death of Christ is thought of especially with reference to the foundation of the New Covenant congregation. It is not only the Shepherd's voice that gathers together the scattered sheep and constitutes them one flock (10. 16); the laying down of his life is also necessary to this end (10. 11, 15, 17).

---

[1] *The Bible and the Greeks*, pp. 93 ff.; cf. article on "ἱλασμός" and "καθαρμός" by Büchsel in *T.W.z.N.T.*, iii, pp. 311 and 315.

[2] *Love in the New Testament*, p. 255.

[3] Cf. Vincent Taylor, *The Atonement in New Testament Teaching*, pp. 221 ff.

And although Jesus' death cannot, according to the terms of the allegory, be represented in a sacrificial aspect, the thought is expressed that it avails not only to save the life of the sheep from the wolf's attack (10. 12), but to give them more abundant life (10. 10). How important this conception was for John we see in 11. 50-52: "It is expedient for you that one man should die for the people, and that the whole nation perish not. Now this he said not of himself: but being high priest that year, he prophesied that Jesus should die for the nation; and not for the nation only, but that he might also gather together into one the children of God that are scattered abroad". He here interprets Caiaphas' astute counsel as a prophecy of Jesus' death as a sacrifice for the nation, and more particularly as the covenant sacrifice which constituted the scattered children of God one people.

It is likewise John's own interpretation of Jesus' words which represents his death as the event that draws all men unto him (10. 32, 33). In 17. 19 Jesus represents himself more expressly as the covenant sacrifice which consecrates his disciples as God's people: "For their sakes I consecrate myself, that they themselves also may be consecrated in truth". In view of the fact that Jesus has already entered upon the way to his death, this saying can only refer to his sacrificial consecration to God; and the consecration of his disciples, which he thereby effects, is a consecration to God's possession as a covenant people. This interpretation is confirmed by the meaning implied by the word ἁγιάζειν. It is closely related to ἁγνίζειν, "to make sacred". It therefore means much more than to sanctify. It means to set apart and dedicate a person or thing to the service of God. In the Old Testament the word is used especially in a sacrificial sense.[1] The passage, therefore, means that Jesus is about to establish between God and man a relation which men could never have established themselves, but into which they can truly enter; and into which they will be drawn once it is established by him.[2] This is the equivalent of the Pauline doctrine that Christ

---

[1] See Hoskyns, *The Fourth Gospel*, pp. 596 ff. ; Procksch, *T.W.z.N.T.*, article "ἁγιάζω", i, pp. 112 f.

[2] Denney, *The Death of Christ*, p. 195.

dies our death that we may be drawn into the fellowship of his death. He establishes the reconciliation; we receive it (Rom. 5. 11).

Jesus' death as a covenant sacrifice has reference solely to the covenant people. Although we have seen that his saving work is for the whole world, it is effectual only for those who stand within the covenant relationship. The Old Testament idea of the covenant was essentially that of peculiar and exclusive privilege: the New Covenant was likewise exclusive, though only those who were self-excluded were excluded. The forgiveness of sins was one of the privileges of the Old Covenant, and it was prophetically promised as one of the blessings of the new. It is therefore thoroughly in accord with the Old Testament point of view when John represents that only he who by walking in the light has come into fellowship with God, and stands thereby in fellowship with God's people, can enjoy the cleansing of his sins through Christ's blood (1 John 1. 7). The same conception is postulated in the Old Testament phrase "faithful and just" (1 John 1. 9; cf. Ps. 143. 1). It is only in relation to the covenant that God's mercy in forgiving sins can be characterized as an act of faithfulness and justice; but where the covenant atonement is already provided, and confession of sins is truly made, forgiveness is simply the consequence of God's faithfulness to his promise and his righteousness in observing the covenanted terms.

Christ's sacrifice, like the sacrifice of the covenant (Exod. 24), was made once and for all. Moreover, in the Christian dispensation there is no provision of repeated sacrifices for recurrent sins; for the purpose of Christ's coming was, both by his sacrifice (1. 29) and by his total manifestation (1 John 3. 5), "to take away sins"; and we have seen that, for God's children, sin and the sinful power is already radically overcome and abolished.

It would indeed be strange if the sacrificial idea were ignored in a Gospel which begins with the Baptist's witness to the Lamb of God (1. 29), and ends by representing Christ's death as occurring on the very day, perhaps at the very hour, when the Passover was wont to be slain.[1] Dr. E. F. Scott thinks that the phrase

[1] See Bernard, *St. John*, p. cvi.

"Lamb of God" is a "vague concession to an earlier doctrine".[1]
But it is hardly likely that John would have made a vague concession when first introducing Jesus to his readers. Rather the
fact that he brings the phrase to the very forefront of his Gospel
shows what importance he attached to it. Dr. F. C. Burney
defends it as the actual opinion of the Baptist, though, as always
in this Gospel, it retains the impress of John's own mind.[2]

The phrase itself may be regarded in one of five ways[3]:
(i) As referring to the Lamb at the morning and evening sacrifice
(Exod. 29. 38-46); (ii) as referring to Jeremiah 11. 19; (iii) as
referring to the Paschal Lamb (Exod. 12; cf. John 19. 36);
(iv) as referring to the Messianic leader of God's people in
Enoch; (v) as referring to the Servant of Jahweh (Is. 53. 7, 12).
Dr. Vincent Taylor prefers the fifth interpretation on the ground
that Isaiah 53. 7, 12 easily explains the references to a lamb
and sin-bearing. Furthermore, the identification of the Suffering
Servant with our Lord had already been made in the early
Church (Matt. 8. 17; Acts 8. 32), and was probably derived
from our Lord himself (Luke 22. 37; 24. 26). Jeremias supports
this view[4] in so far as he thinks that ὁ ἀμνὸς τοῦ θεοῦ is a mis-
translation of talyā dēlāhā in the sense of 'ebed 'ᵃdōnai, meaning
"the Servant of God". But Prof. Dodd rejects this suggestion
because tāleh is never translated ἀμνός in the LXX, and there are
no examples of rendering 'ebed as talyā.[5] He inclines to the view
of Spitta "that in the Gospel and the Apocalypse alike, 'Lamb'
is a Messianic title derived from the Apocalyptic figure of the
young wether which leads the flock, whatever sacrificial ideas
may have come to be associated with it". This would accord
with our view that Jesus used the title Son of Man in those
circumstances when he conceived himself as the Head and Founder
of the Kingdom of God.[6]

The difficulty is that αἴρων in 1. 29 probably means "taking

[1] *The Fourth Gospel*, p. 219.
[2] *The Aramaic Origin of the Fourth Gospel*, pp. 104-108.
[3] Cf. Vincent Taylor, *Jesus and His Sacrifice*, pp. 226 f.
[4] *T.W.z.N.T.*, i, p. 343.
[5] *J.T.S.*, xxxiv, p. 285.
[6] See pp. 142 f.

away" whereas φέρειν in Isaiah 53. 6 means "bearing sin". In the Fourth Gospel αἴρειν never means "to carry", but always "to lift up" in order to remove something (cf. 2. 16; 10. 18; 11. 39; 11. 48; 15. 2; 19. 31). And, according to Strack and Billerbeck,[1] it is never used in the LXX with the sense of "bearing sin". Hence the primary meaning of the passage cannot refer to Jesus as a piacular sacrifice.

Nevertheless, whatever the phrase meant to the Baptist, it is difficult not to believe that in the mind of John Jesus was both the Passover Lamb and the Lamb mentioned in Isaiah 53. In John 12. 38 our Lord is actually identified with the Suffering Servant and, as we have suggested, this was the interpretation given to his Person and work by Christ himself. "It is not too much to say that the conception of Christ's death as a sacrifice for sin, put thus at the very beginning of the Gospel, is meant to convey decisively the Evangelist's own conception of Jesus and his work. He is here to put away sin—that sums up his vocation; and he does not put it away by denunciation, like the Baptist, but by the sacrificial method, in which it has to be borne."[2]

vi. *The Sacraments*

Jesus represented his death as a covenant sacrifice when at the Last Supper he took the cup and said: "This is my blood of the Covenant".[3] The phrase is clearly a reproduction of Exodus 24. 8. Mark 14. 24 adds, "which is shed for many", and Matthew still further (26. 28), "for the remission of sins". St. Paul (1 Cor. 11. 25) and Luke (22. 20) unite in calling it "the cup of the New Covenant in my blood"; and this conception was firmly rooted in the Church. We cannot point to any single sacrifice of the Old Testament cultus as the exclusive type of Christ's sacrifice: it fulfilled the idea of sacrifice in general.[4] It was in particular the foundation of a covenant; but many of the

---

[1] Quoted by Rigg in *The Atonement in History and Life*, p. 158.
[2] Denney, *The Death of Christ*, p. 184.
[3] See Vincent Taylor, *Jesus and His Sacrifice*, pp. 74, 136-139. The following authorities omit the word "new": ℵ B C D L etc.
[4] Cf. Hicks, *The Fulness of Sacrifice*.

sacrifices recorded in the Old Testament beside that of Exodus 24
were of this character. The Passover (Exod. 13) was a covenant
sacrifice of an earlier date and more primitive type; and many
of its inspiring ideas have survived in the Christian Eucharist.
It represented not merely a national, but a family covenant, and,
like every covenant sacrifice, its benefits were shared only by
those who ate it.[1] The Passover is also more closely a type of
Christ's sacrifice because of its particular reference to deliverance
from death.

John, however, does not record the Institution of the Christian
Passover. The reason for this may have been, as Dr. W. F.
Howard suggests, because "the upper room was no place for
doctrinal polemic".[2] Dr. W. L. Knox suggests that the omission
at the Last Supper was in order to comply with the Hellenistic
tradition that the actual words of the mysteries should not be
made public.[3] In our opinion the best explanation is to be found
along the lines already suggested in the Introduction. John seeks
to guard against any isolation of God's activity in the world.
The Word of God is active and present everywhere. The sacraments merely represent a focus for the divine activity which is
present throughout the world; and it is this wider truth that
John would not have his readers ignore.

Though the Institution of the Eucharist is not narrated as
taking place during the Last Supper there is an indubitable
reference to it in John 6. The whole traditional Eucharistic
terminology is to be found in the chapter: εὐχαριστεῖν (6. 11, 23),
διδόναι, ἄρτον, φαγεῖν, πίνειν, ὑπέρ (6. 51). The fourfold τρώγειν
(6. 54, 58) would seem to imply the idea of real eating, but in
Hellenistic Greek it is merely present suppletive for φαγεῖν.[4]

[1] Robertson Smith comes to the following conclusion after a comprehensive survey
of the idea of sacrifice : " The one point that stands out clear and strong is that the
fundamental idea of ancient sacrifice is sacramental communion ". " The leading
idea in the ancient sacrifices of the Semites . . . was not that of a gift made over to
the god, but of an act of communion, in which the god and his worshippers unite
by partaking together of the flesh and blood of the sacred victim " (*Religion of the
Semites* (1927), p. 439). According to Dr. Buchanan Gray, however, all Hebrew
sacrifices were primarily gifts to the Almighty ; see *Sacrifice in the Old Testament* (1925).
[2] *The Fourth Gospel in Recent Criticism and Interpretation*, p. 214.
[3] *Some Hell. Elements in Prim. Christianity*, p. 66.
[4] See Moulton and Milligan, *Vocabulary of New Testament Greek*, p. 644.

The use of σάρξ instead of σῶμα is probably to be explained, as Bernard suggests,[1] "because he wishes to emphasize the fact of the Incarnation as against the nascent docetism of the age".

Doubt is, however, cast upon certain verses in this chapter and so upon the presence of any sacramental reference in it. Thus Loisy surmises that 6. 26, 27, 32, 33, 47, 48, and 6. 51, 53-58, which he calls "the poem on the Bread of Life", is independent of the chapter.[2] Dr. J. E. Carpenter says of 6. 51-58: "I cannot avoid the conviction that in 51, 58 language on a very different plane compared with that in 32-50 has been embodied".[3] An entirely different view is taken by Kreyenbühl, who, according to Dr. Odeberg,[4] maintains that the section really speaks of the Eucharist, not by way of advocating it, but by way of strong rejection of the sacrament. The object of the Evangelist, according to Kreyenbühl, is to put against the sacrament of the Church his own spiritual understanding. The real flesh and blood of the Son of Man are his teaching, his religion, his life in God and of God, and these only are potent to eternal life. Dr. G. B. Stevens represents another school of thought when he says: "Whatever, therefore, be the exact meaning of 'flesh' and 'blood' in our passage, and whatever may be the distinction between them, the discourse as a whole directly relates neither to the Eucharist nor to the death of Jesus, but to his person as the medium of the supreme revelation of God, from which his teaching is, of course, quite inseparable. Those who spiritually receive him as the bread of their souls, enter into loving fellowship with him and make him their guide and inspiration, thereby attain eternal life".[5] Bauer draws attention to the fact that the idea of the celestial food which nourishes eternal life can be traced to the Greek world as far back as Homer, and is also characteristic of the East. The underlying idea of the Eucharist, he says, which in the sixth chapter is represented as the eating of the flesh and blood of Christ, is that by consuming the Deity, embodied in some edible object, man

---

[1] St. John, p. clxx.

[2] Le Quatrième Évangile, p. 233.

[3] The Johannine Writings, p. 428.

[4] The Fourth Gospel etc., p. 237.

[5] The Theology of the New Testament, pp. 226 f.

enters into communion with God and thereby becomes a sharer in eternal life.[1]

Those views which reject the sacramental idea as being unworthy of John are based upon a fundamental misunderstanding of the Fourth Gospel. They are based upon the supposition that John proclaimed a purely spiritual Gospel and the idea that sacramental notions are therefore upon a lower plane of religious insight. This is not the place to argue the relevance of a sacramental religion in a sacramental universe,[2] but we have already argued that John opposed such a false spirituality and that he maintained an even balance between the spiritual and the material. "The conscience of the Church has been right in regarding the Evangelist as the advocate and apostle of the Christian sacraments. There is in him, curiously intertwined, a keen recognition that after all man is not a pure spirit, and that to have full effect spiritual teaching must be combined with the visible and material."[3] In the opinion of Dr. Nolloth, "the true significance of the Eucharist only became manifest when the discourse in the Synagogue at Capernaum was published. The Sacrament is shown to be rooted in the fundamental relations of God and man and to be the application of the principle of the Incarnation to the spiritual needs of the individual".[4]

The discourse is, therefore, an excellent illustration of that subjective-objective point of view which was discussed in the Introduction. In verse 40 it is "he that beholdeth the Son, and believeth on him, hath eternal life"; whereas in verse 54 it is "he that eateth my flesh and drinketh my blood" who hath eternal life. For this reason the sacraments could have been discussed just as appropriately in the chapter where we discuss the subjective appropriation of salvation or eternal life. But as Jesus' objective sacrifice is the element which is the ultimate explanation of the life-giving effect of his manifestation, it seems proper to discuss the subject here. It is the eating of the sacrificial

---

[1] *Das Johannes Evangelium*, pp. 95, 96 ; cf. Jevons, *Introduction to the History of Religion*, pp. 214 ff.

[2] See Temple, *Nature, Man, and God*, ch. xix.

[3] Gardner, *The Ephesian Gospel*, p. 210.

[4] *The Fourth Evangelist*, pp. 142 f.

flesh which conditions communion with Christ (6. 56); the gift
of eternal life (6. 53, 58); the resurrection from the dead (6. 54);
and the escape from death (6. 50). "What the believer receives
is Life in Christ glorified and exalted through death." [1] This
chapter shows, therefore, how fundamental is the notion of the
death of Christ in John's estimation.

To sum up: this discourse refers to the Eucharist, to the
sacramental eating of the flesh and blood of Jesus. It is not
the momentary eating, however, that is of primary importance,
but the permanent abiding in Christ. The sacrament is normally
necessary, but it is the communion that is vital. This explains
why John separates the teaching of the Eucharist from the Last
Supper. That believers should "take" and "eat" he does not
deny, but the one thing that matters is that we should "feed
upon him in our hearts", for "it is the spirit that quickeneth; the
flesh profiteth nothing: the words that I have spoken unto you
are spirit, and are life" (6. 63).

It remains to discuss whether John also regards Baptism as a
means of obtaining eternal life. We have already discussed in
an earlier chapter the teaching about New Birth [2]; here we are
concerned with the objective necessity of Baptism. The important
passage is 3. 5, and the crucial words are ἐξ ὕδατος καὶ πνεύματος.
The predominant view seems to be that we are to read into
these words a reference to Baptism. Bauer argues that the
rite is an essential element in the New Birth and that Baptism
is the real point of the argument. [3] Dr. P. Gardner sees in
this passage a contrast between the Baptism of the disciples of
John the Baptist, and the Christian rite which accompanied an
illumination of the whole being by means of the Spirit. [4] Dr.
Carpenter says: "According to the current text the Evangelist
recognized the partnership of both water and spirit in bringing
it [i.e. the New Birth] about". [5]

It is, however, argued that the introduction of Baptism at

[1] Vincent Taylor, *The Atonement in New Testament Teaching*, p. 223.
[2] See pp. 44 f.
[3] *Das Johannes Evangelium*, pp. 50 f.
[4] *The Ephesian Gospel*, p. 200.
[5] *The Johannine Writings*, p. 417.

this point of the discourse breaks the continuity of the theme, which is concerned, not with contrasting the Baptism of John with Christian Baptism, but with contrasting the birth from above as a condition for entering the Kingdom or eternal life with the birth from below. The supposed difficulties of assuming the authenticity of a reference to Baptism here have led some scholars [1] to regard the words ὕδατος καὶ as an interpolation. But it is just as easy to claim that the passage is set in a framework controlled by the significance of water. The mention of Baptism in the section immediately following (3. 22-4. 2) and the contraposition in 1. 33 of the Baptism of John ἐν ὕδατι and the Baptism of Jesus ἐν πνεύματι ἁγίῳ are suggestive. Dr. Odeberg is to be numbered among the few who reject any reference to Baptism in this passage. He thinks that John is here referring to Rabbinic speculations about "celestial waters", according to which "water" is regarded as a generative power which accomplishes a new life in man. Dr. Strachan, who accepts the suggestion of Dr. Odeberg, sees no reason why John should not be referring to both the "celestial waters" of Rabbinic speculations and Christian Baptism. "The water of baptism might well symbolize the 'water of the Spirit'." That such a double meaning should lie behind the words "water and spirit" would be thoroughly in accordance with the mind and method of John.[2] The waters of Christian Baptism are made potent by the activity of the Holy Spirit so that the New Birth may be accomplished in all who believe in Jesus.

Assuming, therefore, that there is here a reference to Baptism, we go on to note that John also brings the water of Baptism into association with the blood of the Atonement. "This is he that came by water and blood, even Jesus Christ; not with the water only but with the water and with the blood" (1 John 5. 6). Brooke points out [3] that of the many interpretations given to this passage there are only three worthy of consideration: (i) There is the theory that the passage refers to the two Christian sacraments.

[1] E.g. Bernard, *St. John*, ad loc.

[2] See Odeberg, *The Fourth Gospel* etc., pp. 49 ff., and Strachan, *The Fourth Gospel*, pp. 134 ff.

[3] *The Johannine Epistles*, pp. 132 f.

According to this view, the water refers to Baptism (3. 5), and the blood is symbolized and applied in Holy Communion (6); and the Spirit by his divine power is perpetually making them effective. (ii) The second theory is that the passage symbolizes the life-giving and cleansing work of Christ; (iii) and the third, that it refers to the Baptism of Jesus by John the Baptist and the death on the cross by which the work of Jesus was consummated.

There is truth in each one of these interpretations, and it is possible to combine them. The Baptism of John and the death of Christ on the cross are referred to in the verse, but in such a manner as to concentrate attention upon the significance of water and blood in general rather than upon particular incidents. This is in harmony with the allusive references to the sacraments elsewhere in the Fourth Gospel. In the context the author is alluding to the way in which Jesus conquered sin and empowered his disciples to share the fruits of victory (cf. 1 John 2. 13, 14). Water symbolizes purification, and the blood life released in death. Both the perfect life and the sacrificial death of Jesus were necessary for the victory over sin. Not merely the purity of his life, but also his death upon the cross, are the sources of the victory over sin and the cause of the rebirth: "not with the water only, but with the water and with the blood". To this the Spirit bears perpetual witness in the experience of the converted. The Spirit, the water and the blood bear witness to the perfect sacrifice of Jesus and to the benefits which are secured by it. They are the means by which eternal life is communicated to men, and of this communication Baptism and the Eucharist are effective symbols.[1] The sacraments are, therefore, an integral part of the Johannine scheme of salvation.

[1] Cf. Hoskyns in *New Commentary*, pt. iii, pp. 668 f.

8

ETERNAL LIFE

i. *Introduction*

In the previous chapter we considered some of the consequences of the manifestation of the light in the world: the judicial discrimination which was effected amongst men; the judgement of the world which did not apprehend the light, and the election out of the world of a covenant people, who through Christ's death enjoy forgiveness and cleansing from sin and access to God. These considerations have to do predominantly, though not exclusively, with the objective aspects of salvation. The predominating emphasis of John's representation lies, however, with the subjective appropriation of salvation, which is also the more positive conception, because it deals not with what man is saved from, but with what he is saved to—with the positive realization of salvation in the children of God, rather than its mere conditions. Nevertheless we must remind ourselves that, although we have separated the objective considerations from the subjective for the sake of clearness of treatment, they are not thus separated by John, but the subjective appropriation of eternal life is so closely associated with the objective significance of Christ's work that the same fact is at one and the same time regarded from both points of view.

Salvation is a negative term, and as such is unsuited for the expression of John's positive conception. He prefers to use the term eternal life, and this is the key-note of this chapter. In due course we shall consider the whole range of ideas with which it is most characteristically associated. In this chapter we shall limit ourselves to a consideration of God's action in making eternal life available for men, and discuss in the chapter which follows the subjective appropriation of God's gift.

The sequence of John's thought may be summarized as follows: The Son of God revealed the Father to men, and thus made possible for them that true communion with God which is the very fruition of eternal life. As John says, the mutual knowledge of the Father and the Son is perfect (10. 15); and life eternal is knowledge of the only true God and Jesus Christ (17. 3). "Here the language of the Fourth Gospel approximates to that of contemporary Hellenistic mysticism, which taught that by *gnosis* man might enter into union with God, and so become divine and immortal." [1] But it is only an approximation to Hellenistic thought. The ceremony of ἐποπτεία, which was a characteristic of the Mystery Religions and at which this union with God was accomplished, has no place in the books of the New Testament. The meaning of John is that it is only possible for a man to enjoy perfect communion with God and so enter into eternal life if God reveals himself to men. In the person and work of Christ there was revealed the divine love and holiness of God. Such knowledge inspires men to obey the commandments of God and fulfil his purposes. As they thus enter into union with the Father and the Son they enjoy the gift of eternal life. There is no single passage which so completely sums up this message as the penultimate verse of the First Epistle: "We know that the Son of God is come, and hath given us an understanding, that we know (διάνοιαν ἵνα γινώσκωμεν) him that is true, and we are in him that is true, even in his Son Jesus Christ. This is the true God, and eternal life".

This saying in its most significant part is the reproduction of an Old Testament promise: "I will give them an heart to know me, that I am the Lord" (Jer. 24. 7). In the same verse the consequence of God's self-disclosure of himself in the very hearts of men is expressed in this, that "they shall be my people, and I will be their God". This mutual approach and appropriation on the part of God and his people constitutes a New Covenant,

---

[1] Dodd, *Apostolic Preaching and its Developments*, p. 160 ; see Bousset, *Kyrios Christos*, pp. 163 ff.

which rests upon a new and intimate knowledge of God. Another passage, which is in many respects parallel, expressly promises the establishment of a New Covenant, in the place of the one which had been broken, upon the basis of the forgiveness of sins, and of such knowledge of God as shall make his law an inward revelation, written upon the heart (Jer. 31. 31-34). We see, therefore, that the sequence of Johannine thought is not based upon the Hellenistic mystery cults, but has its roots in the Old Testament.

In the very nature of the case, revelation represents an action that proceeds from God to man. The knowledge of God has to be given to men from without. God is remote and invisible, but makes himself known in various ways. It was God's revelation of himself on Sinai which, more positively than the sacrifices there inaugurated, brought Israel into covenant relation with God; and God's covenant with the Patriarchs rested upon a new revelation of his name (Gen. 32. 29; Exod. 6. 3). According to the Hebrew idea, a name ought to be descriptive of the object named. In the words of Giesebrecht,[1] a name according to ancient conception means "a something parallel to the man, relatively independent of its bearer, but of great importance for his weal or woe, a something which at once describes and influences its bearer". And what was true of a human name was also true of the divine name. Hence the divine name in the Bible gives in broad outline the course of revelation.[2] John retains this pregnant Hebraism, recording Jesus' profession of the accomplishment of his mission thus: "I manifested thy name unto men whom thou gavest me out of the world" (17. 6); and his prayer, "Holy Father, keep them in thy name" (17. 11). The name by which God has made himself known to the Church is most adequately expressed by St. Paul: "The God and Father of our Lord Jesus Christ" (Eph. 1. 3; Col. 1. 3; 2 Cor. 11. 31); and John's idea is substantially the same when he records that unique saying in which Jesus made over to his disciples the conception of the divine Fatherhood which he had hitherto so highly exalted by appropriating it to

---

[1] Quoted by E. Kautzsch in *H.D.B.*, article "Religion of Israel", extra vol., p. 640.
[2] Cf. Westcott, *The Epistles of St. John*, p. 243.

N

himself: "My Father and your Father, my God and your God" (20. 17).[1]

Old Testament prophecy was at one in the expectation that the Messianic age would be distinguished by a more profound and general knowledge of God (Is. 11. 9; 59. 21; Joel 3. 1 ff.) so that, all being taught by God, none would need a human teacher (Jer. 31. 34); and that there would be wrought therewith a radical change in the heart of the nation (Is. 1. 27; 29. 23; 32. 1 ff., 15 ff.; Ezek. 11. 19; 36. 25 f.; Zeph. 3. 12). But the prophetic ideas differed very much in respect of the means by which this new revelation was to be brought about. Jeremiah thought, rather, of quickening and deepening the religious consciousness, which did not require an actual manifestation of God; other prophets expected such a divine revelation of the divine glory as would surpass even the manifestation upon Sinai (Is. 40. 5). The inauguration of the era of salvation would be unquestionably God's work, but, as in the establishment of the old covenant, it would be accomplished through chosen instruments; hence it is a prophet that is expected (Deut. 18. 15-18); or, especially, a Messianic King who would realize God's will upon earth by the establishment of God's kingdom (Jer. 33. 15, 21). This diversity in conceiving the nature of the coming age explains the variety of views which Jesus encountered in the Messianic expectation of the Jews. It also furnished a problem for Christian theology to solve. For from the beginning the Church was confident that it possessed in Jesus all that God had promised; and it had therefore to show how the diverse lines of prophecy terminated in him.

It is John's distinction to have solved this problem more adequately than any other writer in the New Testament. He

---

[1] In view of our identification of the creative Word of God with the Logos the following conclusion by Kautzsch is suggestive: "We are thus entitled . . . to regard the theologumenon of the 'name of Jahweh' as one of the most significant attempts at distinguishing between the real essential being of Jahweh and his more or less perfect manifestations—analogous to the angel, the face, the glory of Jahweh" (op. cit., p. 641). Is it possible that John also regarded the name of God as revealed in Jesus because he was in some way identified with the "name" of God on the same lines as with the creative "Word" of God?

represented Jesus not only as prophet and as king. He represented him as God: the Word of God become flesh, manifesting the divine glory in his own person, and thus imparting the vision of God to men. The significance of this revelation of God in Christ is that the knowledge of God thereby made known to men produces eternal life in those who believe and are born again. This knowledge of God is no mere intellectual enlightenment, but carries with it a divine energy. As the Evangelist declares, "This is life eternal, that they should know thee the only True God, and him whom thou didst send, even Jesus Christ" (17. 3). It is only the other side of the same thought when he says in the Prologue, "the life was the light of men". To share in eternal life imparted in Christ is to attain true knowledge; for life and light are inseparable and no one can tell which of them creates the other. By knowing God we share in his life; by sharing in his life we know him. Christ came to men both as revealer and as life-giver; but while we may think of him under one or other of these aspects we must never forget that they are essentially one and the same.[1] This conception, so far from being a strange departure from the Old Testament type of thought, is, rather, more than any other representation of the New Testament, the most faithful to the prophecy of the Messianic age, which likewise pictured salvation predominantly in the terms of revelation and knowledge of God.

ii. *The Nature of Eternal Life*

There is no more compendious statement of John's idea of eternal life than this: "And the witness is this, that God gave us eternal life, and this life is in his Son" (1 John 5. 11). To understand what eternal life is, and how it is mediated to men, is to know the whole Gospel. We have already seen that life—or at least deliverance from the common judgement of death—is dependent upon men's belief in Christ and upon Christ's death upon the cross. The gift of eternal life as the positive content of salvation is particularly the theme of this section.

[1] Cf. E. F. Scott, *The New Testament Idea of Revelation*, pp. 183 ff.

The phrase ζωὴ αἰώνιος (hayyē 'ōlām) first meets us in the LXX version of the Book of Daniel in connexion with the coming reign of the Messiah.[1] The Kingdom of God is to be eternal, his dominion everlasting (Dan. 7. 14). And it is added that in the great convulsions to come the dead shall awake, "some to everlasting life, and some to shame and everlasting contempt". Here eternal life as the reward for the good Israelite is clearly life in the kingdom of the future, though it does not necessarily mean everlasting.[2] The word αἰώνιος is found some hundred and fifty times in the LXX, and it usually means "age-lasting" and not "endless" (cf. Prov. 22. 28; 23. 10; Ps. 77. 5; Lev. 23. 14, 21, 31, 41; Gen. 17. 8; 48. 4). The idea of everlasting life rests on grounds which are independent of the word before us.

When we turn to contemporary non-Christian literature, the evidence for the use of the term is slight. It occurs only once in Philo (De Profugis, 78): "Is not the flight to true being life eternal?" He compares wisdom, the divine word, to a well bestowing life (De Profugis, 97). The parallel phrases ζωὴ ἀθάνατος, ζωὴ ἀίδιος, ζωὴ ἄφθαρτος, are found only rarely.[3] The word ζωή often occurs in the Hermetic writings,[4] but in a manner which is very different from the use made of it in the Johannine books. The common features in the two conceptions are that "life comes to man from God, and through a spiritual revelation of God, which at the same time creates an entirely new man".[5]

On the other hand, eternal life is a characteristic gift of the Torah. For example, in T.B. Keth. 3 a, we read that "every one who makes use of the light of the Torah, him the light of the Torah makes living, and every one who does not make use of the Torah, to him the light of the Torah does not give life". Also in

---

[1] For a summary of the evidence see Dalman, *The Words of Jesus*, pp. 156 ff.; Charles, *Eschatology*, pp. 176 ff.; F. von Hügel, *Eternal Life*, pp. 48 ff.

[2] See Charles, *Eschatology*, p. 181 n.

[3] ἀθάνατος, *De Mund. Op.* 155 f.; *De Post. Cain.* 39, 68 f.; *De Plant.* 44; *De Profugis*, 55; *De Spec. Leg.* 1, 31, 345. ἀίδιος, *De Profugis*, 97. ἄφθαρτος, *Quod det. pot. ins. sol.* 49; *De Gig.* 14; *De Profugis*, 59.

[4] See, e.g., *Corp. Herm.* 1. 9, 12, 17, 21, 32; 13. 9, 18 f.

[5] F. Büchsel, quoted by W. F. Howard in *Christianity according to St. John*, p. 190.

Sifre, '*Ekebh*. 37 *c.d.* we have: "The words of the Torah are likened unto water. Just as water is life to the world, so the words of the Torah are life to the world".[1]

The belief has its origin in the Old Testament itself. For example, in Leviticus 18. 5 the Jews are promised that if they keep God's statutes and judgements, they shall live in them. And in Deut. 32. 46, 47 they are bidden: "Set your heart unto all the words which I testify unto you this day; which ye shall command your children, to observe to do all the words of this law. For it is no vain thing for you; because it is your life, and through this thing ye shall prolong your days upon the land, whither ye go over Jordan to possess it".

And Jesus did not deny this, for in John 5. 39 he says: "Ye search the scriptures, because ye think that in them ye have eternal life; and these are they which bear witness of me". This verse does not mean that, because the Jews maintained that the Scriptures contained all that was necessary for eternal life, they did not think it necessary to go to Jesus for eternal life. But it means, rather, that the means of the attainment of eternal life is to be found in the Scriptures, for they testify of Jesus as the bringer of eternal life. Yet in spite of this witness to Jesus the Jews do not come to him for eternal life. Their relation to the Scriptures is a mere external one: they study and expound the words of the Scriptures; but they are altogether deaf and blind to the divine witness of the Torah.[2]

The phrase occurs in a few passages in the Synoptic Gospels. In one scene, recorded by all three writers (Matt. 19. 16; Mark 10. 17; Luke 18. 18), Jesus is asked by a wealthy young man what he must do to acquire eternal life. The answer is familiar: "Thou shalt not kill, etc.". The same question is asked on another occasion (Luke 10. 25) and the right answer was, "Thou shalt love the Lord thy God, etc.". These questions appear to have reference, as the phrase in Daniel, to the future Kingdom of the Messiah. Both eternal life and the

---

[1] See Odeberg, *The Fourth Gospel* etc., pp. 143 and 158 ; Bultmann, *T.W.z.N.T.*, ii, pp. 856 ff.

[2] For a different interpretation see Bernard, *St. John*, pp. 252 f.

Kingdom of God express the realization of salvation.[1] To enter
into life and into the Kingdom of God are treated by Mark as
identical expressions (9. 45, 47). And in the Fourth Gospel to
"see" or "enter into" the Kingdom of God (3. 3, 5) is the same as
to "have eternal life" (3. 15, 16). Though the "Kingdom of God"
appears only twice in the Fourth Gospel, "eternal life and the
Kingdom are correlative and complementary terms".[2]

This identification of the Kingdom with eternal life is
significant, for it is a characteristic conception of the Fourth
Gospel that eternal life may be a present possession. Jesus
is represented as the direct dispenser of the divine life which
he possesses in himself (5. 26). "Verily, verily, I say unto
you, He that believeth *hath* eternal life" (6. 47); "He that
heareth my word, and believeth him that sent me, *hath* eternal
life, and cometh not unto judgement, but *hath* passed out of
death into life" (5. 24). This is in harmony with one aspect of
the Synoptic conception of the Kingdom of Heaven. With the
coming of Jesus the Kingdom is regarded as having also come in
some real sense, taking men by surprise (Matt. 12. 28; Luke 11.
20). The mighty works, the casting out of demons and the
fall of Satan from his position of power, are all evidences that
the Kingdom of Heaven is in the midst of men (Luke 17. 21).
The verb $\phi\theta\acute{a}\nu\epsilon\iota\nu$, used in "the Kingdom of God is come upon
you" (Matt. 12. 28), signifies in Hellenistic Greek that a person
has already arrived at his goal. Similarly the verb $\grave{\epsilon}\gamma\gamma\acute{\iota}\zeta\epsilon\iota\nu$, used
in Mark 1. 15, "the Kingdom of God is at hand", in the LXX
means to arrive. It is because the $\check{\epsilon}\sigma\chi a\tau o\nu$ already confronts men
in the person of Jesus that the final choice between good and evil
must be made now; it is this that makes the call to repentance
so urgent. Christ is himself the bringer of final salvation.

This conception of eternal life as a present possession is also
found in the Epistle. Thus it is said: "And this is the promise
which he promised us, even the life eternal" (1 John 2. 25).
Again: "We know that we have passed out of death into life"

---

[1] Life, according to Charles, indicates the good of the individual, the Kingdom
that of the community ; see *Eschatology*, p. 315.

[2] Ibid., p. 368.

(1 John 3. 14). Further: "God gave unto us eternal life, and this life is in his Son. He that hath the Son hath the life; he that hath not the Son of God hath not the life. These things have I written unto you that ye may know that ye have eternal life" (1 John 5. 11 ff.).

But there does not appear in the Epistle the further conception that this eternal life in Jesus is assured for the believers in all ages by the coming of the Paraclete. The promise of Jesus' return was, according to the Fourth Gospel, fulfilled by his resurrection and the coming of the Paraclete. This is the distinctive contribution of the Evangelist to the problem of our Lord's coming again. "His theme is life eternal, that is to say, in eschatological language, the life of the Age to Come, but life eternal as realized here and now through the presence of Christ by his Spirit in the Church." [1] We shall discuss this characteristic of John more fully when we come to consider his doctrine of the Holy Spirit. At the moment we wish to confine ourselves to a consideration of the nature of eternal life, which, in the Johannine view, is the equivalent of the Synoptic Kingdom of God.

John's most frequent form is ζωὴ αἰώνιος (3. 15, 16, 36; 4. 14, 36; 5. 24, 39; 6. 27, 40, 47, 54, 68; 10. 28; 12. 25, 50; 17. 2; 1 John 3. 15; 5. 11, 13, 20). He also uses ἡ αἰώνιος ζωή (17. 3); ἡ ζωὴ ἡ αἰώνιος (1 John 1. 2; 2. 25); and ζῆν εἰς τὸν αἰῶνα (6. 51, 58). Bishop Westcott in a careful analysis of these forms [2] distinguishes ἡ αἰώνιος ζωή, the special Messianic gift brought by Christ, from the general conception ζωὴ αἰώνιος; and he says that in the phrase ἡ ζωὴ ἡ αἰώνιος the two elements in the idea are regarded separately. He also sees a shade of difference between ζωή and ζωὴ αἰώνιος in John 3. 36, but this is perhaps too precise a distinction to make with Hellenistic Greek.

There is general agreement that eternal life in the Johannine writings does not mean "an endless duration of being, but being of which time is not a measure".[3] It is what St. Paul

---

[1] Dodd, *Apostolic Preaching*, p. 157.

[2] *The Epistles of St. John*, pp. 10 and 243 ff.; cf. also the suggestive remarks by Loisy in *Le Quatrième Évangile*, pp. 151-199 and 420-481.

[3] Westcott, *The Epistles of St. John*, p. 215.

calls ἡ ὄντως ζωή (1 Tim. 6. 19) and ἡ ζωὴ τοῦ θεοῦ (Eph. 4. 18).
"Eternal life is fulness and richness of being, the realization of
the divinely appointed goal of existence through union with God
and likeness to Christ." [1] It is an entirely new gift, superadded
to man's creaturely and physical life. Those who perceive the
glory of Jesus are drawn to him and this movement of the soul is
rewarded by the divine gift of New Birth which gives them
power to become the children of God. They are born into the
spiritual world and there become partakers of the divine life.
The Johannine conception of life is not, therefore, drawn from
Greek sources where eternal life is regarded as belonging by
right to the natural man (cf. Plato's *Republic*, 10. 608-610; *Phaedo*,
passim). It is a life given by God to men in response to their belief
in Jesus. It is, moreover, a life enjoyed on another plane of
existence when they are born again into the divine world. The
life possessed is the life of the living Son, living through the
Father. The mutual indwelling of Christ and the believer is the
assurance of the continuous acquisition of this life which is
eternal. Eternal life can therefore be said to become constitutively part of a man's soul only in so far as that life is his *true* life.

John does not define his idea of life any more than his idea
of light. The significance of these essentially symbolic terms
lies in the fact that they exceed and defy definition.[2] As the figure
of light represented to John the totality of the divine perfection,
so did the figure of life denote the totality of blessings in and
through Christ. For this reason, in the sentence, "this is life
eternal, that they should know thee the only true God, and him
whom thou hast sent, Jesus Christ" (17. 3), our Lord is not stating
"wherein eternal life consists in its essence, but wherein lies the
means of obtaining it".[3] The revelation of the truth in Jesus,

---

[1] Stevens, *The Theology of the New Testament*, p. 233.

[2] Cf. Bernard, *St. John*, p. 293 : "The phrase τὸ φῶς τῆς ζωῆς may mean the
Light which imparts life or illuminates life ; or it may mean the Light which issues
from life. . . . They are qualities or aspects of Absolute Being, and it is beyond our
powers to define them adequately or explain their mutual relation."

[3] Wendt, *The Teaching of Jesus*, i, p. 244. Bernard appears to regard the verse as
a definition of life (*St. John*, p. 561). The practical difference between the two interpretations is not great ; see Stevens, *The Theology of the New Testament*, pp. 229 f.

and the consequent knowledge of God, is at once the means of imparting life to men and one of the peculiar privileges of the children of God. This is sufficiently clear from our study of the significance of Christ's Person in general, and in particular from John's conception of faith as the apprehension of the revelation of the divine in Jesus. Both knowledge and faith are constantly associated with life, but chiefly as the conditions of life.

John's whole theology turns on the point that, though God is the source of all life, the Logos, being the revelation of the Father, was also the light of the world: the life which he shares with the Father becoming life for the world. In the words of Dr. Scott: "The whole teaching of the Gospel is determined by this thought, that life is bound up with the Person, and that the work of Christ consists in the last resort in the communication of himself".[1] The reason for this is that the revelation of God through Jesus' word and work, being appropriated by faith, issues in that knowledge of God which is the condition of eternal life. Hence Jesus is represented to us as the Way to Life just because he is the Truth (14. 6). The mission of Jesus is essentially a "witness", a recounting of the "heavenly things" which he had seen with his Father (3. 11, 12); and it is his interpretation of the invisible (1. 18), his message concerning the nature of God (1 John 1. 5), which is for John the chief end of Jesus' manifestation.

We have seen that, according to one line of thought, Jesus is the medium of life to the world (10. 28; 17. 2; 1 John 4. 9; 5. 11, 12) owing to the fact of his sacrificial death; along the line of thought which we are now pursuing, Jesus is the life of the world because he is the revelation of God. He is the life manifested (1 John 1. 2), and the revelation of the divine nature which in him has been brought within the apprehension of human faculties—heard, seen, beheld, handled—is the foundation of the Christian fellowship (1 John 1. 3) and the ground of Christian joy (1 John 1. 4).

It is not only the total manifestation of God in the Logos, nor the expression of the divine nature as light, which is life-giving.

[1] *The Fourth Gospel*, p. 283.

Jesus' several sayings, his words (ῥήματα) are also life-giving (6. 63-69); his commandment is eternal life (12. 50); and abiding in his word, or keeping it, ensures deliverance from death (8. 51). Walking or abiding in the Truth as it is revealed in Jesus (1 John 3. 19; 2 John 4; 3 John 3-4) is the same as walking or abiding in the Light.

There is another term which properly comes in between the knowledge of the truth and life: it is the term fellowship. "Eternal life stands in closest relation to the apprehension of that which is true through fellowship with 'him that is true'." [1] A true knowledge of God is necessary to a true fellowship with him; but fellowship with God cannot but issue in a fuller knowledge. Fellowship, like knowledge, is a condition of life, but it is also, and far more adequately than knowledge, the fruition of it. In 6. 56 f. the life which is to be had by participation in the flesh of Jesus is associated with personal communion with him, and through him with the Father; similarly in the Epistle (1 John 2. 24, 25): "If that which ye heard from the beginning abide in you, ye also shall abide in the Son, and in the Father. And this is the promise which he promised us, even life eternal" (cf. 1 John 5. 20). So also, in 1 John 1. 3-4, the message of the Gospel is the condition of fellowship with the Father and the Son; and this constitutes the fulness of joy. Next to eternal life, it is fellowship with God which most commonly serves to describe the peculiar blessedness of the children of God. There is no conception which John develops more richly than this; beside the expression "to have fellowship with him" and the whole range of terms which represent God (Son or Holy Spirit) as "coming" and as "dwelling" in men, we have the formula of mystical union "being in him" and "dwelling in him". As Christ's mystical union with the Father is the ground and content of his own life (6. 57; 14. 10, 19 ff.), so must his corresponding communion with his disciples impart to them the same life which he possesses through the Father's abiding in him (15. 1-5). It is for this reason that eternal life may be said to be derived from the knowledge of God, because such knowledge is a condition of communion with God.

---

[1] W. F. Howard, *Christianity according to St. John*, p. 188.

The revelation of the truth in Jesus is, therefore, life, because it is the way to the Father (14. 6).[1]

This eternal life which is enjoyed in communion with the Father through the Son—and which is, in fact, participation in the divine life—cannot be thought of as subject to decay or death. Therefore, in the sixth chapter, quite parallel to the expression, "he that eateth my flesh hath eternal life" (6. 54), we have "if any man eat this bread he shall live for ever" (6. 51, 58), and, "that a man eat thereof, and not die" (6. 50). Eternal life has in itself the potency of continuous existence; it is indifferent to death and the dissolution of the body, and is the earnest of an everlasting existence in plenitude of life.[2] "Eternal life forms a continuum in the mind of the writer."[3] Thus it is said: "He that believeth on me, though he die, yet shall he live" (11. 25).

The consideration of the consummation of life after death was of less importance for John because he conceived of it as effecting no change which was not in the nature of mere development of that which the believer already possessed. As he here and now enjoys eternal life in communion with God, and refers this in turn to knowledge of God, we have the double consequence that wherever there is faith in Christ as the Son of God there is eternal life, but, as faith grows deeper and knowledge richer, the possession and fruition of that life becomes ever richer and fuller. From the knowledge which is by faith, to that which consists in beholding God (17. 24; 1 John 3. 2), there must be such a progress as to make eternal life almost a new possession. We are not, however, to think of a higher life taking the place of a lower, but eternal life is, in its

---

[1] Cf. F. von Hügel : " The social organically connected and variously graduated life of the Spirit, Christ and God, so deeply embedded in our Lord's teaching, and so clearly articulated by St. Paul, is here explicitly insisted upon by Christ himself : ' I am the true vine, ye are the branches, and my Father is the husbandman ' (15. 1-5) ", *Eternal Life*, p. 78.

[2] On the time factor in eternal life see pp. 71 f. above.   Cf. Howard in *Christianity according to St. John*, p. 124 : " The Hebrew approach . . . seems to involve three propositions : (*a*) the time process is a reality, (*b*) closely related to ' eternity ', and (*c*) which includes it rather than extends it, still less overshadows it ".

[3] R. N. Flew, *The Idea of Perfection*, p. 96.

very conception, the same heavenly blessing, in this world and for ever.

iii. *The Paraclete*

We have hitherto considered the significance of the Incarnation and the death of Christ, and the close connexion between the revelation of God in Jesus and the gift of eternal life. But the same Gospel whose earlier part treats of the Light coming into the world (1. 9; 3. 19; 12. 35, 46) treats towards the end of Jesus' departure out of the world (13. 1). It would be a poor fulfilment of the prophecy which promised an enduring covenant, and an abiding presence of God among his people, with the consequent possibility of eternal life for all who had faith and knowledge, if, with Jesus' ascension, the newly given privilege came to an end, and remoteness again succeeded to the close relation of fellowship which Jesus had established. Jesus' departure from the world was in fact a turning-point of great importance. The sensible, visible manifestation of God before men came thereby to an end. That Jesus was the light of the world as long as he was in the world (9. 5) signifies that for the world at least his departure meant the disappearance of the light and the closing in of darkness (12. 35, 36). Because the world has neither recognized nor received God's revelation (17. 25; 1 John 3. 1) it falls back into the dominion of darkness (12. 35). The illumination which is experienced in Christ is, however, an enduring one for those who by faithful reception of the light have broken the bonds of darkness (12. 46; 8. 12), and become the children of light (12. 36). For them the true light continues to shine (1 John 2. 8); they are in the light (1 John 2. 9), and "walk in the light, as he is in the light" (1 John 1. 7).[1]

Jesus' departure out of the world had, moreover, the effect of revealing him more clearly as the Son of Man from heaven (3. 13), and of removing the causes of stumbling which were due to an imperfect recognition of his nature (6. 61, 62). But,

---

[1] ἦν in John 1. 4, 10 indicates continuous existence. Many Old Syriac texts, not realizing this, replaced ἦν with ἐστίν.

above everything else, the "lifting up" of the Son of Man (3.14)
serves to make him accessible to the faith of all (3. 15). We have
seen the double meaning attached to this expression.[1] John
finds in it a hint of the mode of Jesus' death (12. 33; 18. 32).
He also sees in it a revelation of Jesus' glory and dignity (8. 28),
and of his love for the Father and obedience to him. But above
all, it denotes his transcendence of earthly limitations which
enables him to exercise universal rule and make his saving work
effectual for all (12. 32). As Loisy says, "The glory of the
Father, which is the salvation of all the children of God, could
not be fully realized by God under the conditions of his earthly
activity, because that was an external existence subject to all the
limitations of human action. When, however, the action of
Christ, wholly spiritualized in the divine glory, should become
spiritual and universal, instead of being limited to a useless
preaching to the Jews, then the Son would be able to exercise the
full powers given him for the benefit of humanity".[2]

The departure from the world which is accomplished through
his death and ascension is therefore anything but a breaking
off of his relation with the world. Only as one who gives his life,
in order that he may take it again (10. 17; 12. 24), does Jesus
attain to the universal significance which his mission demands
(10. 16; 11. 52). Jesus' revealing work not only continues, but
in becoming more spiritual, more inward, is able to lay aside
the restrictions which clung to his earthly teaching (16. 25). It
is precisely as he is exalted to heaven that Jesus is able to come
into the most inward and direct relation with his disciples: "I
in them and they in me".

The conception of Jesus' continued presence among his
disciples is founded upon his "coming again". Jesus will not
leave his disciples orphaned. He will come and, though hidden
from the world, he remains for them an enduring vision. The
primary reference to this coming again of Christ is no doubt to
the resurrection appearances, which were confined to those who
had been chosen out of the world. But the vision of the glorified
Christ is not limited to the resurrection appearances. In the

---

[1] See pp. 145 ff. above.   [2] *Le Quatrième Évangile*, pp. 441 f.

words of Hoskyns: "The Resurrection inaugurates a new era; and the day of the Resurrection is extended in the experience of all who love the Lord, and whose love is exposed in the possession and performance of his commands".[1]

Now this advent of Jesus, and his abiding for ever with his disciples, is explicitly referred to as the gift of the Holy Spirit. And this introduces us to one of the most profound elements in the teaching of the Fourth Gospel. The Jews had believed that the coming of the Son of Man would be cosmic and catastrophic. There would be changes in the sky, the sun darkened, the moon turned to blood, the stars falling, the seas roaring, the mountains moved, and men's hearts failing them for fear of what would happen. The dead would be raised: those who persecuted the Jews to condemnation; but the righteous Jews to a life of peace and prosperity on the earth.

These apocalyptic hopes reappear in the Synoptic Gospels. And Schweitzer argued that the ministry of Jesus was dominated by the sense of the imminence of the inauguration of the Kingdom of God. Jesus believed that he was the Son of Man and that his coming in the clouds of glory, the resurrection of the dead, the last judgement, and the establishment of God's Kingdom would all take place within the lifetime of his disciples. His words and works were all controlled by this hope from the beginning of his ministry. The ethical teaching of Jesus was, therefore, only of temporary importance, an interim-ethic, intended to meet the needs of the disciples during the short interval that was expected before the consummation of all things.[2]

Recent criticism has shown that Schweitzer's view was exaggerated, although it had the effect of demolishing the liberal conception of the Jesus of history. Prof. Dodd in his books, *The Apostolic Preaching and its Developments*, and *The Parables of the Kingdom*, has argued that the early Christians were convinced

---

[1] *The Fourth Gospel*, p. 541.
[2] See *The Quest of the Historical Jesus*, Eng. Trans., 1910. The grounds for the assumptions made in this volume are set out at length in *The Mystery of the Kingdom of God : the Secret of Jesus' Messiahship and Passion*, 1901, trans. W. Lowrie, 1925.

that they were already living in the new era of the Kingdom of God and that the thought of a future coming was secondary to this belief. He thinks that such evidence as exists in the Synoptic Gospels for the future coming of Jesus in glory was based upon a misunderstanding of the teaching of our Lord.[1] It was largely due, he says, to the traditional Jewish eschatology, examples of which have found their way into the Synoptic Gospels. With this point of view Otto agrees; he says: "What distinguishes his eschatology [i.e. Jesus'] from that which preceded it is, on the one side, that he already lives in the present miracle of the final age, that with clear vision he sees this as something which is already coming into being and growing up around him. . . . On the other side, by his works, speech, parables, charismatic conferring of power, he mediates to a circle of disciples following in his steps, a contact with this miracle of the transcendent as a personal possession".[2]

It is readily agreed that Jesus proclaimed that the spiritual power of the ἔσχατον, the final order of the Kingdom, had already broken in through his coming. Nevertheless it is impossible to eliminate all references to the future coming of Christ in glory from the Synoptic Gospels. Dr. C. J. Cadoux acknowledges that Jesus thought and spoke of the Kingdom as already present in his person and ministry.[3] But he also argues that Jesus expected his own return in glory when the Kingdom of God would be established with power. "The presence of the Kingdom in the work Jesus was then engaged on was at most only an *initial* presence; and however successful and hopeful he might be in it, he would not regard it as in any way a *full or sufficient* presence of the Kingdom." [4] Similarly, Dr. T. W. Manson shows that the idea of the future manifestation of the Kingdom in power is an integral part of the earliest records of the Gospels. "The consummation is to be something which will take the world by surprise. This is the testimony of Mark (13. 32-37), Q (Luke 12.

---

[1] *Apostolic Preaching*, pp. 79 ff.
[2] *The Kingdom of God and the Son of Man*, p. 155.
[3] *The Historic Mission of Jesus*, pp. 128 ff.
[4] Ibid., p. 195.

39; 17. 23-30), and L (Luke 21. 34-36). That being so, it follows that it is not to be thought of as a peaceful reformation of the existing order, but as a drastic revolution by which a new order of things is introduced." [1]

In the early Church we find a tension between the belief that Christ has ushered in the Kingdom of God and the hope of the future coming of Christ in Glory. The early Christians were firmly convinced that the New Age had already come upon them. "This is that which was spoken by the prophet" (Acts 2. 16, 25). By virtue of the resurrection Jesus was believed to have been exalted at the right hand of God, as Messianic King of the New Israel. "God has made him Lord and Christ" (Acts 2. 33-36). The prophecies had been fulfilled, the Messiah had come; he had been exalted at the right hand of God; he had given the Spirit which the prophets had foretold would accompany the New Age. All that remained was the completion of that which was already in being. This would be accomplished by the second coming of Christ, which might be expected at any moment.[2]

But as the years went by the Lord did not come in the way the disciples expected. Had the disciples misunderstood our Lord? It cannot be doubted that our Lord had taught the disciples that, as the Son of Man, he would come again from heaven in glory, and come to reign as the true Messiah in the Kingdom of God. Yet the apocalyptic picture of a physical descent upon a material earth is not the only way in which the Messiah may truly come to reign amongst men. Our Lord had reinterpreted two other elements in the Jewish Messianic hope, and it is probable that he also reinterpreted the manner of his coming. The conception of the Kingdom as held by the Jews in our Lord's day was national and material. The teaching of our Lord in the Synoptic Gospels is that the Kingdom of God is spiritual and that it comes by a surrender of the will to God, who is at once both righteous King and loving Father (Luke 17. 20, 21). In the teaching of Jesus "the *Parousia* and the Judgement are essentially and exclusively the victory of good over evil and the

---

[1] T. W. Manson, *The Teaching of Jesus*, p. 269.
[2] Cf. Dodd, *Apostolic Preaching*, ch. 1.

elimination of the latter from the world".[1] It is in keeping with this loftier teaching on the nature of the Kingdom that Jesus also reinterprets the Jewish conception of the Messiah. The new interpretation came from the application of Isaiah 53 to himself. This Scripture had never been regarded by anyone as Messianic. Even after the crucifixion, in which the prophecy of the Suffering Servant found its supreme fulfilment, the disciples were still at a loss to understand what had befallen. They had been taught a new meaning, but it was a hard saying, and they had not been able to learn.

The picture of the Kingdom and the portrait of the Messiah are distinctively Christian. But the picture of the Son of Man and of his coming again is entirely Jewish and inconsistent with the new teaching on the nature of the Kingdom and the purpose of the King. It is highly probable, therefore, that Jesus had re-interpreted the conception of the coming again so as to be in line with the new teaching on the Messianic Age and the Suffering Messiah, but that the disciples had failed to grasp his meaning. This was not surprising, nor was it an irremediable error. The Holy Spirit, the Spirit of Truth, would lead them out of error and misconception into all truth.

And what we find in the early history of the Church is just such a groping towards a truer conception of the manner of our Lord's coming again. In the Acts the coming of the Holy Ghost at Pentecost is identified by the quotation from Joel with the Messianic and apocalyptic Day of the Lord. St. Paul recognizes that the presence of the Spirit in the Church was evidence of the actual presence of Christ. The "communion of the Holy Spirit" was also "the communion of the Son of God" (1 Cor. 1. 9). The fellowship which had been formed by the Spirit was also the body of Christ. Prof. Dodd points out that as St. Paul developed the idea of Christ's presence in the Church, his interest in the speedy advent of Christ declined. The futurist eschatology of his earlier phase was replaced by a Christ-mysticism.[2]

But it was not until the Fourth Gospel was written that the

---

[1] T. W. Manson, *The Teaching of Jesus*, p. 275.
[2] *Apostolic Preaching*, p. 148.

O

"crudely eschatological elements in the *kerygma* are quite refined away".[1] There we find that the promise of a second coming is reinterpreted to mean the coming of the Spirit. The Evangelist asserts that only if Christ goes can the Comforter come (16. 7), and this Comforter is identified with the Holy Spirit (14. 26). Then, after having made it clear that the Comforter can only come after Christ has ascended, and that Christ will certainly send the Holy Spirit of Truth, the Evangelist proceeds to mention the coming again of our Lord himself. This coming will be in a little while. The stress laid upon "a little while" is strange in a Gospel written not less than sixty years after the ascension. Christ had promised that he would come again before the passing of the first generation of Christians (Matt. 24. 34; Mark 13. 30; Luke 21. 32). This little while, therefore, is intended to refer back to the generation of the first disciples. The Evangelist wishes us to understand that Christ's promise had been fulfilled, but in a manner quite different from the expectation of the early disciples. He deliberately interprets the second coming as a spiritual and invisible coming, a coming by the Holy Spirit into the hearts of believers. This teaching is emphasized time and again in the central chapters 14-16. The spiritual interpretation is presented in the story of Nicodemus and confirmed in the story of Thomas, both of whom were at fault in demanding the physical instead of the spiritual reality. This profound reinterpretation of Christian eschatology "appears to do fuller justice to the teaching of Jesus Christ than the naïve thinking of the primitive Church".[2]

The continued presence of Christ is, therefore, assured for all who believe on him, by the coming of the Holy Spirit. For this reason the Holy Spirit occupies an integral place in the Johannine scheme of salvation and justifies the inclusion of this topic under the general heading of "Eternal Life". We must not make the mistake of Dr. E. F. Scott, who thinks that the Johannine teaching about the Holy Spirit is superfluous. "The more closely we examine the Johannine doctrine of the Spirit," he says, "the more we are compelled to acknowledge

---

[1] *Apostolic Preaching*, p. 155.   [2] Dodd, *The Johannine Epistles*, p. liv.

that there is no place for it in the theology as a whole." The reason for this is that John "regards the Spirit as the power of Christ still in action in the Christian life, and pervading it throughout . . . under the light of his Spirit the whole life of Christ will disclose its inner meaning, and sayings and events which were little thought of at the time will come out in their true grandeur".[1] It would be more accurate to say that the Holy Spirit is the abiding *representative* of Christ, in whom he himself returns to his flock. For John makes it quite clear that in his own mind it is "another Paraclete" who shall be with his disciples when Jesus withdraws his visible presence (14. 16; 16. 7).[2] The judgement of Dr. H. B. Swete seems conclusive: "It cannot be maintained that Christ is speaking in John 14-16 merely of a new operation of divine power in man (cf. Ps. 139) or of his own spirit as perpetuating itself in the lives of his disciples. For he proceeds to distinguish both from the Father and from himself. . . . The differentiation is perfect; the Spirit is not the Father, nor is he the Son; as a person he is distinct from both".[3]

In the broader sense, in the sense that was current in the Old Testament, the Spirit of God was said to be bestowed upon Jesus to equip him for his work (3. 34; 11. 32). In the Epistle this earlier conception of the Holy Spirit is the dominant one (1 John 3. 24; 4. 6, 13; 5. 6-8). There is no indication of the deeper theological ideas contained in the Gospel. The Evangelist is consistent in his representation that the Spirit, in the deeper sense, could not be given until Jesus was glorified (7. 39; cf. 20. 22). He explains the earlier references to the Spirit as prophecies of that which was yet to be given. The phrase in 7. 39 ("for the Spirit was not yet") has from the earliest times caused some difficulty, e.g. D adds the explanation ἐπ' αὐτοῖς and B adds δεδόμενον. But the difficulty is to some extent mitigated if we understand by Spirit (without the article) a gift or dispensation of the Spirit as an interior motive working in men's lives, and not

---

[1] *The Fourth Gospel*, pp. 347 and 388 ; cf. Gardner, *The Ephesian Gospel*, p. 159.
[2] The Sinai Syriac renders : "He will give you another, the Paraclete".
[3] *H.D.B.*, article "The Holy Spirit", ii, p. 408. The manner in which the neuter Πνεῦμα is connected with the masculines ὅς, ἐκεῖνος, and αὐτός is very striking.

in the sense of the Person of the Holy Spirit. "When Jesus spoke there was as yet no spiritual force in the world such as was brought into it at the Pentecost and afterwards swept like a great tidal wave over the face of the earth. And the reason for this was that Jesus was still in the flesh, was not yet glorified." [1] But the phrase is quite easy to understand when it is recognized that John interprets the gift of the Spirit from heaven as the fulfilment of the promise that our Lord would come again in the clouds. The same conception is found in Luke, who regarded the gift of the Spirit as belonging exclusively to the exalted Christ (Luke 24. 49; Acts 2. 33). It was only then (Acts 1. 5) that he justified the testimony of the Baptist that he should baptize with the Holy Spirit (Mark 1. 8).

John lays greater stress than any other Evangelist upon the work of the Holy Spirit, and more clearly than any other Evangelist he shows what constituted the distinctive operation of the Holy Spirit. The comparative silence of Jesus on the Holy Spirit in the Synoptic Gospels has suggested to some that the prominence given to the doctrine in the Fourth Gospel is a reading back of later experience. But, as Dr. Strachan remarks,[2] it may have been as difficult for Jesus to speak about the Spirit as about his own Messiahship. The Old Testament conception of the Spirit needed to be revised in the light of the death and resurrection of Jesus. No doubt the Evangelist's distinctive teaching about the *Parousia* served to bring the doctrine of the Holy Spirit into prominence.[3]

Dr. A. J. Macdonald draws attention to a distinction which should be observed between πνεῦμα with the article and without the article.[4] An examination of all the relevant passages in the New Testament shows that the article is invariably used when the Holy Spirit is regarded as an agent operating upon man from the outside, as it were, or as a divine Being. When

---

[1] Swete, *The Holy Spirit in the New Testament*, p. 145.

[2] *The Fourth Gospel*, p. 288.

[3] There is also the fact that during the public ministry of Jesus he himself revealed the life of the Spirit. There was not therefore the need to speak about the Holy Spirit.

[4] *The Interpreter Spirit and Human Life*, pp. 66 ff.

the article is omitted the Holy Spirit is regarded as an inward inspiration working as an impersonal divine power within men. The Fourth Gospel is no exception to this rule, and it is important to notice that in chapters 14-16, where the distinct personality of the Holy Spirit is most clearly described, the article is used in every case.

The difference in meaning between the two uses may be illustrated by quoting in full the passages where πνεῦμα is used both with and without the article. In 3. 5, 6, 8 we have: "Except a man be born of water and Spirit (πνεύματος), he cannot enter into the Kingdom of God . . . for that which is born of the Spirit (τοῦ πνεύματος) is spirit (πνεῦμα). . . . The wind bloweth where it listeth . . . so is every one that is born of the Spirit (τοῦ πνεύματος)". As the gift received in Baptism becomes part of the nature of a man and works within him it is described without the article. But when the Holy Spirit denotes the agent by which the New Birth is brought about the article is employed. Similarly, in 7. 38, 39 Jesus says: "He that believeth on me, out of his belly shall flow rivers of living water. But this he spake of the Spirit (τοῦ πνεύματος), which they that believed on him were to receive; for Spirit (πνεῦμα) was not yet given". Here the contrast is between the Holy Spirit as a personal agent and the spiritual endowment which would proceed from him.

It is as Paraclete that the Spirit is most characteristically represented by John. The term is used only five times in the New Testament, and that only in the Johannine writings (14. 16, 26; 15. 26; 16. 7; 1 John 2. 1), and it is translated in two ways: by Advocate in the sense of pleader or defender, and by Comforter in the sense of consoler.[1] According to the strict etymological use of the word it should always be used in "the sense of advocate, counsel, one who pleads, convinces, convicts in a great controversy, one who strengthens on the one hand and defends on the other, meeting formidable attacks".[2]

---

[1] See Westcott, St. John, pp. 211 ff. ; Hastings in H.D.B., iii, pp. 665 ff. ; A. Jülicher, Ency. Bib., 3567 ff. ; Field, Notes on the Translation of the New Testament, pp. 102, 103.

[2] Westcott, St. John, p. 212.

This is the sense in which the word is used in Philo.[1]   For
example: "I grant forgiveness for all that you have done against
me; you need no one else as intercessor" (De Joseph., 40).   "It
was indispensable that he who was consecrated to the Father
of the world should employ as his advocate the Son, most perfect
in virtue, for both the forgiveness of sins and the supply of
unlimited blessings" (De Vit. Moys. 3. 14).   Similarly, in the
Talmud and the Targums the Greek word appears in the form
p^eraqlet or p^eraqletā, and always in the passive sense of helper or
advocate.[2]   For example: "R. Eliezer b. Jacob says: He that
performs one precept gets for himself one advocate (p^eraqlet),
but he that commits one transgression gets for himself one
accuser.   Repentance and good works are as a shield against
retribution" (Aboth 4. 11).

On the other hand, the prevailing interpretation among
the Greek Fathers is that of "consoler" (ὁ παρακαλῶν).   For
example, Origen says: "Paraclete in the Greek has the two
meanings, 'intercessor' and 'consoler'. . . . Paraclete when used
of the Holy Spirit is generally understood as 'consoler' " (De
Princ. ii. 7. 4).   Cyril of Jerusalem says: "παράκλητος . . . διὰ
τὸ παρακαλεῖν" (Cat. 16. 20).   And Gregory of Nyssa: "τὸ ἔργον
ποιῶν παρακλήτου . . . παρακαλῶν" (Adv. Eunom. 2).   This interpretation is probably due to the context in which the word appears in
the Fourth Gospel.   The Paraclete is promised to the disciples to
console them for the forthcoming loss of their Lord.   But this can
hardly have been the purpose for which Jesus sent the Paraclete,
for the disciples needed no consolation in view of the resurrection.
Even before the Paraclete came they "returned to Jerusalem with
great joy" (Luke 24. 52).

Windisch offers a much more complicated explanation
for the term Paraclete.[3]   He points out that there are five

---

[1] It should be noticed, however, that " the παράκλητος of the Gospels has nothing
in common with that of Philo but the name and the idea of advocacy implied in it.
Neither can the conception of πνεῦμα as it is found in Philo be regarded as in any sense
parallel to the Johannine Spirit " (E. F. Scott, The Fourth Gospel, p. 331).

[2] See Schlatter, Der Evangelist Johannes, p. 297.

[3] " The Five Johannine Sayings about the Paraclete ", in Festgabe für Adolf
Jülicher, pp. 11-137.

Paraclete sayings which together form a unity, namely, 14. 15-17; 14. 25, 26; 15. 26, 27; 16. 5-11; 16. 12-15. In these five sayings he distinguishes three different meanings of the word Paraclete: (i) as a vindicating and punishing witness; (ii) as one who assists and supports; and (iii) as a counsellor and tutor. His conclusion is that the Paraclete represents the figure of a prophet who bears witness, bestows counsel, teaches and discloses the future.[1] This describes well enough the function of the Paraclete, but he says that the Paraclete is only the Christ-Spirit which inspires and guides the Christian Church. This weakens the representation of John and seems quite contrary to the statement that the Paraclete is "another comforter".

These different interpretations must not be allowed to obscure the primary significance of the Paraclete. This is that God perpetuates through another representative the close union with his people which they had enjoyed in the presence of Jesus. The bodily ministry of Jesus had only been for a time. The dwelling of the Paraclete in the Church is unending, εἰς τὸν αἰῶνα. The presence of God becomes even closer, for the Paraclete abides not only with his people, but in them (14. 17). Jesus' departure is therefore an advantage, since it is the condition of the coming of the more, and more universally, effective Paraclete (16. 7), who at the same time assures believers of the presence of Jesus in power. The Paraclete shall guide the disciples unto all truth (16. 13) and reveal to them what they were unable to bear from Jesus' lips (16. 12). There is even a beholding of the Spirit, which is the special privilege of God's people in contrast to the world (14. 17).

This conception of the Paraclete, as the teacher of the truth, constitutes a most important element in John's doctrine of the Spirit, and brings it into line with his philosophy of salvation. Notwithstanding the mystical note in John's teaching, namely, his conception of the Spirit as dwelling in the disciples, he does not represent him as operating upon the will in an irrational manner, but, like Christ himself, through the whole personality by the revelation of the truth. The Paraclete as the Spirit of Truth is

[1] Ibid., p. 127.

no abstract moral quality, but signifies the revelation in history of the ultimate truth of God.[1] The work of the Paraclete "is more than a reminiscence of the *ipsissima verba* of the Son of God: it is a living representation of all that he had spoken to his disciples, a creative exposition of the Gospel".[2] As Jesus' saving work is predominantly represented as a revelation of the truth, so likewise is that of his representative, God's other advocate. He is "the Spirit of truth" (14. 17; 15. 26; 16. 13; 1 John 4. 6), or, as it is said in 1 John 5. 6, "the Spirit is the truth". As the Spirit of truth, he is a witness to Christ (15. 26), and a guide unto all truth (16. 13), and under whatever name he is referred to he is constantly regarded as a teacher. In 14. 26 he is called the Holy Spirit, but his work here is likewise expressed in the same terms: "He shall teach you all things". Even when John speaks of the Spirit under the Old Testament symbol of an "unction", the effect of this anointing from the Holy One (i.e. Christ) is that we know all things (1 John 2. 20, 27). As it is Jesus' revelation of the truth which is virtually the inception of eternal life, so it is only by a birth from above, by water and the Spirit, that one can enter into the Kingdom of God (3. 5) or eternal life. Revelation, Spirit, and Life are expressly brought into connexion with one another in the saying of Jesus: "It is the spirit that quickeneth; the words that I have spoken unto you are spirit and are life" (6. 63). The "words" of Jesus are, of course, the means of revelation. Hence, according to John's conception of the Spirit's work, Christian Baptism may be viewed as an illumination, as it was also called in the early Church.[3]

iv. *The Spirit and Water*

The association of the Spirit with the gift of life is very subtly intimated in the Fourth Gospel under the Old Testament symbolism of water. John's explanation of one of Christ's sayings as referring to the Spirit who "was not yet" (7. 39)

---

[1] Cf. Hoskyns, *The Fourth Gospel*, p. 552.

[2] Ibid., p. 543.

[3] Cf., e.g., Justin, *Dial.* 61 : καλεῖται δὲ τοῦτο τὸ λουτρὸν φωτισμός. Cf. Heb. 6. 4 and 10. 32.

justifies us in seeing this reference in other sayings of the same character. This interpretation of Jesus' words as a prophecy of the Spirit is connected directly with the saying, "He that believeth on me, as the Scripture hath said, out of his belly shall flow rivers of living water" (7. 38). And John's interpretation is justified by Isaiah 44. 3 (cf. Joel 3. 18 and Zech. 14. 8), which was probably the Scripture Jesus had in mind, and which expresses the pouring out of the Spirit under the image of a pouring out of water upon a thirsty land. It was, however, directly from Jesus that thirsty souls were called upon to drink (7. 37). Furthermore, those whose desires are satisfied by faith in Jesus will in turn become a well of water to others. "He who drinks of the Spiritual Rock becomes in turn himself a rock from within which the waters flow to slake the thirst of others." [1] Jesus' words are spirit and life, and they were therefore "living water" (4. 10), "a well of water springing up into eternal life" (4. 14). We can probably see in this another reason why John dwells with so much emphasis, and with so great mystery, upon the flowing water from Jesus' pierced side (19. 34, 35; cf. 1 John 5. 6-8). That well of living water, which in Jesus had begun to spring (4. 14),[2] was not sealed up by his departure, but chiefly then it flowed like a river from his exalted body.

In Rabbinic literature the expression "living water" is seldom discussed, but "water" is sometimes referred to as symbolizing the Holy Spirit. For example, with reference to the House of Libation, R. Yehosua b. Levi says: "It is called this, because from there they drew the Holy Spirit" (*T.B. Šuk.* 55 a). The Old Testament simile of the pouring out of water for the gift of the Spirit is retained in the Rabbinic interpretation (e.g. *Targum to Isaiah* 44. 3). But the usual interpretation is that water means the Torah. For example, "The words of the Torah are likened unto water, just as water is life to the world, so the words of the Torah are life to the world. . . . Just as water is priceless, so the words of the Torah are priceless. And just as one may say, does

[1] Westcott, *St. John*, p. 123.
[2] The contrast between φρέαρ in verse 12, which gives the suggestion of shallowness, and πηγή in verse 14, which suggests depth and inexhaustibleness, is significant.

not water make glad the heart of a man, so one may say, do not the words of the Torah make the heart glad" (*Sifre*, '*Ekebh*. 37 *c.d.*).[1]

In the Jewish Apocrypha water is identified with wisdom. For example, "And in that place I saw the fountain of righteousness which is inexhaustible: and around it were many fountains of wisdom; and all the thirsty draw of them, and were filled with wisdom" (1 Enoch 48. 1). "For wisdom is poured out like water . . . because the Elect One standeth before the Lord of Spirits . . . and in him dwells the Spirit of wisdom" (1 Enoch 49). "For he that feareth the Lord doeth this, and he that taketh hold of the Law findeth her. And she will meet him as a mother, and as a youthful wife will she receive him; and she will feed him with the bread of understanding, and will give him the water of knowledge to drink" (Ben Sira 15. 1-3).

Because of the frequency with which water is identified with the Torah and with wisdom in contemporary literature, Dr. Odeberg thinks that the water given by Jesus as contrasted with the water given by the Samaritan woman indicates the teaching of Jesus.[2] But, as we have seen, John himself interprets living water as meaning the Spirit (7. 39). In the words of Canon W. L. Knox, "The Evangelist takes over the standing equation of wisdom with the waters of the Old Testament, and identifies wisdom, not with the Torah, but with the Holy Spirit".[3]

Although the Holy Spirit takes the place of Christ and carries out his work, John does not intend to represent that the revelation given by the Spirit makes a material advance beyond the revelation given by Jesus, or that any other is in the same sense as he the mediator of truth to men. For as, in the Epistle, the gift of the "unction" is to the effect that the disciples abide in Christ (1 John 2. 27), so, in the Gospel, the teaching of the Paraclete is simply a witness to Christ (15. 26), a calling to remembrance of his words (14. 26), a drawing from his

---

[1] See Odeberg, *The Fourth Gospel* etc., p. 158 ; Strack-Billerbeck on John 4. 10 ; Schlatter, *Der Evangelist Johannes*, pp. 119, 200, 201.

[2] *The Fourth Gospel* etc., p. 168.

[3] *Some Hell. Elements in Prim. Christianity*, p. 64.

fulness, a taking of his things to declare them unto his disciples
(16. 14). The Spirit indeed "shall declare things to come"
(16. 13); but his principal witness is to the past, to the historic
fact of Jesus' manifestation, and his witness is in this case co-
ordinate with that of the water and the blood (1 John 5. 8) and
with that also of the Apostles themselves (15. 26).

This witness is so complete that it may be said that Jesus
himself is present wherever the Spirit is. The coming of the
Spirit is also the advent of Jesus. Thus Jesus remains in a unique
sense the mediator of truth and life to believers, and it is thus
made possible for those also "who have not seen and have
believed" (20. 29) to enjoy a teaching from God, and in some
sort a vision of Christ.

In the relative independence which John ascribes to the
Paraclete we see reflected the high significance of the Spirit as
the medium of revelation which Jewish theology had already
dimly recognized, and which the Christian theology expressed
in the Trinitarian formula. To quote Dr. W. F. Howard,
"Though with St. John we are still in the pre-dogmatic stage
of the Trinitarian teaching, the sayings about the Paraclete
carry us a degree farther than any other writing in the development of the New Testament doctrine of the Godhead".[1]

[1] *Christianity according to St. John*, p. 80.

9

THE APPROPRIATION OF ETERNAL LIFE

Hitherto our attention has been directed almost exclusively to the consideration of God's work in the salvation of men. And this is the emphasis which we find in the Johannine writings. Having considered the work of God in Jesus Christ to bring about the salvation of man, we must now consider the part which man has to play in the process of salvation—namely, how he appropriates the divine gift of eternal life.[1] It is not enough that God's work is accomplished; man too has a work to perform. Salvation is primarily the establishment of a relation between God and man, and this demands a mutual work, because it is a relation between person and person. Hence "the actual impartation of the actual life of God is the core of Johannine soteriology. It is this that marks the Gospel as a gospel, and Christ as the mediator of a real salvation".[2]

i. *Knowledge and Faith in Contemporary Thought*

However, before considering the means by which eternal life is appropriated according to the conception of John, it will be well to discuss the idea of salvation in contemporary thought, and especially the ideas of knowledge and faith, as these are also prominent conceptions in the Johannine writings. This will enable us to appreciate the distinctive contribution which John makes to religious thought in this matter.

We have already seen how John refutes the Gnostic teaching of Cerinthus in the emphasis he lays upon the "Word made flesh". But Gnosticism is also a way of salvation.[3] According

---

[1] The Sacraments, which are also the means by which eternal life is appropriated, were considered at the end of Chapter 7, in connexion with the death of Christ. In this chapter we consider the subjective attitudes to Christ which are essential before men can receive this gift from God.

[2] R. Law, *The Tests of Life*, p. 56.

[3] See Nygren, *Agape and Eros*, pt. ii, vol. i, pp. 77 ff.

to the various Gnostic sects, salvation consisted in the escape of the spirit from the prison-house of the soul, which was the body. The human spirit must somehow break away from the sensible and material world, until, freed from all contamination of sense, it becomes altogether spiritual. This salvation is achieved through knowledge (γνῶσις), which is imparted by a divine being who descends to the earth and reveals the saving truth. In the *Hermetica* the divine revealer is Hermes Trismegistos. Some of the Gnostic sects adopted certain Christian ideas and terminology; the Valentinian Gnostics especially made considerable use of the Fourth Gospel in an attempt to commend Christianity to the Alexandrians.[1] In this Christian Gnosticism the part played by Hermes Trismegistos in the *Hermetica* is taken by Christ. It was in respect of this later Gnosticism that Dean Mansel remarked [2]: "The distinctive feature which marks Gnosticism in all its schools as a religious heresy, and not merely a philosophical extravagance, is the presence of the idea of a redemption of the world, and the recognition in a perverted form, of the person and work of Christ as taking part in this redemption". The Christ of the Fourth Gospel is, of course, different from that of the Gnostics. Because of the inherent evil of matter the Gnostics could not conceive of a Christ who had a real body of flesh such as that proclaimed by John. The death of Christ was of no importance to the Gnostics, for salvation was mediated by teaching and revelation and not by death. The task of the Gnostic Christ was to awaken men's souls rather than to save them.[3] In absolute contrast to the Johannine conception that a man must be born from above (ἄνωθεν, 3. 3),[4] Nygren emphasizes that the essence of the Gnostic way of salvation was upwards from below, κάτωθεν ἄνω (Hippol., *Elench.* 7. 22. 8).

Owing to the presence of this idea of redemption and of a saviour in Gnostic thought it was once thought to be a peculiarly Christian movement. According to Harnack the Gnostics were

---

[1] See Sanders, *The Fourth Gospel in the Early Church*, pp. 47 f.
[2] *The Gnostic Heresies*, p. 4.
[3] Nygren, op. cit., p. 85.
[4] Westcott supports the rendering " anew ", *St. John*, p. 63 ; cf. Schlatter, *Der Evangelist Johannes*, p. 87, and Büchsel, *T.W.z.N.T.*, i, p. 378.

the first Christian philosophers who brought about an acute secularizing of the Gospel.[1] The suggestion was that the Gnostics were mere intellectualists and barren of practical morality. In the words of Dean Mansel: "The motto of the Gnostic might be exactly given in the words of a distinguished and modern philosopher, 'men are saved, not by the historical, but by the metaphysical' ".[2] Recent research has, however, served to mitigate the hardness of this view. The appearance of the Hermetic literature and fuller knowledge regarding the Mystery Religions show that Gnosticism was not in origin Christian and was in fact world-wide. In particular, Norden points out [3] that the essence of Gnosticism was not philosophy or speculation, but spiritual vision. "Gnosticism can very easily lose itself in cosmological speculation, speculation about aeons and so on, but it is always speculation on a practical religious basis and with a practical religious aim." [4] The actual translation of the word γνῶσις by knowledge "is quite inadequate and misleading, for such gnosis is not so much an attainment of human reason as a supernatural endowment communicated from above".[5]

Such a verdict is borne out by an examination of the instances in which the word γνῶσις occurs in the Hermetic literature. For example, "We thank thee . . . for thou hast bestowed upon us mind, speech and knowledge . . . knowledge that having come to know thee, and found salvation in the light thou gavest, we may be filled with gladness" (Asc. 41 b; Scott, i, p. 375). "The knowledge of God is man's salvation . . . and by this alone can a man become good" (Libellus 10. 15 a; Scott, i, p. 197). In Libellus 10. 10 a, we have, "knowledge is the perfection of science and science is the gift of God". Scott, however, thinks that ἐπιστήμη has slipped into the text from a marginal note (Corp. Herm. ii, p. 247; cf. also Exc. 2 b. 2; Scott, i, p. 391 and 13. 8 b. and 9; Scott, i, p. 245). In the words of Clement of Alexandria (Excerpta ex Theodoto 78. 2), gnosis is knowledge of "who we

---

[1] *The History of Dogma* (Eng. Trans.), i, p. 226.
[2] *The Gnostic Heresies*, p. 4.
[3] *Agnostos Theos*, pp. 69 ff.
[4] Nygren, op. cit., p. 78.
[5] Macgregor and Purdy, *Jew and Greek Tutors unto Christ*, p. 313.

are and whence we come; whither we hasten, whence we are redeemed; what our birth is and what our rebirth". This knowledge is not attained through the processes of rational thought, but through religious ecstasy: "Not yet are we able to open the eyes of the mind and to behold the beauty, the imperishable, inconceivable beauty, of the Good. For you will see it when you cannot say anything about it. For the knowledge of it is divine silence and annihilation of all senses. . . . Irradiation of the whole mind, it shines upon the soul and draws it up from the body, and changes it all into divine essence" (*Corp. Herm.* 10. 5-6). We may therefore say that the word is "constantly used . . . to denote an immediate vision of truth as contrasted with that wisdom that comes by seeking".[1]

Philo implies that life is dependent upon knowledge. In his allegory of Nadab and Abihu true life in God is attained by fleeing from the world and empty opinion (*Leg. Alleg.* 2. 57). Knowledge of God is the climax of happiness and age-long life (*De Spec. Leg.* 1. 345). Such knowledge is not barren intellectualism any more than it is in the Hermetic literature, for Philo knows that life is impossible without virtue (*De Post. Cain.* 68; *De Spec. Leg.* 1. 31).

With this background of contemporary thought it is not surprising that in Johannine thought knowledge "is never a purely intellectual process. It is acquired by the exercise of all the faculties".[2] According to Mr. Sanders,[3] the Gospel represented a true restatement of the true Christian *kerygma* in the terminology and to some extent the ideology of Hellenistic speculation. It was written at a time when knowledge was not yet condemned as "falsely so-called" (1 Tim. 6. 20). John is, however, nearer to the Biblical tradition than to the Hellenistic ideas. To know God is to experience his love in Christ, and to return that love in obedience.[4] Bultmann points out that the distinctive characteristic of the Hebrew conception of the know-

---

[1] E. F. Scott, *E.R.E.*, article "Gnosticism", ii, p. 231.
[2] Brooke, *The Johannine Epistles*, p. 29.
[3] *The Fourth Gospel in the Early Church*, pp. 65, 66.
[4] Cf. Dodd, *The Johannine Epistles*, p. 31.

ledge of God is that it is attained through the activity of God manifested in nature and history. The Gnostics, on the other hand, regarded knowledge as a direct gift from God to the soul, supplied in the course of religious ecstasy. Whereas the Greeks observed the object of knowledge from a distance, and endeavoured to ascertain its essential qualities, to grasp its reality (ἀλήθεια). They therefore seek to know God as the ultimate reality.[1] In common with the Gnostics John believed that it is God's will to be known and upon this fact depends man's hope of salvation. He also believed, in common with the Greeks, that God is the only True, the ultimate reality. But with his emphasis upon the moral walk [2] he introduced an ethical element into his conception of knowledge which is absent from both the Greek and Gnostic ideas and which brings him into line with the Hebrew conception.

In the *Poimandres*, faith, according to Prof. Dodd, is hardly to be distinguished from *gnosis*.[3] But as πίστις occurs only twice in the Hermetic literature it would not appear to have acquired any special significance in Hellenistic mysticism. Philo also identifies faith with knowledge. Faith is γνῶσις εὐσεβείας, κλῆρος εὐδαιμονίας, ψυχῆς ἐν ἅπασι βελτίωσις (*De Abr.* 268). We shall see that likewise in the Johannine writings there is a very close connexion between faith and knowledge. In the above passage, which describes the faith of Abraham, Philo reveals that he understands the word in the Hebrew sense of trust. He compares the instability of all other faith with the firmness or stability of trust in God. "It is best to trust completely (πεπιστευκέναι) to God and not to misty reasonings and unstable imaginations of men." [4] In later Gnosticism, however, faith was regarded as a much inferior virtue. It was suitable only for the ψυχικοί, or animal men, who were incapable of higher things. It was the privilege of the πνευματικοί, or spiritual men, not to believe but to know. According to Clement of Alexandria a similar distinction could be made even among Christians. A Christian at the stage of faith clings to the letter of the Scripture, while its spiritual meaning is hid

---

[1] *T.W.z.N.T.*, i, pp. 692 ff.
[2] See below, pp. 240 ff.
[3] *The Bible and the Greeks*, p. 199.
[4] See Abbott, *Johannine Vocabulary*, 1472.

from him. The true Gnostic is a Christian of higher rank and
may even be called a god.[1] But the New Testament as a whole
knows no such antithesis between faith and knowledge. If any
distinction were to be made in the Johannine conception we
may say that John's teaching is nearer the *credo ut intelligam* of the
saints rather than the *intelligo ut credam* of the philosophers.[2]

We have already seen that in the Hebrew the words *'ōmen*
and *'emeth* express faithfulness and reliability[3]; we now observe
that the same words express even faith itself. Prof. C. H. Dodd
points out that in the LXX πίστις and πιστεύειν nearly always
render Hebrew words having the root *'mn*.[4] This suggests
that in the LXX πιστεύειν contains the idea of trust and confidence rather than mere belief, for the basic idea underlying the
root is that of firmness and fixity. This was so even in classical
Greek. Prof. Dodd illustrates this from a passage in Xenophon
(*Mem.* 1. i. 1-5) which makes it clear that πιστεύειν θεοῖς means
something more than just νομίζειν εἶναι θεούς.[5] Prof. Dodd's conclusion is that the New Testament carries over this idea and that
the dominant meaning of faith is supplied by the Hebrew *'mn*
implying faith and trust in God rather than mere belief. We
shall see that John is no exception to this rule, and he emphasizes
the fact by using the phrase πιστεύειν εἰς as being a more literal
translation of the Hebrew phrase *he'emīn be*.[6]

ii. *Believing and Knowing in Johannine Literature*

In the Synoptic Gospels, when Jesus is asked what a man
must do to inherit eternal life, the answer is given in terms of
moral conduct, and with express reference to the Law (Matt. 19.
16-21; Mark 10. 17-21). The same question recurs in the
Fourth Gospel, but the answer is different. Jesus interprets the
visit of 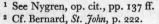Nicodemus, and his acknowledgement of him as "a

---

[1] See Nygren, op. cit., pp. 137 ff.
[2] Cf. Bernard, *St. John*, p. 222.
[3] Pp. 38 ff.
[4] *The Bible and the Greeks*, p. 70.
[5] Ibid., pp. 66, 67.
[6] In the LXX neither εἰς nor ἐπί is used with πιστεύειν. Sometimes ἐν is used
(Ps. 78. 22). The usual construction is with the dative.

P

teacher come from God" (3. 1, 2), as a request for instructions about the conditions of entrance into the Kingdom of God (3. 3, 5), and he answers it by a demand for moral regeneration which is, however, traced back to belief in the Son of Man (3. 15). This question explicitly recurs in 6. 28, "What must we do, that we may work the works of God?" And the ruling conception of life and salvation is conclusively expressed in Jesus' reply, "This is the work of God, that ye may believe on him whom he sent" (6. 29).

This last quotation has the effect of disposing of the question which so engrossed St. Paul and St. James (Gal. 3. 5; Jas. 2. 24). For St. Paul it was an alternative between faith and works; for St. James it was faith with or faith without works: for John the contrast simply did not exist; faith is the work which is required for participation in life. With no writer less than John, however, is faith viewed as a work meritorious in itself, and deserving of salvation on account of its moral quality as an act. Belief in all its various forms is never regarded as an end or ultimate object. There is no thought of "believing in believing".[1] Jesus' striking saying in 6. 29 does no doubt express the fact that believing is more than passive receptivity. It is with the labour which is required for earthly sustenance that he compares the work required "for the meat which abideth unto eternal life"; but on the other hand this is the meat which is not in any wise to be earned, but "which the Son of Man shall give unto you" (6. 27). Christ's gift to the world is primarily the revelation of the truth; and this of itself produces in man eternal life and its consequent fruits. But it is not enough that the truth which is the light should shine upon men; it must be received into them. Inasmuch as the truth which Christ reveals is not a bare philosophical conception, but is distinctly within the moral sphere, it can be received only by a moral act, by an act of the will, which is the expression of the deepest disposition of the heart. In the words of Bernard[2]: "An act of faith in Christ at a definite crisis is a good thing, but a better (and a harder) thing is to keep in perpetual contact with Christ, and nothing less than this is what is

---

[1] Abbott, *Johannine Vocabulary*, par. 1549.   [2] *St. John*, p. 193.

needed εἰς ζωὴν αἰώνιον". [In this sense, faith is a work: it expresses a positive activity on man's part.]

Nevertheless, as the condition of salvation, it is regarded with complete abstraction of the intellectual or moral difficulties that have to be overcome, and of the active element of moral choice which it involves; from this point of view the question is simply whether one has the truth; and therefore seeing God and knowing him are, as conditions of life (17. 3; 1 John 3. 6), precisely on a par with believing on him. So far, therefore, is this saying of Jesus from substituting the work of faith for the works recognized by the law as conditions of life, that it rather does away altogether with the legalistic conception of works. As Bernard points out, Jesus will not allow the Jewish enquirers to begin by speaking of the working of the works of God. They must get away from the legalism which counted up good works as meriting from God the recompense of eternal life. There is one ἔργον τοῦ θεοῦ which must precede all others, because it places the man in his true relation with God, namely, faith in Christ.[1] The antithesis between justification by works and justification by faith, which was so radically important in the Pauline system, and which proved itself so liable to misunderstanding, simply does not emerge in the Johannine theology. This is not merely because the idea of justification is completely strange to his thought; but because he was not conscious of the rather barren analysis of faith and works, which so puzzled the readers whom St. James addressed. He did not feel the antithesis between salvation by law and by grace. This was due partly to the fact that by this time the breach with the synagogue had ended the Judaistic movement in the Church. John, furthermore, had not passed through a spiritual crisis such as St. Paul had experienced. Therefore, without thinking of the Law as in any sense the antithesis of the Gospel, he expressed the Gospel in the terms of the Law. Yet as soon as he had come to regard Jesus' revelation of love as the Law, and as the new commandment, the Law in the contemporary Jewish sense was as completely done away as it was for St. Paul.

[1] *St. John*, p. 192.

We see in this instance, as in so many others, how the more mature thought of John resolves the apparent contradictions of the earlier apostolic teaching. St. James' discrimination between faith which is accomplished by works and faith without works was simply impossible for one who, like John, conceived of faith as imparting true life, and producing the appropriate moral fruits of life just in proportion as it was the apprehension of a true knowledge. The possibility that moral conduct might in any way be divorced from the idea of salvation did not occur to the mind of John, as it did to St. Paul (Rom. 3. 8; 6. 1). His system as a whole was so constituted as to render transparent, beyond the possibility of misconception, the relation of faith to salvation: it is simply the willing reception of the light of life. "He that believeth hath eternal life" (6. 47).

There is a point to be noticed about John's language which serves materially to prevent ambiguity in his conception of faith. It is that the word faith itself (πίστις) occurs but once in the writings we are considering (1 John 5. 4). Instead of the substantive, he uses the verbal forms to believe (πιστεύειν), and for the negative, to believe not (μὴ πιστεύειν). There are scholars who say that the reason for this is because πίστις had acquired a definite Gnostic import from which it could hardly be dissociated.[1] It would seem more likely, however, that the word had come to suggest a fixed deposit of faith, whereas John preferred to use the verbal form in order to lay emphasis neither upon the object, nor upon the act, but upon the fact that the object is appropriated by the subject.[2] It is true that he frequently uses the verb absolutely, as far as grammatical construction is concerned (1. 7, 50; 4. 42, 53; 5. 44; 6. 64; 11. 15); but it is never used absolutely in sense: an object is always clearly implied, and the more obviously because for John there is but one object of faith, namely Jesus.

The ambiguity attaching to the word "faith" is seen in the single case of John's use of it in 1 John 5. 4, 5. We are at a loss to decide whether the faith that overcometh the world is the creed "that Jesus is the Son of God", or the act of moral

---

[1] Cf. E. F. Scott, *The Fourth Gospel*, p. 194, and Bernard, *St. John*, p. lxv.
[2] Cf. Howard, *Christianity according to St. John*, p. 155.

surrender to him.   In the next verse, however, John returns to
the verbal form, and disposes of this apparent alternative by a
conception which in a measure includes both of the ideas which
have been mentioned: "And who is he that overcometh the
world, but he that believeth that Jesus is the Son of God?"
The orthodox creed is not a victorious power except it is received
by faith; still less has the act of faith any moral significance apart
from its object.   Dr. E. F. Scott is, therefore, very misleading
when he says that faith "implies not so much an inward disposition of trust and obedience, as the acceptance of a given
dogma.   To believe is to grant the hypothesis that Jesus was
indeed the Christ, the Son of God".[1]   The verbal form implies
rather that faith is the act of the whole personality by which
eternal life is appropriated.   It "stands for the active exercise of
the higher judgement, with a certain moral force, in so far as it
involves the taking up of a personal attitude to Christ".[2]

In order to appreciate the important place which the idea
of faith occupies in the mind of John we have only to recall
what was said above about the division wrought among men by
the manifestation of the light.   The ruling motive of the Johannine
narrative is the representation of the reception which Jesus encountered from the various classes of men with whom he came
in contact.   John, in striking contrast with the Synoptists,
represents this in terms of faith: they believed or believed not.
Unbelief is not a mere negative conception, though even from
this point of view this consequence can only mean death, because
it forgoes the gift of life.   But it is more than not knowing God;
it is the active rejection of him (15. 24).   It therefore not only
involved condemnation (16. 8, 9) but justified it, inasmuch as
the refusal argues an evil life (3. 19, 20).   We have already
seen that for John the most deadly sin is "that they believe not
in me".   Believing in him, on the other hand, is the condition
of a begetting from God (1. 12, 23).

The idea of faith is as simple as it is fundamental.   Although
John employs the term in manifold relations, although it is a

---

[1] *The Fourth Gospel*, p. 267.
[2] Howard, *Christianity according to St. John*, p. 155.

progressive term,[1] corresponding at each stage to the believer's
appreciation of the significance of Jesus' Person, progressing in
steadfastness as well as in content, its fundamental significance is
the acceptance of his relation to the Father. The attitude of men
towards Jesus is expressed in a variety of ways, although faith
strictly has no synonym in the New Testament. Men's attitude
towards the light is expressed by receiving it or not receiving it
(1. 5), by coming to it or not coming; by hating it or loving it
(3. 20, 21); and even by believing in it (12. 36). We have also
the expression, hearing his voice (10. 4, 5), coming unto him
(5. 40; 6. 35, 37, 44, 45, 65), following him (8. 12; 10. 4, 5, 27;
21. 19, 22), knowing him (10. 14; 14. 17; 17. 3), seeing him
(14. 9), and, of course, pre-eminently, believing in him.

Jesus as the object of faith is distinguished from all others by a
form of expression which is highly significant of John's idea of
faith as a personal relation. It is in regard to Jesus alone that men
are said to believe in (or unto) him (εἰς αὐτόν).[2] It is no contradiction of this that men are said to believe in the light (12. 36),
for the light is Christ himself. This phraseology corresponds to
the Semitic affinities of John's language and thought. The construction with εἰς makes the Name an object of faith precisely the
same way as Jesus is himself, for the name is the expression of the
person.[3] The significance of this construction is expressed by
Dr. Moulton as follows: "It would seem, therefore, that the
substitution of εἰς or ἐπί for the simple dative may have obtained
currency mainly in Christian circles where the importance of the
difference between simple belief (he' ᵉmīn lᵉ) and personal trust
(he' ᵉmīn bᵉ) was keenly realized. The prepositional construction

[1] Cf., e.g., the following stages recorded in the incident of the Woman of Samaria:
(a) 4. 21, "Give credence to me", πίστευέ μοι; (b) 4. 39, "Many of the Samaritans
believed on him", διὰ τὸν λόγον τῆς γυναικός; (c) 4. 42, "Now we believe, . . .",
αὐτοὶ γὰρ ἀκηκόαμεν καὶ οἴδαμεν.

[2] π. εἰς αὐτόν, εἰς τὸν Ἰησοῦν, εἰς υἱὸν τοῦ θεοῦ, 2. 11; 3. 16, 18, 36; 4. 39;
6. 29, 35, 40; 7. 5, 31, 38, 39, 48; 8. 30; 9. 35, 36; 10. 42; 11. 25, 26, 45, 48;
12. 11, 37, 42, 44, 46; 14. 1, 12; 16. 9; 17. 20; 1 John 5. 10, etc. π. εἰς τὸ ὄνομα
αὐτοῦ, 1. 12; 2. 23; 3. 18; 1 John 5. 13.

[3] Abbott is surely mistaken when he interprets "believing in the Name" to mean
believing in Baptism, and says that trusting in his Name is inferior to trusting in him
(*Johannine Vocabulary*, 1483 ff.); cf. Kautzsch, *H.D.B.*, extra vol., p. 641, and Schlatter,
Der Evangelist Johannes, p. 19.

was suggested no doubt by its being a more literal translation of the Hebrew phrase with b^e".[1]

With reference to God the construction is not so uniform. Either with the name God, or with such a paraphrase as "him who sent me", the construction is usually the simple dative; but there are two exceptions, in which Jesus speaks of believing in God. In both cases the construction is determined by the fact that Jesus would represent the close connexion, we might rather say identity, of faith in him and faith in God (12. 44; 14. 1).

Even in relation to Jesus the simple dative construction is often used; but in these instances we see that the change in construction denotes a change in sense, and that, instead of the profound New Testament idea of trusting, we have the simple classical sense of giving credence to one (4. 21; 5. 46; 8. 45, 46; 10. 37, 38; 14. 11). Belief in Jesus' words and works is expressed by the dative, though we have one instance of π. εἰς τὴν μαρτυρίαν (1 John 5. 10). The construction with ὅτι is not uncommon; but it is false to conclude that the object of faith is, therefore, a proposition about Christ, rather than Christ himself; for it is worthy of note that the content of these object clauses is always a proposition which expresses in the most essential terms what Jesus is, and therefore equivalent to a definition of what he is as an object of faith—believing in Jesus Christ as the Son of God (20. 31).[2]

We have finally the expression, to believe through someone or something (διά τινος or τι). The very vision of Jesus as the light ought to be sufficient to elicit faith; but inasmuch as men are able to see only gradually what he is, he does not discard the testimony of external witnesses. It was in the first place through the Baptist that men believed in Jesus (1. 7)[3]; it was through Jesus' works that they learned to believe in him (10. 38); through the word of the Samaritan woman (4. 39) men were led to a faith which was afterwards confirmed through his own word (4. 42);

---

[1] *Grammar of New Testament Greek*, i, p. 68 ; cf. Oepke, *T.W.z.N.T.*, ii, p. 430.

[2] See Brooke, *The Johannine Epistles*, p. 128.

[3] This may mean " through the light ", i.e. through Jesus Christ ; cf. 1 John 4. 9, ἵνα ζήσωμεν δι' αὐτοῦ, and see Abbott, *Johannine Vocabulary*, 1482, and *Johannine Grammar*, 2302-2304.

and finally, he looks forward to the time of his departure from the world when men shall believe in him through the word of the disciples (17. 20).

The whole purpose of the Gospel was that "ye might grow in the belief (πιστεύητε) that Jesus is the Christ the Son of God" (20. 31). The ministry of Jesus was a schooling of the disciples in faith though they attained but slowly to an adequate appreciation of his nature and dignity. Nevertheless even an imperfect recognition of him is called not unbelief but faith. Every acknowledgement of him which reveals a movement towards the truth Jesus greets as faith (4. 48). Even the Twelve did not attain to a complete knowledge of the fulness of Christ's person until after his resurrection; it was Thomas the Doubter who made the first adequate confession, "My Lord and my God" (20. 28). There was also a strengthening of faith that went hand in hand with its enrichment. Faith is not an attainment; there is constant growth.[1] John refuses to consider the possibility that anyone who had really seen and known Jesus could fall back again into sin; but no such finality is involved in faith; it might not only exist imperfectly, but cease altogether or, as in 8. 30-40, turn to murderous hate. Not even does the faith of the Apostles continue constant: in their confession of faith just before the passion they say, "By this we believe that thou camest forth from God", and Jesus answers, "Do ye now believe?", not suggesting a doubt in the reality of their present faith but suggesting that the hour approaches when they will no longer believe (16. 30-32).

This insecure and changeable faith was very far from the goal of Jesus' purpose. It had to attain a fixed and constant quality; and this was only reached after the resurrection. To express this faith as an abiding, though growing condition, rather than a momentary act, the ordinary construction with the verb does not suffice; and therefore Jesus uses the substantive expression, "Be not faithless, but believing" (μὴ γίνου ἄπιστος, ἀλλὰ πιστός), for the first and only time on the occasion of Thomas'

---

[1] The tense of μὴ γίνου in 20. 27 implies that faith is a process which is continually going on.

recovery to faith (20. 27). With faith thus perfected in content
and constancy, the first draft of the Gospel fitly ended.[1]

Closely and emphatically associated with the idea of believing
is that of knowing. The idea of knowledge is, in accordance with
the whole character of the Fourth Gospel, one of John's most
important concepts.[2] As in the case of faith, the substantive is
never used. The object of knowledge is not a proposition about
God or Christ, but the person himself. John does not speak of
knowledge about God, but of knowing him. It is true that
knowing, like believing, is often expressed with an object clause
(γινώσκειν ὅτι), but the propositions which are thus grammatically
expressed as the objects of knowledge are in content identical with
those which are represented as the objects of faith: "that I am"
(8. 28), "that thou didst send me" (17. 25), "that I am in the
Father" (14. 20); as these are believed so are they known.
Therefore the propositions which are thus expressed as the objects
of knowledge are such as define the essential character of the
person known, and John's highest and most characteristic
expression is that of the verb with the direct personal object: to
know Christ or to know God (14. 7; 17. 3; 1 John 2. 4, 13;
4. 6, 7, 8; 5. 20). There is thus a distinctly personal relationship
involved. "It is not mere theoretic knowledge, but a knowledge
which carries the whole nature with it, so that God becomes the
supreme object and ruling power in life."[3] The ethical and
spiritual content of knowing is seen in 1 John 2. 3-6; 4. 7, 8, 12, 13.
How far John is from thinking of a mere theoretical knowledge is
seen in his characteristic employment of εἶδον, which denotes such
knowing as comes through seeing; and of θεωρεῖν αὐτόν, to behold
him (6. 40; 12. 45).

A distinction is to be observed between γινώσκω and οἶδα.[4]
The former means to know by experience, knowledge which
is acquired, and by a natural extension, to understand. The
latter means to know anything in an absolute sense, to know

---

[1] See Bacon, *The Fourth Gospel in Research and Debate*, pp. 190 ff., 211 f., and
Moffatt, *I.L.N.T.*, pp. 570 ff.

[2] Cf. Bultmann, *T.W.z.N.T.*, i, pp. 711 ff.

[3] Stevens, *The Theology of the New Testament*, p. 230.

[4] See Westcott, *St. John*, p. 46, and Abbott, *Johannine Vocabulary*, 1621 ff.

all about anything.[1] The difference between the two words is made plain when we examine the passages in which both words occur: 8. 55, "Ye have not known him (ἐγνώκατε, i.e. have no understanding); but I know him (οἶδα, i.e. have absolute knowledge), and if I say that I know him not (οὐκ οἶδα), I shall be like unto you a liar; but I know him (οἶδα)"; 13. 7, "What I do thou knowest not now (οἶδας); but thou shalt understand hereafter (γνώσῃ)"; 14. 7, "If ye had known me (ἐγνώκειτε, understood), ye would have known my Father also (ᾔδειτε, absolute knowledge)". It is therefore with irony that Jesus says of the Jews (7. 28), "Ye both know me and know whence I am (οἴδατε)"; the fact is, as he says later, "ye know not (οὐκ οἴδατε), I know him (ἐγὼ οἶδα αὐτόν)". Again, in 8. 14, he says, "I know (οἶδα) whence I came . . . but ye know not (οὐκ οἴδατε)". In 8. 19 he says, "If ye knew me (ᾔδειτε, i.e. knew all about me), ye would know my Father also (ᾔδειτε ἄν, i.e. know him absolutely)".

In view of this meaning of οἶδα one would have thought that John would have always used it of the relationship between the Father and the Son. The Evangelist, however, uses γινώσκω in 10. 15: "Even as the Father understands me and I understand the Father". The reason for this is that Jesus wishes to show that his relationship with the people of God as the Good Shepherd is the same as that of himself with the Father. He wishes to show that there is common ground between them. The one relation is the measure of the other. He therefore uses a word which suggests mutual knowledge and sympathy, instead of one which suggests absolute distinction.[2]

Believing, so far from being contrasted with knowing, seeing, and beholding, is expressly associated with them. As we have already observed, there is no antithesis between faith and knowledge. The multitude demand of Jesus a sign in order that they may "see and believe" (6. 30); we have in 1 John 4. 16, "we know and have believed", in 6. 69, "we have believed and know", in 10. 38 the disciples are required to believe in order

---

[1] Bultmann observes that the perfect ἔγνωκα is to a great extent displaced in later Greek by the use of οἶδα (T.W.z.N.T., i, p. 689).

[2] Cf. Westcott, St. John, p. 155.

that they "may know and understand",[1] and in 6. 40 we have
"he that beholdeth the Son and believeth in him". The two ideas
of believing and knowing are, however, by no means synonymous,
and they are in fact distinctly discriminated. Believing is referred
pre-eminently to Jesus, whereas the relation of men to God is
expressed more commonly as knowing him. The profound
breach between God and the world, which expresses itself in
their unbelieving treatment of Jesus, is not called unbelief in
God, but ignorance of him (7. 28; 8. 55; 15. 28; 16. 3; 17. 25).
The result which accrues from knowledge of Jesus is not faith in
God, but knowledge of him (8. 19; 14. 7). Similarly, when
reference is made to the Holy Spirit, it is not believing that is
spoken of, but knowing and beholding (14. 17; 1 John 4. 2, 6).
Even in relation to Christ, the idea of believing recedes, and that
of knowing takes its place, in view of his ascension and the consequent beginning of his more perfect and spiritual relationship
with his disciples. Whereas in view of his earthly manifestation
Jesus demanded, "believe that I am" (8. 24), in view of his
glorified condition it is said, "When ye have lifted up the Son of
Man, then shall ye know that I am" (8. 28). "In that day shall
ye know that I am in my Father" (14. 20). It is also highly
significant of the relation of these two ideas that, while there is
emphasis upon Jesus' knowledge of God (8. 29, 55; 10. 15; 18.
25), there is no mention of his faith in God. This is the more
remarkable because Jesus represents his own relation to the
Father as the perfect pattern, according to which that of his
disciples is to be fashioned. As he is in the Father and the
Father in him, so are his disciples in him and he in them; as he
knows the Father, so do they know him; as he abides in the
Father's love, so do they in his; as he keeps the Father's commandments, so do the disciples keep his. But with all these
parallels there is no analogous comparison between his faith in
the Father and the disciples' faith in him. Jesus' relation to God
is never expressed in terms of faith.[2]

[1] γνῶτε καὶ γινώσκητε suggests to know once and for all, and to go on knowing.
[2] It may also be pointed out that truth and love are represented as objects of
knowledge and not of faith (8. 32 ; 1 John 2. 21 ; 3. 16).

Both of these conceptions, therefore, have their own special sphere of application, and the mark which distinguishes them is this—that believing connotes a characteristic exercise of the will. We have seen that the fundamental idea of faith, both in the Old Testament and in New Testament Greek, is that of trust. The use of πιστεύειν in 2. 24 is indeed unique, but the idea of trust appears very clearly in the single instance in which we have the expression "to believe in God" (εἰς τὸν θεόν, 14. 1). Faith is here contrasted with trouble of heart at Jesus' departure. The construction with εἰς is significant, for, when in view of his forthcoming death, which seems to render him unavailable as an object of faith, he urges his disciples to turn their faith towards God. As the disciples had, through faith in him, been led to a true faith in God, so now he hopes that their trustful faith in God will carry them through the supreme crisis, and preserve their faith in him—"Believe also in me". Faith has, in this instance, as in so many others, a special reference to difficulties to be overcome. It is for this reason that man's relation to God is expressed rather in terms of knowledge than of faith. Whatever difficulties a man has to overcome in making a personal surrender of himself to God, they are not such as are represented by the idea of faith.

If God is known, he is, by that very fact, manifest as man's supreme good; and the reasonableness of surrender to him is immediately apparent. But in the case of Jesus, whose divine majesty is obscured by his earthly manifestation in the flesh, the act of surrender is impossible except through an act of trust, and more especially on the part of those who on account of their ignorance of God have many hindrances and objections to overcome. It is therefore not without significance that the first man whose faith in Jesus is mentioned should be a man whose prejudice showed itself in the objection, "Can any good thing come out of Nazareth?" (1. 46 ff.). And the original Gospel ended with the faith of Thomas, whose trust in Jesus had been so profoundly shattered that even the testimony of his fellow disciples could not convince him (20. 26 ff.). The victory which overcometh the world (1 John

5. 4), which triumphs over every inward and outward obstacle, and apprehends Jesus as the Eternal Word, is an act of trust, and from this the idea of faith gains a significance which differentiates it from knowledge which implies rest and attainment.

IO

THEOLOGY AND ETHICS

i. *Introduction*

We have already had occasion to note [1] that John's teaching is essentially a theology. The history he records is in every detail a revelation of God, and his ethics are resolved into the imitation of God. The divine life in God's children is both manifested and tested by filial likeness to God. Christian ethics from this point of view are the spontaneous fruit of the true life; though they are also directly conditioned by a true knowledge of God. It is, as we might expect, in the Epistle rather than in the Gospel that the ethical bearing of John's teaching is most clearly expressed. The Epistle seeks to make plain for practical purposes the profound teaching already presented in the Gospel. The Epistle "presupposes in its readers acquaintance with a compact body of teaching like that which we find in the Fourth Gospel".[2] It is no less theocentric than the Gospel. In the words of Robert Law, the Epistle "bids its readers try themselves not as to the fulness and fruitfulness of their spiritual life, but as to their exhibiting those qualities which belong essentially to the life of God. God is righteous, therefore whosoever has the divine life in him doeth righteousness. God is love, therefore his life in men exhibits itself in love. God is conscious of himself in his only begotten Son Jesus Christ, therefore his life is manifested in men by their belief—their perception of the divine in Jesus".[3]

The idea of fellowship is exhibited in the double form of fellowship with the Father and the Son, and with the brethren.

[1] See p. 32 above.
[2] Sanday, *The Criticism of the Fourth Gospel*, p. 245. Prof. Dodd also shows that the author was acquainted with a body of traditional sayings similar to those which we have in the Synoptic Gospels (*The Johannine Epistles*, pp. xxxviii ff.).
[3] *The Tests of Life*, pp. 208 ff.

These two aspects of the Christian fellowship are not separable, even in thought: "that they may all be one; even as thou, Father, art in me, and I in thee, that they also may be in us" (17. 21). It is one indivisible fellowship; and while on the one hand a man can remain in this community only by abiding in Christ the Vine (15. 6), it is on the other hand no less truly a condition of fellowship with God that the fellowship of believers with one another be realized by observing the commandment of brotherly love (1 John 3. 24). This is justified by the consideration: "He that loveth not his brother whom he hath seen, cannot love God whom he hath not seen" (1 John 4. 20). The idea of children of God includes two moments of thought: the filial and the brotherly relationship. From John's emphasis upon the latter we may see how far he was from regarding eternal life as the mere contemplative knowledge of God. It is a life which is to be exercised in the sphere of Christian brotherhood, and finds its satisfaction in the fellowship with the brethren as well as in the fellowship with God. The Christian fellowship and eternal life are the two ideas into which John has analysed the Kingdom of God; as eternal life represents the blessings of the Kingdom, so does the brotherhood represent its sphere. Love, the principle of fellowship, directed towards the Father and towards the brethren, is the complete expression of the moral life, the fulfilment of the law of the Kingdom. It is at once the duty and privilege of fellowship. This was something new in the Hellenistic world. As Stauffer says: "It is the spirit of *Caritas* which set the tone for the relation of the brethren with one another. And so, in the midst of a world which was to a very large extent overwhelmed by the power of 'Eros', and was searching for a means of escape from itself by some kind of sublimated erotic, there appeared young bands of 'brethren', there emerged a church, which knew of a love which gives, but does not desire. Here it is that the half-sensuous, half-supersensuous, twilight of the mystery religions yields to the sure clarity of the μυστήρια τῆς ἀγάπης".[1]

This love which forms the fellowship of all Christian believers

---

[1] *T.W.z.N.T.*, i, p. 55.

is indeed regarded as a commandment; but more characteristically as the spontaneous fruit of the true life. As the Father
is love, and as the Son has manifested this love to the world, the
life which he thereby imparts to men can be nothing else but
a life of love. Likeness of the children to the Father, filial and
brotherly affection, is the consequence of their begetting from
God, and the natural expression of their condition as children.
Love is therefore the test of the presence of the true life in men;
and in the assurance of meeting this test lies the filial confidence
which casts out all fear. As Dr. Moffatt remarks, "The love
relation between the Father and the Son is organically connected
with the divine love for men; there is repeated concern to show
that it is not a detached piece of celestial speculation, like some of
the gnostic elaborations of the tie between heavenly aeons. The
love of the Father and the Son is bound up with the message
of God's love to the world of men; the significance of it is missed
when it is detached and isolated".[1] In a word—the ethics of
John spring from the fundamental ideas of his theology. As
Prof. Dodd says in regard to this Epistle, "nowhere is there less
excuse for the reader to suppose that Christian theology can stand
apart from Christian ethics, or Christian ethics apart from
theology".[2]

ii. *Ethics, Practical*

Because of this complete integration of the love of God and
its manifestation in love towards the brethren, John's whole
system is in the highest sense practical, and it is capable of being
brought to bear upon every individual problem of the moral life.
If there is a problem raised by lack of harmony in the brotherhood, he judges the quarrel in the light of God's nature
revealed in Jesus: "He that loveth not knoweth not God, for
God is love". If the brotherhood is tempted to sin, the denunciation comes with the absoluteness of one who has seen the purity
of God in the Person of Jesus. He refuses to give assent to the

---

[1] *Love in the New Testament*, p. 259.
[2] *The Johannine Epistles*, p. xxxii.

fiction that love can be divorced from practical problems or confined to the experience of a certain "feeling" towards God. He does not, however, discuss in the Epistle the application of love to special problems: as in his Gospel he sums up his theology in a few general ideas, so in his Epistle he dwells upon the great central conceptions of morality. Christian morality is summed up in the idea of likeness to God, and is expressed particularly by love. John does not extol love more highly than St. Paul, but it is because he includes under this one term the whole catalogue of Christian virtues that he justifies the title Apostle of Love. Nothwithstanding his strong emphasis upon the moral walk, he mentions in the Epistle but one concrete case of conduct: "But whoso hath the world's goods, and beholdeth his brother in need, and shutteth up his compassion from him, how doth the love of God abide in him?" (1 John 3. 17). This example serves to display the discrepancy between love which is only in word and tongue, and love in deed and truth which is ready to lay down life for the brethren, as Jesus laid down his life for us (1 John 3. 16, 18).

This instance recalls the Epistle of St. James (2. 15, 16), though the single point of contact rather serves to direct attention to the contrast which is so marked between these two Epistles. There is in fact no greater contrast within the New Testament than that between the Epistle of St. James, with its many moral precepts unrelated to any moral theory, and that of John, with its single precept of love as the outcome of his whole theology. The concrete examples of discipline, admonition, and exhortation with which the Pauline Epistles abound stand also in strong contrast to the generalities of the Johannine Epistles. This may perhaps be explained in part from the fact that the aim and destination of the Epistle was too general to allow of reference to the particular situation of any individual community.

iii. *Imitation of God*

The writers of the New Testament, except the Evangelists, make little use of the acts and words of Jesus when setting before their readers the pattern of Christian living. This should not

Q

be exaggerated, however, as the example of Jesus' earthly life is implied in the following passages: 1 Cor. 2. 1, 2; 1 Thess. 1. 6; 2 Cor. 8. 9; 10. 1; Rom. 15. 2, 3; Phil. 2. 2-8; 1 Tim. 6. 13; 1 Pet. 2. 21; Heb. 12. 3, 4. Nevertheless it would appear that St. Paul, for example, prefers to consider Jesus as he is at present in his glorified life; and he exhorts us not only to imitate him and to model ourselves after him, but to transform ourselves into him. He invites us to put on Christ, to fill ourselves with the thought of Christ and to live from the life of Christ. These expressions suggest that it is less the direct imitation of Christ that St. Paul has in mind than the effort to assimilate to ourselves the divine nourishment of grace which makes Christians another Christ. In the same way John, in his Epistle, does not adduce the traits of Jesus' earthly life as the pattern for the disciples' example. He mentions only casually the Incarnation, the Baptism, the holiness and the love of Jesus. This by no means implies that he is ignorant of the details of the earthly life of Jesus, for he expressly declares that he has been an eye and ear witness of Jesus' ministry. The words and deeds of the historic Jesus are not, therefore, ignored, but as it is the imitation of God that is the rule of the Christian life (cf. Matt. 5. 48), it is just those features of Jesus' life in which he most conspicuously transcended the normal human standards and manifested the divine that are set forth as the disciples' example. John sees love exemplified not in Jesus' kindly intercourse with his disciples, but in the gift of his life for them (15. 13; 1 John 3. 16), and in God's gift of his Son (3. 16; 1 John 4. 9). It is therefore Christ's sacrifice that is the example of love for the world. As the love which Jesus displayed on the cross is essentially one with the love of the Father, it is not human goodwill or a martyr's devotion to his cause that is set before the disciples as their example, but a *divine* charity that burns in the heart of God. This is the distinguishing mark of Christian ethics. When John expresses the ideal Christian conduct under any other terms, it is by such general conceptions as walking in the light as he is in the light (1 John 1. 7), or "he that saith he abideth in him ought himself also to walk as he walked" (1 John 2. 6).

iv. *Righteousness and Purity*

There is another general conception under which John represents the conduct required of Christians: that is the Old Testament conception of righteousness. As he emphasizes the righteousness of the Father (17. 25; 1 John 1. 9), and of Christ (1 John 2. 1), so he says, "If ye know that he is righteous, ye know that every one also that doeth righteousness is begotten of him" (1 John 2. 29). Righteousness is an ethical conception with John, the chief element in it is brotherly love. It is used in quite an untechnical sense and there is no trace of St. Paul's idea of imputed righteousness.[1] Indeed, he seems to warn his readers against the misinterpretation to which this idea was so liable: "Children, let no man lead you astray: he that doeth righteousness is righteous, even as he is righteous" (1 John 3. 7). In the Old Testament the prophets had protested against the view which identified righteousness with the punctual observance of feasts and fasts, instead of with justice and humanity. St. Paul's doctrine that the Christian was justified by grace had suggested to some the possibility of remaining in sin that grace may abound. Such an idea implied that one might be righteous without practising righteousness.[2] But John insists that being righteous should be interpreted in the sense of the Hebrew prophets—righteousness is doing right.

To this conception we must add the ideas of consecration and purity as characteristic elements in the Christian life. In 17. 17 Jesus prays the Father to consecrate the disciples in the truth. This does not refer so much to internal and subjective purification as to the external hallowing by which God sets a man apart for his service. Attention has already been drawn to the fact that in the Old Testament the word is used in a sacrificial sense.[3] That this is so may be inferred from the fact that Christ uses the same word in verse 19 of himself: "For their sakes I consecrate myself". There can be no reference to internal

---

[1] Cf. Moffatt, *Love in the New Testament*, p. 287, and R. Law, *The Tests of Life*, pp. 67 ff.

[2] Cf. Dodd, *The Johannine Epistles*, pp. 72 f.

[3] P. 181.

purification in this case, but rather the constant dedication of his life to the work of redemption. And it is to such dedication that God calls those who believe on Christ. The idea of freedom from moral defilement is found in 1 John 3. 3, where the command to "purify oneself" is equivalent to "love not the world, neither the things that are in the world" (1 John 2. 15). The Greek ἁγνός means the same as the Hebrew ṭāhōr, Levitically clean,[1] and ἁγνεία is that element in the Christian character which is achieved by the discipline of temptation. The Christian is to purify himself, even as Jesus who, though tempted at all points as any other man, was and is pure (1 John 3. 3).

v. *The New Commandment*

We shall now consider in more detail what is meant by the New Commandment (13. 34). As the divine life which was in the Logos was manifested as love, and so was the light of men (1. 4), so must also that eternal life which is imparted to believers manifest itself as light and love. This must be displayed in the lives of Christ's followers not only in such a way as will satisfy themselves of the reality of their possession of life, but more especially that the world may know that they are Christ's disciples (13. 35). Thus love is regarded as the spontaneous fruit of life. It is therefore strange at first sight that John should express it also in terms of the law, as a commandment. There are few ethical precepts attributed to Jesus in the Fourth Gospel, yet Jesus is represented as repeatedly calling upon his followers to keep his commandments. And this exhortation appears still more frequently in the Epistle. John has indeed no aversion to the expression of Christian morality in the terms of commandment. He had, however, as completely superseded the legalistic standpoint as had St. Paul himself. His idea of the "new commandment" had nothing in common with the "new law" which early in the second century was used to designate the Christian revelation as the successor and counterpart of the Old Testament. By including all commandments under the one

---

[1] See Hauck, *T.W.z.N.T.*, article "ἁγνός", i, p. 123.

commandment of love, John dissolved the whole conception of Jewish legalism. In the words of Stauffer: "The imperative is in no wise cancelled out . . . but its firm anchorage in Jesus' act of love permits its influence to permeate beyond the bounds of nomistic ethics, as also far beyond the bounds of mysticism— the latter because the final decision of the Father's will always prevails".[1]

Though there is no hint of Jewish legalism in John's conception of the "new commandment", he has contact with Old Testament thought in his strong emphasis upon the moral walk. He had no sympathy with the notion of contemplative knowledge of God which found in itself its end and satisfaction. To know God was to keep his commandments (1 John 2. 3). Nor did he regard love as mere feeling which found its end solely in religious adoration. To love God is to keep his word and his commandments (1 John 2. 5; 5. 2; 2 John 6). True love is shown in work ($\dot{\epsilon}\nu$ $\ddot{\epsilon}\rho\gamma\psi$, 1 John 3. 18), as God's love was also displayed in work (3. 16; 1 John 4. 9). Love to Christ shows itself by keeping his commandments (14. 21, 23), as his love to the Father was shown by fulfilling his commandment (14. 31). No one was better aware than John that the tree of knowledge was not the tree of life; that it is not knowing but doing that makes blessed (13. 17). It is not sufficient to possess the commandments of Jesus; there must be the doing of them (12. 47). One of the purposes of the light being in the world is to urge men to walk in the light (12. 35). Similarly, as God has revealed to men his truth, so it is his commandment that they walk in the truth (2 John 4). "Therefore obedience, not ecstasy or an esoteric mysticism, and apostolate, not prophecy, are the ground of the Church's authority. Here is the root distinction between the Fourth Gospel and all Gnosticism and Philonism and Neo-Platonism." [2]

It is characteristic of John's mind that he should include all commandments in the one commandment of love to the brethren. "The Christian commandments are not a miscellany of arbitrary

---

[1] *T.W.z.N.T.*, i, p. 47.
[2] Bauer, quoted by Hoskyns, *The Fourth Gospel*, p. 600.

requirements or by-laws; they are practical applications of the one Divine Law to the outstanding facts and situations of human life." [1] In the commandment of love, John sums up the whole message (1 John 3. 11), and it is characteristic of his ethical conception that he should represent righteousness as equivalent to brotherly love (1 John 3. 10). We have noticed how John saw the revelation of God not only in Jesus' words but in his manifestation as a whole; so in his ethical teaching, rather than in individual precepts, it was in the total impression of his life, as love unto the end, that he found the guiding principle of the Christian life.

In common with most commentators, Archbishop Bernard regards the essential obligation of the ἐντολὴ καινή as brotherly love.[2] From this point of view the commandment is new because it was enjoined according to a new measure, or rather was measureless: "as I have loved you" (13. 34). Jesus loved his own εἰς τέλος—"greater love hath no man than this, that a man lay down his life for his friends" (15. 13). Hence we are introduced to a new definition of love, "Hereby know we love, because he laid down his life for us: and we ought to lay down our lives for the brethren" (1 John 3. 16). Love is therefore no mere sentiment but an enduring passion, not the correlative of dislike, but of hate and murder—"not as Cain was of the Evil One and slew his brother" (1 John 3. 12). The commandment is therefore new because whereas "the Old Testament demanded that men should love their neighbours as themselves, the New Law is that they should love the brethren better than themselves and die for their friends".[3] Similarly, Bultmann draws attention to the entirely new situation that was created by the coming of Jesus. His message was a "call for a Utopia of neighbourly love in a world of hard reality". This new situation was brought about, says Bultmann, by Jesus' proclamation of the forgiveness of sins, "and whosoever experiences this forgiveness finds welling up within him an utterly new, overflowing, love".[4]

---

[1] R. Law, *The Tests of Life*, p. 212.
[2] *St. John*, p. 527.
[3] Hoskyns, *The Fourth Gospel*, p. 527.
[4] *T.W.z.N.T.*, i, p. 47.

But while all this is true it does not seem to go deep enough to explain the solemnity with which Jesus spoke of the New Commandment. The whole trend of the narrative in which the saying occurs (13. 1-35) appears to require that ἐντολὴ καινή shall break new ground and not be simply a restatement of familiar teaching. Schrenk realizes the need for a deeper interpretation of the New Commandment. He says: "'newness' consists not in the commandment of love in general, not in a new degree of loving, but rather in the *novel Christological* reference: they are to love one another as they are loved by Jesus. They are to realize the love of which Jesus lays the foundation. Thus the loving act-of-giving of Jesus himself will become the foundation and strength of the new ἀγαπᾶν." [1]

This theory of the embodiment of the New Commandment in the Person of Jesus rather than in any new idea about the content of the word love may be carried further. After Judas had departed from the Upper Room, Jesus found himself at last alone in the company of his true disciples, whom he had gathered out of the world, and whom he had finally purified. In the constitution of this little company he sees his earthly work finished, himself and his Father glorified (13. 31). This was the New Israel brought to birth by the creative power of God. As one family they had just partaken of the New Covenant meal. When, therefore, he gives to his disciples a commandment which shall distinguish them from all the world (13. 35), what can this mean but the New Law for the New Covenant? It is old because it was foretold by Jeremiah and had been the intention of God from all eternity (Jer. 31. 33; 32. 40). It is new because now for the first time it could be written on the hearts of men who abide in Christ. The ancient covenant failed because, as St. Paul says, the external law had no power to make alive (ζωοποιῆσαι). It was due to the insight of the prophets that they foresaw a New Covenant which would be written not on tables of stone but upon the heart and vitally appropriated by the elect children. Thus the ἐντολὴ καινή

[1] *T.W.z.N.T.*, ii, p. 550.

is the καινὴ διαθήκη.[1] In contrast to the ritual use of blood by
Moses in establishing the ancient covenant, the Mediator of the
better covenant gives his own life to be appropriated by the
elect in order that they may abide in him and be fruitful in good
works. Thus, as Schrenk says, the significance of the New
Commandmant is to be found in the novel Christological
reference. For Jesus is not only the embodiment of the ἐντολὴ
καινή; he is also the sacrifice which establishes the καινὴ διαθήκη.
Through his sacrifice life is released so that it may be shared
by the faithful. One of the means by which this life is appropriated by the faithful is the Sacrament of the Body and Blood
of Christ. The New Commandment is therefore parallel to the
New Covenant ratified by "my blood" (1 Cor. 11. 25), and "the
New Covenant blood" (Matt. 26. 28). But John, in his characteristic manner, emphasizes the spiritual side of the sacrament—
the spirit of love without which the *opus operatum* is valueless.[2]
It is the spirit that quickeneth, and this is the redemption of the
failure of the first covenant: it enables men to love one another,
as he gave commandment.[3]

It is noteworthy that in the Johannine writings there is
no commandment to love either God or Christ. In the Old
Testament this was the commandment which held first place
(cf. Matt. 22. 38). This was no doubt due to the formal relations
that existed between the people and God under the old covenant;
and Jesus had actually to remark upon the lack of love to
God on the part of the Jews (5. 42). But under the New
Covenant the relation of the Christian community to God
is no longer external; it is real and inward, founded not only
through the election of God, but by his begetting the children.
Because of this immediate experience of God, love towards God
is a matter of course, and throughout the Johannine writings
it is simply assumed. It is a matter of course that every child

---

[1] Cf. Schlatter, *Der Evangelist Johannes*, p. 288 : " ἐντολὴ καινή is implied in
b^erith h^adāshā = διαθήκη καινή, which from now on determines the relation of God to
humanity ".

[2] Cf. Macgregor, *The Gospel of John*, p. 284.

[3] See Abbott, *Johannine Grammar*, 2093, 2094 ; cf. an article entitled " Ἐντολὴ
Καινή " by R. P. Brown in *Theology*, April 1933.

of God "loveth him that begat" (τὸν γεννήσαντα), and it is a consequence of this that he "loveth him also that is begotten of him"[1] (1 John 5. 1). The two relationships are really one: "for he that loveth not his brother whom he hath seen, cannot love God whom he hath not seen" (1 John 4. 20). As the Love of God is the postulate of the Christian community, its very *raison d'être*, only the love of the brethren needs to be enjoined as a commandment. "And this commandment have we from him, that he who loveth God love his brother also" (1 John 4. 21).

This point is illustrated in a striking way by the unusual turn which he gives to some of his sentences. For example, when in 1 John 4. 11 he says, "Beloved, if God so loved us", we might expect him to go on and say that we ought to love him, but instead we have, "we also ought to love one another". Similarly in 1 John 3. 16 he says, "Hereby know we love, because he laid down his life for us: and we ought to lay down our lives"— not for him but—"for one another". This is in harmony with the teaching of the Synoptic Gospels: "Inasmuch as ye did it unto one of these my brethren, even these least, ye did it unto me" (Matt. 25. 40; cf. John 13. 20). The only way in which after Christ's departure (12. 7, 8) the disciples' love can be shown towards him "in deed" is by works of loving-kindness towards his brethren (1 John 3. 17, 18).

As John found in the idea of love the whole conception of Christian morality, it is natural that he should associate with it the ideal of meekness and lowliness of heart which is so prominent a trait in the Synoptic account (Matt. 11. 29). Just before enjoining the New Commandment he narrates the incident of washing the disciples' feet (13. 12-17). In this symbolic act Jesus represents more clearly than any words could have done the character of meekness which he required. It was not thinking lowly of himself, nor adopting a lowly attitude, but assuming a lowly position. It was a yoke, a burden, the willing assumption of the position of a servant, and this not with reference to God— for that would have been only too obvious—but towards one's

---

[1] τὸν γεγεννημένον ἐξ αὐτοῦ may mean either Jesus or the sons born of God; see Moffatt, *Love in the New Testament*, p. 272.

fellow-men. "If I then, your Lord and Master, have washed your feet, ye also ought"—note the same turn of expression—"to wash one another's feet." It was not enough that St. Paul should recognize himself as "a servant of Jesus Christ" (Rom. 1. 1); we must also recognize "ourselves as your servants for Jesus' sake" (2 Cor. 4. 5).

The way in which John brings the idea of reward into prominence corresponds with his presentation of Christian morality in terms of a commandment. The single passage in which he regards hope as the motive of Christian conduct (1 John 3. 3) implies this conception. There is the same implication in the exhortation to abide in Christ, "that we may have boldness, and not be ashamed before him at his coming" (1 John 2. 28); and in 1 John 4. 17, "boldness in the day of judgement" is regarded as the reward of perfected love. The idea of reward is more clearly stated in the Second Epistle verse 8 than in any other passage: "Look to yourselves, that ye lose not the things which we have wrought, but that ye receive a full reward". The reward is probably eternal life. In 4. 36 wages as the reward of faithful work is closely associated with the gathering of "fruit unto life eternal". Even Jesus, who does his work in fulfilment of the Father's commandment (10. 18; 12. 49), looks for the Father's reward. He expects to be glorified because he himself has glorified the Father, and has accomplished the work which he had given him to do (17. 4, 5).

vi. *The Doctrine of Assurance*

We have already discussed John's teaching concerning the knowledge of God. But John uses the words οἴδαμεν and γινώσκομεν in another and quite different way. It belongs exclusively to the Epistle, and is one of its most characteristic features. It was natural for John, who regarded salvation as a present possession, to think of it also as a fact that could be tested and verified. Therefore he says: "These things have I written unto you, that ye may *know* that ye have eternal life" (1 John 5. 13). The same confidence is expressed in the last verses of the Epistle, "We *know* that we are of God, and the whole world lieth in the Evil One. And we *know* that the Son of God is come, and hath given us an understanding, that we *know* him that is true, and we are in him that is true, in his Son Jesus Christ". This emphasis upon knowledge may very well have been prompted by the claim of some Gnostics to possess a superior *gnosis*, of which they deemed the ordinary Christian incapable. John refutes this claim by saying that every Christian has saving knowledge of the truth. "You all possess knowledge" (1 John 2. 21), he says.[1] It is the privilege of all Christians to apprehend the fundamental truths of the Gospel, and, above all, to be convinced that they are thereby saved.

This knowledge or assurance of salvation is not intuition, nor does it rest upon any subjective grounds. As Robert Law remarks, no place is found in the Epistle for any immediate, self-certifying, consciousness of regenerate life.[2] The test is essentially practical. His fundamental maxim is this: "If ye know that he is righteous, ye know that every one also that *doeth* righteousness is begotten of him" (1 John 2. 29). The orthodox faith is certainly emphasized as the test for discerning between the spirits of error and the spirit of truth (1 John 4. 1), but it is never expressly mentioned as the ground for a disciple's certainty of possessing eternal life. As love is the test whereby the world may know the disciples of Christ (13. 35), and as the false brother is marked out by his lack of compassion towards a brother in need (1 John 3. 17), so each disciple has to judge of the reality of his own salvation by the same objective proof of a love which is "in deed and truth" (1 John 3. 18). "We know that we have passed from death into life, because we love the brethren" (1 John 3. 14). In 1 John 2. 3 we have a characteristic expression, "Hereby know we that we know him, if we keep his commandments" (cf. 1 John 2. 5).

There is a test of a different character, and that is the witness of the Spirit. This is as objective as the witness of brotherly love. For the Spirit is not regarded as bearing immediate and self-evidencing testimony of the divine sonship of the believer.

---

[1] οἴδατε πάντες, ℵ B P. See Dodd, *The Johannine Epistles*, p. 53.
[2] *The Tests of Life*, p. 279.

The Spirit witnesses to the historic Christ, and it is the acknowledgement of faith in Christ that provides the assurance that God abides in men. Thus the words, "And hereby we know that he abideth in us, by the Spirit which he gave us" (1 John 3. 24), do not signify the intuition of a fact, but rather the inference from a fact; for the indwelling of God is recognized by the confession that "Jesus Christ is come in the flesh" (1 John 4. 2). Furthermore, in one of the rare instances in which John looks forward to the perfection of the believer's life in the other world, he regards that too as the object of knowledge: "We know that when he shall be manifested, we shall be like him; for we shall see him as he is" (1 John 3. 2). But as the future life is only the perfection of that which we now have, and advances to perfection by increasing in the knowledge of God, a man may be assured of the future life by the verification of eternal life in the present.

vii. *Prayer*

John brings the idea of prayer into close connexion with the doctrine of Christian assurance which we have just considered. "If our heart condemn us not, we have boldness toward God; and whatsoever we ask, we receive of him, because we keep his commandments, and do the things which are pleasing in his sight" (1 John 3. 21, 22). "And this is the boldness we have toward him, that, if we ask anything according to his will, he heareth us: and if we know that he heareth us, whatsoever we ask, we know that we have the petitions which we have asked of him" (1 John 5. 14, 15). These two passages taken together show that Christian prayer is not a cry of helplessness in the face of great odds, but rather the expression of confidence that God will answer the petitions of the man whose will is in harmony with the will of God. The word παρρησία "stood in ancient Greece as the most valued right of a citizen in a free state, the right to 'speak his mind'; and, although the meaning of the word became wider and vaguer in course of time, yet there always hangs about it this special association with the thought of freedom of speech, unhampered by fear or shame. In our relation to God such freedom of speech is not an inherent

right, but is strictly dependent upon an equally frank and straight-
forward obedience to the divine will".[1] It is the will of God that
the eternal life of truth and righteousness shall grow and multiply;
when we will this together with him we have the absolute assurance that God will answer our prayers. It is the characteristic
of him who is "begotten of God" that he seeks to do the will of
God. Our prayers are answered because our will is in inward
harmony with God's, and the evidence of this is that "we keep
his commandments, and do those things that are pleasing in his
sight" (1 John 3. 22). As Jesus himself said: "If ye abide in me,
and my words abide in you, ask whatsoever ye will, and it shall
be done unto you" (15. 7).

In addition to the High Priestly prayer in the seventeenth
chapter there are more references to Jesus' prayers in the Fourth
Gospel than elsewhere in the New Testament. It has often been
noted that the prayers of Jesus are expressed by the verb ἐρωτάω
(14. 16; 16. 26; 17. 9, 15, 20), and those of the disciples by
αἰτέω. Because of this an attempt has been made to discriminate
between the two words. Stählin, for example, says: "Furthermore, αἰτέω seems to presuppose a lesser degree of intimacy of
relationship than ἐρωτάω; for that reason αἰτέω is used of the
disciples' petitions to God, but ἐρωτάω is used of the petitions to
Jesus and of Jesus' petitions to God".[2] But the grounds for
such discrimination in the New Testament are uncertain. In
1 John 5. 16 αἰτέω and ἐρωτάω are both used of prayers made to
God; in John 19. 31, 38 ἐρωτάω is used of requests made to
Pilate, where the Synoptists use αἰτέω. Both words, therefore,
mean to ask,[3] and generally no distinction can be observed in the
New Testament. Furthermore, the papyri quoted by Moulton
and Milligan lend no support to such a distinction.

In one particular way John comes nearer than any other
writer in the New Testament to giving a definite doctrine of
prayer. The possibility of prayer addressed to God was simply

---

[1] Dodd, *The Johannine Epistles*, p. 93.

[2] *T.W.z.N.T.*, i, pp. 192, 193; see also Field, *Notes on the Translation of the New Testament*, p. 101, and Abbott, *Johannine Grammar*, p. 468 f.

[3] Dr. Field deals trenchantly with those who attempt to make the distinction (*Notes*, p. 102); cf. Moulton's *Grammar of New Testament Greek*, i, p. 66 n.

assumed by all Christian writers. Prayer was not a new thing with Christianity; but prayer in the name of Jesus was, and it is this that John emphasizes in a way entirely consistent with his Christology.

Participation in the Messianic salvation was in the Old Testament made dependent upon "calling upon the name of the Lord" (Joel 2. 32). St. Peter and St. Paul agree in interpreting this as calling upon Jesus as one who had been exalted to be Lord (Acts 2. 21; cf. verse 36; Rom. 10. 12 ff.). "Calling upon the name of Jesus" appears together with Baptism as the condition of salvation (Acts 22. 16). And in Acts 9. 14; 1 Cor. 1. 2; 2 Tim. 2. 22, Christians are actually designated as "those who call upon the name of the Lord Jesus Christ". It was thus a characteristic of the Christian community to address their prayers to Jesus as well as to the Father.

This conception also appears in the Fourth Gospel. According to the true text of 14. 14, prayer is thought of as being directly offered to Jesus: "If ye shall ask *me* anything in my name, that will I do".[1] The omission of "me" in some manuscripts was evidently due to the feeling that there is some incongruity in the thought of addressing Jesus himself "in his name". No such incongruity existed in the mind of John. In 15. 16 the phrase "in my name" is connected with "he may give", as appears clearly from the parallel expression in 16. 23: "If ye shall ask anything of the Father, he will give it you in my name". The conception that asking in Jesus' name means direct address to him is made clear in 16. 26: "In that day ye shall ask in my name: and I say not unto you, that I will pray the Father for you". Jesus here explains to his disciples that prayers addressed to him do not have to be passed on, as it were, to the Father. The exalted Christ is so thoroughly the dispenser of all gifts to the Church, that whatever the Father himself gives is given in Jesus' name (14. 26; 15. 16; 16. 23). This is not in any wise to derogate from the Father's supremacy; for in the verse just quoted it is assumed that the Father is pre-eminently the hearer of prayer, and Jesus' power to answer prayers directed to him

---

[1] א B and C, om. A D L. με is rejected by Bernard, *St. John*, p. 544.

is grounded upon the fact that "the Father himself loveth you, because ye have loved me". And in 14. 13 the fulfilment of the disciples' prayers by Jesus is said to be a glorification of the Father in the Son.

There is a contradiction in Jesus' representation of the possibility of addressing prayers to him; whereas he says in 16. 23, "And in that day ye shall ask me nothing ($\dot{\epsilon}\rho\omega\tau\acute{\eta}\sigma\epsilon\tau\epsilon$). Verily, verily, I say unto you, If ye shall ask anything of the Father, he will give it you in my name", we have, on the other hand, in 16. 26, "In that day ye shall ask ($a\dot{i}\tau\acute{\eta}\sigma\epsilon\sigma\theta\epsilon$) in my name", and in 14. 14, "If ye shall ask me anything in my name, that will I do". It has been noted that the verb in the first instance is that which is elsewhere used only in reference to Jesus' prayers, and it may be that John intends in this case to make a discrimination between the two words. But the passage shows how difficult it is to give them any interpretation which does not involve some confusion. We can see, however, in a general way, that John would represent that prayers could be addressed either to the Son or the Father.

This is in accordance with the general trend of Johannine theology. As in the Epistle the reference to personal pronouns seems often to be to the Father or to the Son indifferently, so here we have a neutral expression in regard to prayer: "Ask whatsoever ye will, and it shall be done unto you" (15. 7). In these parting words of Jesus he does not emphasize the fact that the Father is hearer and answerer of prayer; but it was necessary for him to assure his disciples that though they might no longer address him in his exalted state as when he was on earth, yet prayer to the Father constituted intercourse with him, and the Father's gifts were given in his name. Furthermore, they may ask him directly in his name. Hitherto they had talked familiarly with him, but they shall do so no longer (16. 23). The old form of intercourse will be broken off with his departure, but a new form of intercourse will take its place as Jesus ceases to be the object of earthly friendship and becomes the satisfaction of their religious aspirations: "Hitherto ye have asked nothing in my name: ask, and ye shall receive, that your joy may be fulfilled" (16. 24).

This last phrase suggests that Jesus aimed at comforting his disciples with the assurance that the communion which was their joy on earth would be continued though in a new form. Upon his departure they would hold intercourse with him "in his name", that is, in the same manner in which they held intercourse with the Father. This would be proved by experience as they received the gifts which they asked: "Whatsoever ye ask, it shall be done". In the Epistle there is added the qualification "according to his will" (5. 14). The purpose of prayer is thus not to persuade God to act according to our desires, but a means by which our desires might be brought into harmony with the mind of God and become channels for the fulfilment of his will. As the will of God is the final and perfect redemption of men (6. 39, 40), this qualification does not limit the exercise of true prayer, but rather displays the breadth of its scope and the certainty of its fulfilment. In the verse following there is a thought which doubtless John often recalled to mind as he considered the apparent failure of his own prayers: "And if we know that he heareth us whatsoever we ask, we know that we have the petitions which we have asked of him". The force of the "we have" instead of "we shall have" is that though the fulfilment may not yet be apparent, it exists in the sphere of the divine thought, which is the sphere of reality, and only awaits manifestation. It is thus characteristically Johannine in thought.[1]

John reveals his close dependence upon Hebrew thought in his expression to "ask in his name". The more usual phrase in the New Testament is to "call on the name of the Lord Jesus". But John's expression stands much nearer the Hebrew formula *liqᵉrō' bᵉshēm 'ᵃdōnai* (Gen. 4. 26), which is strictly "to call in the name of Jahweh". The usual interpretation of the phrase "to call (or ask) in the name of Jesus" is to take it as the concluding formula of a prayer addressed to the Father, indicating the ground of confidence for approaching the mercy-seat of God. But the correct text of 14. 14 shows that this interpretation fails

---

[1] See R. Law, *The Tests of Life*, p. 302. The Greek translated literally means, " We know that we possess the requests we have made " ; see Dodd, *The Johannine Epistles*, p. 135.

to afford an adequate explanation of the expression, "ask me in my name". We have here an explicit reference to prayer addressed to Jesus, and it is significant that it should be expressed by so striking an Hebraism. It is true that in the Old Testament we have no precise parallel such as to "call upon me in my name Jahweh", but such an expression would not be foreign to the profound conception of the "name" in Hebrew thought. Whether or not we can interpret this phrase in the sense of direct prayer to Christ, we are obliged to recognize in it the pregnant force of the Hebrew idea. And just because in Hebrew the significance of the "name" is so large and inclusive, there is nothing unusual in the transition from "asking in my name" to "receiving in my name", which appears to some to be sudden and harsh (16. 23, 24).

It is difficult to account for the Johannine use of the word "ask" to the exclusion of the generic word for prayer ($\pi\rho o\sigma\epsilon\acute{v}\chi\epsilon\sigma\theta\alpha\iota$) but it is unlikely that it was intended to exclude adoration and thanksgiving from the notion of prayer—petition being the most specific conception of prayer, it includes all else. The prayer of petition was the most apt to express to the disciples the assurance of continued intercourse with Jesus. For it is only by answer to prayer that the reality of the mutual relation can be proved. Prayer is not merely the expression of man's attitude to God; it is a means of communication with him and involves a reciprocal response on God's part. It is in fact part of John's doctrine of fellowship. What prompts prayer is the fact that "the Father himself loveth you" (16. 27). And the condition of prayer is that "ye abide in me, and my words abide in you" (15. 7). It is therefore as the assurance of continued fellowship with Jesus that the answer to prayer is said to fulfil the disciples' joy (16. 24). This is an expression which is almost invariably associated with the perfection of fellowship in one or other of its forms—with one another or with God in Christ (15. 11; 16. 20, 22; 1 John 1. 4). Prayer is not only the fulfilment of the joy of fellowship with the Father and the Son; it is also associated with the fellowship which exists among the brethren. It is with the same idea of fellowship in mind that John considers the subject of inter-

R

cessory prayer: "If any man see his brother sinning a sin not unto death, he shall ask, and God will give him life". The brother who sins is cut off from the Christian fellowship. All sin separates from God; but "there is a sin not unto death" (1 John 5. 17): sin, that is, which, though it cuts one off from life, does not do so irretrievably. As the sinner is thus cut off from fellowship, and can therefore no longer pray in the covenant name of Jesus, it is the duty of the brother to intercede for him, and God will give him life.

viii. *Conclusion*

It has been the contention of this chapter that the ethical precepts of John are all dependent upon his conception of God. This is a characteristic of all the writers of the New Testament. In the early Church two aspects of the Christian message may be discerned. There was the declaration of what God had done through Jesus Christ, and there was the preaching of what kind of behaviour was required of those who accepted Christ. The *kerygma* and the *didache* were two parts of one whole. "The two are intimately united, though distinguishable. The distinction and the relation between the two appear in the structure both of the Gospels, which interweave the story of Jesus and the record of his teaching, and of the Epistles, several of which are divided into a 'theological' part, expounding the implications of the *kerygma*, and an 'ethical' part, developing and applying the Law of Christ (see Romans, Galatians, Ephesians, Colossians, 1 and 2 Thessalonians, Hebrews—with an attenuated 'ethical section'— and 1 Peter)."[1]

In the Johannine writings these two parts of the Christian message are completely integrated. It is this comprehensive unity of the teaching of John that we have endeavoured to display throughout this book. The different parts of his message all dovetail into one another and are dependent upon one another to such a degree that they cannot be understood in isolation. The great unifying idea is that God is love. The whole of John's theology and ethics are based upon this fact which he learned

---

[1] Dodd, *The Johannine Epistles*, p. xxxi.

through the ministry, death, and resurrection of Jesus Christ. It is this that gathers all the varied details of Johannine thought into one whole. "God so loved that he gave" is the heart of the Johannine conception of God. God is love; therefore he must impart himself. It is almost a necessity in the Divine Being that God should go forth in Creation and Incarnation. The manifested life of the Logos in Creation and Incarnation is only an illustration, as it were, of forces and principles which dwell eternally in God.

The Evangelist therefore begins with the nature of the divine Logos: "the Word was God", and from this postulate the details of the Gospel are unfolded step by step. The Logos dwells with the Father in a relation of eternal intercommunion; within the Godhead he is perpetually going forth; he is essentially self-communicating, for such is the nature of God. It is by reason of this same self-giving impulse that he goes forth in creation; the impulse which ever draws him to the Father causes him to fashion a world, in which to pour forth the fulness of his love. It is the nature of light to shine, so it is the nature of the Logos to impart himself. He sustains, informs, and guides the world process. It was the same impulse that brought about the Incarnation: God so loved the world that he gave; it was inevitable once we grasp the nature of God as revealed in Jesus. The unfolding process of the self-communication of God is grounded at every stage in the essential and absolute nature of God as love. This is the grand ruling conception in the mind of John. He finds the sanction for the most commonplace duties of life in this fact. The fellowship of the brethren is brought about because they share this love that gives rather than desires. The life that pulsates through the Church is the life that God gives through his Son. The appropriation of that life depends upon the surrender of our life in faith and love to God. Without a clear grasp of this fundamental characteristic of divine love it is impossible to appreciate the unity of Johannine thought. John is a theologian in the exact sense of the word; for he traces everything back to its origin in the Divine Being.

BIBLIOGRAPHY

See also Rabbinic Literature on page xv, and index of Names

Abbott, E. A.—
>   *Johannine Vocabulary*, 1905.
>   *Johannine Grammar*, 1906.
>   *The Son of Man*, 1910.

Abrahams, Israel, *Studies in Pharisaism and the Gospels*, i, 1917; ii, 1924

Adam, James—
>   *The Religious Teachers of Greece*, 1908.
>   *The Vitality of Platonism*, 1911.

Angus, S., *The Mystery Religions and Christianity*, 1925.

Apuleius, *The Golden Ass* (*Metamorphoses*), in Loeb Classical Library.

Aurelius, Marcus, *Meditations*, Trans. by Rendel, 1898.

Bacon, B. W.—
>   *The Fourth Gospel in Research and Debate*, 1910.
>   *The Gospel of the Hellenists*, 1934.

Bauer, W., *Das Johannes Evangelium*, 2nd Ed., 1925.

Bernard, J. H., *St. John* (I.C.C.), 1928.

Bevan, E. E., *Stoics and Sceptics*, 1913.

Black, Matthew, *An Aramaic Approach to the Gospels and Acts*, 1947.

Bousset, W., *Kyrios Christos*, 2nd Ed., 1921.

Brandt, W., *Encyclopaedia of Religion and Ethics*, vol. viii. (art. " Mandaeans "), 1915.

Bréhier, E., *Les Idées Philosophiques et Religieuses de Philon d'Alexandrie*, 1925.

Brooke, A. E., *The Johannine Epistles* (I.C.C.), 1912.

Broomfield, G. W., *John, Peter, and the Fourth Gospel*, 1934.

Burkitt, F. C.—
>   *The Gospel History and its Transmission*, 1906.
>   *Church and Gnosis*, 1932.

Burnet, J., *Early Greek Philosophy*, 1920.

Burney, F. C., *The Aramaic Origin of the Fourth Gospel*, 1922.

Cadoux, C. J., *The Historic Mission of Jesus*, 1941.

Caird, E., *The Evolution of Theology in the Greek Philosophers*, 1904.

Carpenter, J. E., *The Johannine Writings*, 1927.

Charles, R. H.—
  Eschatology : Hebrew, Jewish, and Christian, 1899.
  The Book of Enoch, 1893.
  The Revelation (I.C.C.), 1920.
Cicero, *De Natura Deorum*, in Loeb Classical Library.
Colwell, G. C., *The Greek of the Fourth Gospel*, 1931.
Copleston, F., *A History of Philosophy*, i, 1944.
Cornford, F. M., *The Cosmology of Plato*, 1937.
Cornutus, *Theologia Graeca*, in Bibliotheca Scriptorum Graecorum et Romanorum Teubneriana, Ed. C. Lang, 1881.

Dalman, G., *The Words of Jesus*, Eng. Trans., 1902.
Diogenes Laertius, in Loeb Classical Library.
Dodd, C. H.—
  The Background of the Fourth Gospel, 1935.
  The Bible and the Greeks, 1935.
  The Apostolic Preaching and its Developments, 1936.
  The Parables of the Kingdom, 1936.
  The First Epistle of John and the Fourth Gospel, Reprint from *Bulletin of John Rylands Library*, 1937.
  The Johannine Epistles (Moffatt Commentary), 1946.
Drummond, J.—
  Philo Judaeus, 1888.
  The Character and Authorship of the Fourth Gospel, 1903.

Ely, M. R., *Knowledge of God in Johannine Thought*, 1925.
Epictetus, *Discourses*, in Loeb Classical Library.

Field, F., *Notes on the Translation of the New Testament*, 1899.

Gardner, P., *The Ephesian Gospel*, 1915.
Gardner-Smith, P., *St. John and the Synoptic Gospels*, 1938.
Gould, E. P., *D.C.G.*, vol. ii, art. " Son of Man ", 1908.
Granger, F., "The Poimandres of Hermes Trismegistos ", in *J.T.S.*, 1904.
Grill, J., *Untersuchungen über die Entstehung des vierten Evangeliums*, i, 1902; ii, 1923.

Harnack, A.—
  Über das Verhältniss des Prologs des vierten Evangeliums, 1892.
  The History of Dogma, Eng. Trans.

Harris, Rendel, *The Origin of the Prologue to St. John's Gospel*, 1917.

Heitmüller, W., *Das Evangelium des Johannes*, 1908.

Heraclitus, *Quaestiones Homericae*, in Bibliotheca Scriptorum Graecorum et Romanorum Teubneriana, Ed. Soc. Philol. Bonn., 1910.

Hoare, F. R., *The Original Order and Chapters of St. John's Gospel*, 1945.

Holland, H. S., *The Fourth Gospel*, 1923.

Hort, F. J. A., *The Way, the Truth, the Life*, 1897.

Hoskyns, E. C., *The Fourth Gospel*, 1940.

Howard, W. F.—
> *The Fourth Gospel in Recent Criticism and Interpretation*, 1931.
> *Christianity according to St. John*, 1943.

Hügel, Baron F. von—
> *Eternal Life*, 1929.
> *Encyclopaedia Britannica*, vol. xv., 11th Ed., art. " The Gospel of St. John ", 1910.

Inge, W. R.—
> *Christian Mysticism*, 1899.
> *Personal Idealism and Mysticism*, 1907.
> *Cambridge Biblical Essays*, " The Theology of the Fourth Gospel ", 1909.
> *Dictionary of Christ and the Gospels*, vol. i, "The Fourth Gospel", 1907.

Jackson, H. L., *The Problem of the Fourth Gospel*, 1918.

Kennedy, H. A. A., *Philo's Contribution to Religion*, 1919.

Kirk, K. E., *The Vision of God*, 1931.

Kittel, G. (Editor), *Theologisches Wörterbuch zum Neuen Testament*, 3 vols., 1933-1938.

Knox, W. L., *Some Hellenistic Elements in Primitive Christianity*, 1944.

Krebs, Engelbert, *Der Logos als Heiland im ersten Jahrhundert*, 1910.

Law, Robert, *The Tests of Life*, 1909.

Lebreton, J., *The History of the Dogma of the Trinity*, Eng. Trans., 1939.

Lewis, F. W., *Disarrangements in the Fourth Gospel*, 1910.

Lightfoot, R. H., *History and Interpretation in the Gospels*, 1935.

Lock, W., *A New Commentary on Holy Scripture* (S.P.C.K.), 1928.

Lofthouse, W. F., *The Father and the Son*, 1934.

Loisy, A., *Le Quatrième Évangile*, 1903.

Lowrie, W., *The Doctrine of St. John*, 1899.

Macgregor, G. H. C., *The Gospel of John* (Moffatt Commentary), 1928.

Mackintosh, H. R., *The Doctrine of the Person of Jesus Christ*, 1912.

Mansel, H. L., *The Gnostic Heresies*, 1875.

Manson, T. W., *The Teaching of Jesus*, 1931.

Manson, W., *Jesus the Messiah*, 1943.

Maspero, G. C. C., *The Dawn of Civilization*, Eng. Trans., 1901.

Milligan, G., *Selections from the Greek Papyri*, 1910.

Moffatt, J.—
   Introduction to the Literature of the New Testament, 1918.
   Love in the New Testament, 1930.

Moore, G. F.—
   Intermediaries in Jewish Theology, Reprint from *Harvard Theological Review*, xv, 1922.
   Judaism in the First Centuries of the Christian Era, 3 vols., 1927-1930.

Moulton, J. H., *Grammar of New Testament Greek*, vol. i., 1908.

Moulton and Milligan, *The Vocabulary of the Greek Testament*, 1930.

Odeberg, H., *The Fourth Gospel interpreted in its relation to Contemporaneous Religious Currents in Palestine and the Hellenistic-Oriental World*, 1929.

Otto, R., *The Kingdom of God and the Son of Man*, Eng. Trans., 1938.

Philo Judaeus—
   Philonis Alexandrini opera quae supersunt, by Cohn and Wendland.
   English Translation of the Works of Philo by Colson and Whitaker in Loeb Classical Library.

Rawlinson, A. E. J.—
   The New Testament Doctrine of Christ, 1929.
   Essays on the Trinity and the Incarnation (Editor), 1928.

Reitzenstein, R., *Poimandres*, 1904.

Rigg, W. H., " The Atonement in the Johannine Writings ", in *The Atonement in History and Life*, Ed. L. W. Grensted, 1929.

Ross, W. D., *Aristotle*, 1923.

Sanday, W., *The Criticism of the Fourth Gospel*, 1905.

Sanders, J. N., *The Fourth Gospel in the Early Church*, 1943.

Schlatter, A., *Der Evangelist Johannes*, 1930.

Schmiedel, P. W., *The Johannine Writings*, Eng. Trans., 1908.

Scott, E. F.—
  The Fourth Gospel: its Purpose and Theology, 1908.
  The New Testament Idea of Revelation, 1935.
Scott, W., *Hermetica*, 3 vols., 1924-1926.
Sextus Empiricus, in Loeb Classical Library.
Siegfried, K., *Philo von Alexandria*, 1875.
Stanton, V. H., *The Gospels as Historical Documents*, iii, 1920.
Stevens, G. B., *The Theology of the New Testament*, 2nd Ed., 1918.
Strachan, R. H., *The Fourth Gospel*, 1941.
Strack, H. L., and Billerbeck, P., *Kommentar zum N.T. aus Talmud und Midrash*, 4 vols., 1922-1928.
Streeter, B. H., *The Four Gospels*, 1926.
Swete, H. B., *The Last Discourse and Prayer*, 1920.

Taylor, A. E., *A Commentary on Plato's Timaeus*, 1928.
Taylor, Vincent—
  Jesus and His Sacrifice, 1937.
  The Atonement in New Testament Teaching, 1940.
Temple, W.—
  Nature, Man, and God, 1935.
  Readings in St. John's Gospel, 2 vols., 1939.
Torrey, C. C., *The Four Gospels: A New Translation*, 1933.

Underhill, Evelyn, *The Mystic Way*, 1912.

Wendt, H. H., *The Teaching of Jesus*, Eng. Trans., 2 vols., 1898-1899.
Westcott, B. F.—
  The Gospel of St. John, 1882.
  The Epistles of St. John, 1892.
Windisch, H., " The Five Johannine Sayings about the Paraclete ", in *Festgabe für Adolf Jülicher*, 1927.
Wright, C. J., "The Fourth Gospel", in *The Message and Mission of Jesus*, Ed. Major, Manson, and Wright, 1937.

Zeller, E.—
  Stoics, Epicureans, and Sceptics, Eng. Trans., 1870.
  Outlines of the History of Greek Philosophy, Eng. Trans., 1931.

INDEX OF NAMES

INDEX OF SUBJECTS